The Real
Kenneth Grahame

The Real
Kenneth Grahame

The Tragedy Behind
The Wind in the Willows

Elisabeth Galvin

WHITE OWL
AN IMPRINT OF PEN & SWORD BOOKS LTD.
YORKSHIRE - PHILADELPHIA

First published in Great Britain in 2021 by
White Owl
An imprint of
Pen & Sword Books Ltd
Yorkshire – Philadelphia

ISBN 978 1 52674 880 5

Typeset by Mac Style
Printed and bound in the UK by CPI Group (UK) Ltd,
Croydon, CR0 4YY.

Pen & Sword Books Limited incorporates the imprints of Atlas,
Archaeology, Aviation, Discovery, Family History, Fiction, History,
Maritime, Military, Military Classics, Politics, Select, Transport,
True Crime, Air World, Frontline Publishing, Leo Cooper, Remember
When, Seaforth Publishing, The Praetorian Press, Wharncliffe
Local History, Wharncliffe Transport, Wharncliffe True Crime
and White Owl.

For a complete list of Pen & Sword titles please contact

PEN & SWORD BOOKS LIMITED
47 Church Street, Barnsley, South Yorkshire, S70 2AS, England
E-mail: enquiries@pen-and-sword.co.uk
Website: www.pen-and-sword.co.uk

Or

PEN AND SWORD BOOKS
1950 Lawrence Rd, Havertown, PA 19083, USA
E-mail: Uspen-and-sword@casematepublishers.com
Website: www.penandswordbooks.com

For my parents

Contents

List of Illustrations

Kenneth on his first day at school, aged 9. (*St Edward's School*)

Kenneth, centre, with his schoolmates in 1870, looking unenthusiastic with head resting on hand. He sits at the feet of Reverend Algernon Simeon, St Edward's charismatic headmaster. (*St Edward's School*)

Inside the Bank of England where Kenneth was employed as 'a paleface quilldriver'. (*The Bank of England Archive*)

The magnificent Frederick James Furnivall, who taught Kenneth how to row on the Thames. (*Mary Evans*)

Kenneth's favourite holiday destination of Fowey in Cornwall, where he visited all his life. (*Mark Camp*)

WE Henley, the editor who gave Kenneth his big break. "I should be a pig if I ever forgot him," said Kenneth. (*Mary Evans*)

Evelyn Sharp (holding placard), editor of *Votes for Women* and Kenneth's early love interest. (*Mary Evans*)

Elspeth Grahame aged 19. Many men fell for her beauty and charm including Mark Twain and Alfred, Lord Tennyson. (© *National Trust Images*)

This poem of Elsie's shows her heartbreak at Kenneth's coldness at the start of their marriage. (© *Bodleian Library, University of Oxford*)

Dandyish portrait of W Graham Robertson aged 28 by John Singer Sargent: he was naked under the coat to make him appear slimmer. (© *Tate*)

Mouse as a young child. Kenneth joked about his "hyacinthine locks". (*The Dorneywood Trust*)

Mouse by the windmill at Littlehampton, aged seven. This picture was discovered in an old photo album discarded behind the squash court at Dorneywood. (*Private collection*)

Woodhall Spa in Lincolnshire, where Elsie tried numerous times to recover from depression. (*Woodhall Spa Cottage Museum, taken from Nicholas M Duke Cox's book Taking the Waters at Woodhall Spa*)

"Have you heard about the Toad?" The first letter Kenneth wrote to his son about the story that became *The Wind in the Willows*. (© *Bodleian Library, University of Oxford*)

Mayfield, where Kenneth wrote *The Wind in the Willows* from the study to the upper right of the front door. (*With thanks to Herries School*)

The willows are as beautiful as ever on the Thames at Pangbourne where illustrator EH Shepard spent an afternoon on the riverbank to inspire him for his *The Wind in the Willows* commission.

The River Lerryn in Cornwall. Could this stretch of water be the one in Kenneth's most famous book – rather than the Thames? (*Mark Camp*)

The day Kenneth was shot at whilst at work made for an amusing cartoon in Punch. (*Mary Evans*)

St Fimbarrus Church in Fowey where Kenneth married Elsie in her white muslin day dress. (*Barbara Woodward*)

EH Shepard's iconic illustrations have endeared readers of *The Wind in the Willows* for all time. But he made a mistake in this image, depicting Rat rowing instead of Mole.

'Coldtonguecoldhamcoldbeefpicklegherkinsaladfrenchrollscresssandwichespottedmeatgingerbeerlemonadeandsodawater'.

The ineffable Constance Smedley, original champion of *The Wind in the Willows*. (*Mary Evans*)

'I have never read anything of yours yet that I haven't enjoyed to the full,' wrote President Roosevelt. (© *Bodleian Library, University of Oxford*)

A true romantic, Elsie wrote valentine cards each year but never received one from the one she loved the most, Kenneth. (© *Bodleian Library, University of Oxford*)

Boham's, the Grahames' beloved farmhouse in the English countryside.

Mouse as an undergraduate of Christ Church College, Oxford. It was the university his father had always longed for.

Kenneth walks with a cane in 1921. He is recovering from his son's untimely death. (© *National Portrait Gallery*)

Elspeth in her late sixties, after a lifetime of anxiety and depression. (*The Dorneywood Trust*)

Kenneth, on his retirement from the Bank of England: his relaxed pose hides the drama of his resignation. (*Mary Evans*)

Pretty Church Cottage in Pangbourne, Kenneth's final home, which is within walking distance of the Thames.

Acknowledgements

L ike many authors, I began writing a book by reading. I will always be thankful to my eldest daughter Mary for sitting patiently for hours while I read and re-read *The Wind in the Willows* to her. Everyone I contacted as part of my research was incredibly helpful and no one declined my requests, which indicates the fondness in which Kenneth Grahame is held by so many. David Gooderson has been deeply supportive by very generously sharing his invaluable insights and research about the Grahame family and writing the fine foreword. I am so grateful to the distinguished expert on children's literature, Professor Peter Hunt, for his wise counsel and encouragement. With indebted thanks to Oliver House and the staff at the Bodleian Libraries' Special Collections without whose help this book could not have been written. Similarly, Rachael Muir, assistant archivist at the Bank of England Archives, worked extremely hard to help me. Tim Price, Gemma Kirk-Stretton, Carole Ambrose and the staff at Dorneywood went to great lengths during difficult circumstances of Covid to assist me with my research, which I am truly thankful for. I'd like to make a special acknowledgement to Julian Fellowes for his time and astute points and Alex Bloch for arranging our interview. I am also much obliged to Gaynor Haliday, Laura Hirst and Aileen Pringle at Pen & Sword; Chris Nathan, archivist at St Edward's School with his colleague Tracy van der Heiden; Fiona Long, headmistress of Herries Preparatory School; Robert Athol, college archivist of Jesus College, Cambridge; Yale University Library; Weston Library, Connecticut; Furnivall Sculling Club in Hammersmith; The River and Rowing Museum in Henley; and St Anne's Church, Dropmore. I greatly appreciate those who helped me in Cornwall including: Barbara Woodward for her fine photographs of Fowey; Sue Reardon; Mark Camp of Visit Cornwall and Walkaboutwest; Royal Fowey Yacht Club; and Fowey Hall Hotel. With grateful thanks to the Woodhall Spa Heritage Committee and Patricia and Nicholas Duke-Cox of Woodhall Spa Cottage Museum for generously sharing their research, knowledge and photographs. I would especially like to thank Richard and Valerie Caesar of Church Cottage for all their kindness. Most importantly I acknowledge the love and support of my family and friends, including my parents Bert and Gay Attwood and my sister Hayley Relph for reading the manuscript, Dr Emma Baldock for so thoughtfully sharing her perceptive psychological insights, Tatiana Morales for donating hours of her time carefully editing the manuscript, and Dale Mulholland and Paul Brogan for their perceptive feedback. Finally, with love and thanks to Sarah Woozley, Miriam Fenster and Linda Mandel, who gave me permission to swim in their beautiful river during Covid, which helped me keep alive the spirit of the Thames as I slowly wrote my way through lockdown.

Foreword

by David Gooderson

I first became interested in Kenneth Grahame in the early 1970s. As an actor and aspiring playwright I was on the lookout for interesting material and the dust-jacket of Peter Green's 1959 biography of Grahame was enough to convince me that here was a rich dramatic seam: the story of an unhappy child who became a conformist adult on the surface while always longing to break free and indulge in dreams and adventures. I was gripped by the drama of a dysfunctional family, in which the father was a famous author, celebrated for two volumes of stories about children and above all for *The Wind in The Willows*, his international bestseller that has enchanted children and adults for more than a century.

My interest soon became a fascination and led me to write a play, *The Killing of Mr Toad*, followed by two adaptations of *The Wind in the Willows* (one a musical version co-written with David Conville and Carl Davis) and then the introduction and notes to a book, *My Dearest Mouse*. Now I'm delighted to be revisiting the world of Kenneth Grahame to commend Elisabeth Galvin's engaging and comprehensive new biography.

'It is the boys that matter most of all,' wrote Grahame, and in *The Wind in the Willows* he celebrates the joys of male companionship. But if it had not been for two women, the book would never have seen the light of day. It is fitting that in the age of '#MeToo' Mrs Galvin's biography gives the women in his life their fair share of the limelight.

The foundations for *The Wind in the Willows* lie in Kenneth's letters to his 7-year-old son, Alastair (nicknamed Mouse). They contain new instalments of a long-running bedtime story that had been a nightly ritual since Mouse was 4. They were written down because Mouse and his new governess, Miss Naomi Stott, were sent away on holiday to Littlehampton during the summer of 1907. Mouse only agreed to go after his father promised him that the bedtime stories would continue by post.

Miss Stott read the letters aloud to Mouse, realised they were special and had the foresight to preserve them. Before leaving Littlehampton she posted them to Elspeth (Mrs Grahame) for safe keeping, 'knowing full well,' wrote Elspeth, 'that if restored to the author they would merely be consigned to the waste paper basket.'

Constance Smedley, the feminist author of *Woman: A Few Shrieks*, who like Toad drove a motor car, lived near the Grahames and was the European representative of the American magazine, *Everybody's*. Kenneth had not written a book for nine years and the editor urged Constance to try to entice him to write something for the magazine. She befriended Mouse and Elspeth and listened in to the nightly ritual of the 'unending' bedtime story. Spurred on by Elspeth, and with Mouse's encouragement, she succeeded in persuading Kenneth to use the letters as the starting point for a book. Once committed to the project he worked quickly and the book was completed by Christmas – only to be rejected by *Everybody's* because it wasn't what the editor was expecting. He wanted a book *about* children, like Grahame's earlier successes, not *for* children, and certainly not about animals.

The most significant woman in Kenneth's adult life was his wife, Elspeth. If some biographers have been over-critical of her, Mrs Galvin certainly redresses the balance. She paints a sympathetic and detailed picture of a talented and sociable woman struggling to cope with the frustrations of a failing marriage and a precocious but difficult child. She adds intriguing new material that throws light on the couple's physical relationship and her book concludes with a moving account of Elspeth (Elsie's) fourteen years as a widow.

One of the drawbacks for a modern biographer is that there is no hope of meeting anyone who knew the Grahames personally. When I was researching the story for my play in the 1970s, I was at least able to contact some of Mouse's contemporaries. I managed to track down the boy who had shared a study with him at School House, Rugby, in the autumn of 1914. The boy, Robert Nisbet, who was by now a twinkly, chain-smoking 78-year-old, still practising as a solicitor, invited me to meet him in his office in Lincoln's Inn. He told me about the school in his day – rife with bullying and beatings for the smallest infringement of the rules.

'Grahame was what I'd call a "bumbler",' said Nisbet. 'He just didn't fit in. Always appeared to be somewhere else – in a world of his own.' (Like father, like son, I thought.) Nisbet remembered noticing him carrying his rifle upside down on a military parade ('something you wouldn't believe possible'). And he was continually playing a childish game with a cup and ball. In the narrow confines of their shared study 'it was,' he remarked with measured understatement, 'rather irritating.' He added: 'We didn't get on at all. We probably scrapped – most people did.'

The sheltered, other-worldly Mouse had cannoned into the real world and after only two weeks his father was summoned to the school. Despite changing studies, Mouse survived for just four more weeks before his parents brought him home. His brief career at Rugby was over.

Even more significant was my correspondence with Michael Parker, a retired bishop, who studied with Mouse at Christ Church College, Oxford, and was one of the last people to see him alive. In tiny, neat handwriting Parker wrote: 'Alastair Grahame was a lonely soul who lived in a kind of dream world. He did not enter into any college activities. On the evening of his tragic death I had coffee with him. He was in good spirits. I learned of his death next morning. It was a great shock to me.'

The loss of their only child just before his twentieth birthday was a devastating blow for his parents, though in one way it brought them closer together, united in their grief. It was a bitter irony that the little boy who had been the inspiration for a delightful children's book died so young.

Some people think that it is best to forget about the tragedy so as not to spoil our innocent enjoyment of the book. But *The Wind in the Willows* is much more than a charming animal adventure. Kenneth poured into it his deepest longings and most profound imaginings. And he wanted his readers to appreciate this, gently berating them when they did not. 'They liked the subject matter,' he told a visiting American professor. 'They did not even notice the source of all the agony, and all the joy.'

In this new biography, Elisabeth Galvin doesn't flinch from describing the pain in Kenneth's life while doing full justice to every aspect of his masterpiece, including an interesting chapter analysing his contribution as an early environmentalist. She gives us, in all his complexity, the real Kenneth Grahame.

David Gooderson
London 2020
www.david-gooderson.co.uk

Introduction

'It seemed as though his pen were dipped in rivers
So silver was his prose'

Elsie Grahame

If Kenneth Grahame had lived during the Covid pandemic of the 2020s, he would have spent as much time as he could on the water. Although he would have missed the comradeship of a morning's fishing or messing about in a boat on the river with male friends, he would have been delighted to know that boat sales skyrocketed in some parts of the world during the epidemic.

With an in-law who was an Eton rowing champion, Kenneth swam well and could handle almost any sort of floating craft from canoe, single scull, fishing vessel, yacht and rowing boat. A life member of the Royal Fowey Yacht Club, he was once part of a lifeboat crew that was called to help after a White Star vessel was wrecked offshore. On another occasion he was mistaken for a Cornish fisherman. He loved the male camaraderie that being on the water brought, and enjoyed nothing better than to spend all night fishing for eels. He could whiff for pollock, sail for mackerel, bait with squid for conger and angle for large fish. The story goes that, during one expedition, off Kynance Cove on the Lizard, he glimpsed the large shadow of a shark.

Kenneth was a master of social isolation; although he was loved by both men and women (he made, perhaps, only one enemy), he was content with his own company, something which his wife never understood. It broke her heart and caused her mind irreparable damage. 'Oddly enough (for he was a most attractive man) Kenneth had few friends. He simply didn't want them,' wrote Kenneth's greatest friend, Graham Robertson.

In 1920, the world was recovering from a global health crisis, the Spanish Flu, which infected a third of the world's population. Kenneth managed not to catch it, but throughout his life he wasn't blessed with good health.

As a child he overcame scarlet fever, which killed his mother and left him with a permanently weak chest; throughout his life he suffered constant bouts of bronchitis, flu and respiratory complaints. Often when he was ill, he sought out the healing balm of the sea; in fact, he was sent away to the coast as a bachelor and came home a married man. Throughout his life and the trials and tribulations that characterised it, Kenneth's soul was nourished with water. He had an unquenchable desire to be refreshed, revived and restored by it.

He had extraordinarily heightened senses and a crystal-clear memory (one of the reasons why he was such a successful author for children is that he could remember exactly what it was like to be a child). Each time he recalled the sight and smell of open water it would soothe him, and he actively sought out rivers, lakes and even fountains wherever he lived or holidayed.

The river followed the ebb and flow of his life; it was Kenneth's vivid impressions of the sea that first inspired him as a young man to write creatively. The river was the subject of his most successful novel, which more than 100 years later remains a cherished part of children's literature; and he breathed his last moments within earshot of the gentle lapping of the river at Pangbourne, Berkshire. Arguably, no other writer has captured so definitively, gracefully and whimsically such an impressionistic essence of the English countryside as seen from a watery perspective. What Wordsworth did for daffodils, Kenneth Grahame achieved for the river and sea – composing such evocative lines as: 'patches of mud that smell like plum-cake'; 'sniffed salt in the air'; and 'the lap and gurgle of waves'.

Kenneth was acutely aware he was one whom Triton held in his spell:

> From each generation certain are chosen whom Nature... leads by the hand one fated day within sight and sound of the sea... Henceforth, that adept is possessed. Desk-bound, pent in between city walls – a fellow, say, fast held in the tangle of Christ Church bells; a solicitor behind wire-blinds in some inland market-town – henceforth the insistent echo will awake and take him betimes, claiming him as one with the trident brand on him. For the Triton knows his man, and whom he has once chosen he never again lets go.

His vivacious yet highly-strung new wife Elsie had to put up with Kenneth spending the majority of their honeymoon rowing and sailing. But eventually she came to accept her husband's great passion, carefully jotting in her personal notebook:

> Loved the sea in all its aspects, loved being by it, in it, swimming, on it, sailing or steaming. Loved gathering shells on the shore – the tiniest always attracting his fancy.
> Loved the river from its banks or in his canoe or bathing in it.

In *The Wind in the Willows,* it is Rat who knows the river best; Badger never comes across it; Toad doesn't appreciate it (calling it 'tongue-tied' and 'uncommunicative'); while Mole loves it immediately:

> The Mole never heard a word he was saying. Absorbed in the new life he was entering upon, intoxicated with the sparkle, the ripple. The scents and the sounds and the sunlight, he trailed a paw in the water and dreamt long waking dreams.

We see that Kenneth notices the very smallest detail about open water, as if he were seeing it for the first time. His memory was extraordinary for remembering how the young feel as they encounter the world afresh:

> 'I beg your pardon,' said the Mole, pulling himself together with an effort. 'You must think me very rude; but all this is so new to me. So – this – is a – a – River!'
> 'The River,' corrected the Rat.
> 'And you really live by the river? What a jolly life!'
> 'By it and with it and on it and in it,' said the Rat. 'It's brother and sister to me, and aunts, and company, and food and drink, and (naturally) washing. It's my world, and I don't want any other. What it hasn't got is not worth having, and what it doesn't know is not worth knowing. Lord! The times we've had together! Whether in winter or summer, spring or autumn, it's always got its fun and its excitements.'

Reeling from his discombobulated childhood, Kenneth always viewed the river as a loyal friend who was more dependable than his family, his wife and even his son: '[Rat] returned somewhat despondently to his river again – his faithful, steady-going old river, which never packed up, flitted, or went into winter quarters.'

Ratty voices Kenneth's obsession with the river:

'Nice? It's the only thing... there is *nothing* – absolutely nothing – half so much worth doing as simply messing about in boats... In or out of 'em, it doesn't matter. Nothing seems really to matter, that's the charm of it. Whether you get away or whether you don't; whether you arrive at your destination or whether you reach somewhere else, or whether you never get anywhere at all, you're always busy, and you never do anything in particular; and when you've done it there's always something else to do, and you can do it if you like, but you'd much better not.'

Hold your breath and dive in for a water-biography of a most extraordinary writer's life.

Chapter 1

Born a Scot

'The most priceless possession of the human race is the wonder of the world.'

Kenneth Grahame

The body of a young man was found on the railway line at the level crossing near Oxford station on 7 May 1920. It was identified as Alastair Grahame, the boy who inspired *The Wind in the Willows*. As a child, his father, Kenneth, had told him bedtime stories about a mole, a water rat and a badger, which he later continued in letter form, and finally published in 1908. The tales became one of the most famous children's books of all time.

Although Alastair would never live to appreciate the success of his father's tribute to him, he became immortalised in this greatest of stories. Kenneth, and his wife Elsie, never recovered from the loss of their son. *The Wind in the Willows* depicts the genteel life of the leisured Edwardian riverbank, yet Kenneth lived through far rougher seas. Just as a swan looks as if it is gliding along serenely, in public this man put on a face of calm poise, but in private he spent most of his life desperately treading water to stay afloat.

Kenneth Grahame was born on 8 March 1859, and it is fitting he made his entrance into the world at this time of year as the spring was always a time of reflection for him. As an amateur naturalist, he describes the season memorably in *The Wind in the Willows* as the Mole awakes from hibernation: 'It all seemed too good to be true. Hither and thither through the meadows he rambled busily... finding everywhere birds building, flowers budding, leaves thrusting – everything happy, and progressive, and occupied.'

In another of Kenneth's books, he personifies Mother Nature as he writes of spring: 'The earth stretched herself, smiling in her sleep; and everything leapt and pulsed to the stir of the giant's movement.'

But Kenneth wasn't born in the countryside, nor even in England. His mother, Bessie, gave birth in the centre of Edinburgh, at 32 Castle Street (currently a pub-restaurant called Badger & Co). It is an elegant granite townhouse, with a view of Edinburgh Castle and opposite the former home of Sir Walter Scott – Kenneth's literary hero and the author he read on his deathbed.

The infant Kenneth was delivered by the leading obstetrician of the time (Queen Victoria's doctor), Dr James Simpson, who some years before had revolutionised childbirth by introducing chloroform as a type of pain relief. By rejecting the commonly held belief that God wanted to punish females by making childbirth painful, Dr Simpson was an early advocate of the empowerment of women. And women would become intrinsic to Kenneth's life and work.

Bessie was the daughter of a wealthy merchant, David Ingles of Lasswade, and was the perfect Victorian beauty with her oval face, rosebud lips and soulful eyes. Her long, glossy, ebony hair and defined arched eyebrows framed her pale skin and gave her a striking look. Apparently, Bessie had a famously joyful laugh – one of her greatest charms – and was described as 'an irreverent angel'. Bessie's popular nature and prettiness captivated one Cunningham Grahame, and they married on 13 March 1855.

Kenneth was their third child after Helen, by then aged 3 (1856), and Thomas William (Willie), just a year old (1858). Cunningham was from a well-respected Calvinist family, descended from Robert the Bruce (King of Scots 1306–29) and a long line of lawyers and accountants, some of whom enjoyed literary pursuits on the side. Kenneth's great great uncle was a poet, and another relation published a history of America.

Cunningham (born 20 July 1830) was a lawyer known for his witty speeches in the Scottish Parliament and was marked for a highly successful career. He and Bessie made a glamorous couple and enjoyed entertaining Edinburgh's great and good. But their happy city life would not last long; shortly after the children were born, Cunningham suddenly left Parliament and was demoted to sheriff-substitute of Argyll in the countryside of Inveraray. The reason was never documented but speculation suggests Cunningham was an alcoholic.

At just 14 months old in May 1860, Kenneth travelled by train with his family from Edinburgh to the rural paradise of Ardrishaig. Astonishingly, this became Kenneth's first memory as he later recalled his seat on the first-class carriage as having 'shiny black buttons, buttons that dug into dusty, blue cloth'. It seems extraordinary that Kenneth could really remember the journey, but being able to accurately recall what it was like to be a child was the talent he was most proud of. Kenneth set sail for his adventure of life, just as the wayfarer in his most famous book: 'Family troubles, as usual, began it. The domestic stormcone was hoisted, and I shipped myself on board a small trading vessel...'

The family moved into Annfield Lodge, in mid-Argyll, which they rented for about a year. It is a handsome granite house with white gabled windows overlooking the spectacular Loch Gilp. The five bedrooms and lush 2-acre garden would have been plenty of space for Kenneth to take his first wobbly steps after the confines of the city. Now a guesthouse, the property has been renamed as *Allt-Na-Craig*, which means 'water from the hill' in Gaelic, and the name of a burn (stream) that runs through the land. An old culvert takes the burn to the loch where Kenneth might have spotted a sea otter; this was the first place he saw a significant expanse of water – other than the puddles of rainy Edinburgh – and would be the first of his many homes by the water. Loch Gilp is a small inlet of Loch Fyne, and of all the lochs in Scotland, Fyne is the deepest, longest and arguably most majestic. It cannot have failed to make an impression on a little boy who would forever be inspired by the beauty of water. As an adult, he wrote of his memories of being 'among the gleaming lochs and sinuous firths of the Western Highlands...' Kenneth remembered the sights and sounds of his home as 'wind-shaken water, [the] whip and creak and rattle of shrouds, [the] flap of idle sails in halcyon spells, [the] cry of gulls at pasture on the pale acres that know no plough... a certain haunting smell of tar and weed.'

Just like a pirate adventure story, Kenneth, his older siblings and their three dogs roamed free with their nanny. Along the banks of the Crinan Canal they discovered voles, which Kenneth called water rats. Playing on the beach, he would later remember 'big blacksided fishing-boats' and 'the ever recurrent throb of [the steamer's] paddle-wheel, the rush and foam of beaten water among the pikes, splash of ropes and rumble of gangways, and all the attendant hurry and scurry.'[1] To their delight, the children were sometimes taken in a rowing boat out into the bay by the kindly local policeman (trying to impress their nanny, his girlfriend).

Perhaps the world owes thanks to this anonymous Scottish law enforcer for introducing Kenneth Grahame to the pleasure of messing about in boats.

In 1861, the family moved to a neighbouring town, Lochgilphead. Like any good children's adventure story, lack of adult spoilsports made Kenneth's early childhood seem all the more idyllic. Bessie, as was customary for well-to-do Victorians, left the majority of the childcare to the family nanny, and Cunningham mostly lived away from the family during the week while he stayed in Inveraray for work. Perhaps these formative early years without his father might have sown the early seeds for Kenneth's fiercely independent and emotionally cold personality. Not seeing her husband much must have been difficult for Bessie, who was used to a busy life in Edinburgh but now confined to a rural fishing village. Children model their behaviour on their parents, and the Grahame children were watching an unconventional marriage.

But after two years, in May 1863, the family was reunited as they moved into the new home built especially for them on the Duke of Argyll's estate in Inveraray – a perk of Cunningham's job. A large house of sandstone with attractive gables, it is surrounded by lawn and gardens that ran right down to the water's edge. Originally called *Tigh na Ruabh*, the property is now the Loch Fyne Hotel. Cunningham and Bessie soon became close again and discovered they were expecting their fourth child. Pregnant and nesting, Bessie enjoyed overseeing the furnishing of the house and had rose cuttings taken from her parents' home in Midlothian, planted in the garden. Eagles, buzzards, deer and, especially, otters would have delighted Kenneth. Human neighbours proved friendly too, when the Grahames were invited that autumn to dine at Inveraray Castle with the duke, duchess and the duke's unmarried sister, Lady Emma. Bessie included an account of the dinner party in her letter to her mother, with the fact that the duke's son, Lord Lorne, knew of her twin brother, David, after they had both been at Eton. David was a rowing star at the college. So well did the dinner party go that Bessie was invited back the very next day with her daughter Helen, to play with the duke's girl of similar age.

Some six months later, Bessie's baby was delivered; another son, Roland, born on 16 March 1864 (almost on Kenneth's birthday). But the Grahames' joy was short-lived. Very soon after the birth, Bessie caught scarlet fever and never recovered. The delivery of her son had weakened her body, and on 4 April she died. Her final words were: 'It's all been so lovely.'

At just 5 years old, Kenneth was left without his beloved mother and the shock would stay with him for the rest of his life. 'Why does a coming bereavement project… [reveal] no shadow of woe to warn its happy, heedless victims?' he reflected as an adult. Yet the worst wasn't over: terrifyingly, Kenneth had caught scarlet fever from his mother and his own life was in serious danger.

Chapter 2

A Barefoot Boy

'I can remember everything I felt then, the part of my brain I used
from four till about seven can never be altered...'

The Golden Age

For an author who made his name from writing about childhood,
Kenneth almost didn't survive his. For several days he slipped
between death and life with scarlet fever; a pandemic had gripped
the United Kingdom and was killing thousands. Perhaps little Kenneth
was weakened by the loss of his mother and his father's raw grief. Help
came in the form of Cunningham's mother, who rushed from Edinburgh
to take care of her grandson. She sat by his bedside, cooling his brow and
flushed cheeks, holding his hand and easing his raging sore throat. Very
slowly, Kenneth began to regain his strength and gradually got better.
But it would not be his only brush with death; the disease permanently
damaged his chest and for the rest of his life he suffered recurrent
bronchial problems, especially during the changing seasons.

Cunningham was devastated by Bessie's death. His beloved wife had
been taken from him just as he had managed to get the family back
together again. Red wine had always been his weakness, but now he
began to slide into an alcoholic abyss. He locked himself away in the
granite house at Inveraray, unable to fulfil his duty as a father to his four
motherless children. It was up to Ferguson, the family nanny, to comfort
them. A Scottish woman of character, she was to become a vital part of
Kenneth's life.

Kenneth never recovered from losing his mother and the resulting
family drama. He was a man who didn't properly grow up; his writing
constantly dwells on childhood, perhaps obsessively. He collected toys,
loved fairgrounds and adored the circus. He would always cling to the
memory of his early life with his mother; from the age of 5, part of his
emotional self shut down and forever after he found close relationships

awkward. He was a bachelor until his forties and failed spectacularly at fatherhood. Kenneth wrote authentically about children – their feelings, experiences and view of the world. Yet in all his stories, parents are absent, shadowy or stylised and he absolutely never mentions his own mother and father. The closest we have to his thoughts of his parents is at the start of *The Golden Age* (his second book, published in 1895): 'Looking back to those days of old... I can see now that to children with a proper equipment of parents these things would have worn a different aspect.' Later, in 1922, he wrote in a magazine story: 'We have learnt by sad experience not to expect very much from any of our relations.' The ultimate insult to his family.

The closest Kenneth got to 'a proper equipment of parents' came in the shape of Bessie's mother, Mary Ingles, who lived in the south of England. A widow in her sixties who was somewhat impecunious, she nevertheless agreed to take in Kenneth, Helen, Willie, and baby Roland who was just weeks old, as well as Nanny Ferguson. The motherless children needed a loving and caring home to help them cope with the loss of effectively both parents; what they received was a strong-minded senior citizen with limited emotional capacity who was a stickler for table manners. As Kenneth wrote in *The Golden Age*: 'they treated us, indeed, with kindness enough as to the needs of the flesh, but after that with indifference...' Bonneted and booted in black silk, the strictly competent Granny Ingles had once been a beauty like her daughter, but age had hardened her looks and whitened her hair. 'I don't suppose she could be described as a child-lover...' Helen later remembered. 'It was hard no doubt at the age of 60, having brought up her own family of five sons and a daughter to have us landed upon her, enough to try anyone's temper...' Kenneth, the diplomat, described Granny Ingles as 'a slight disappointment'. He would always be glad she read him Scottish folktales and ballads from her childhood in Midlothian.

Granny Ingles lived in Cookham Dean, on the edge of Old Windsor Forest, with her son, David (Bessie's twin), and it was he who helped to cheer the children up. Uncle David had been the rowing champion at Eton that the Grahames' neighbours back in Inveraray had been so impressed to hear about. Still a keen riverman, he showed the children the Thames which ran near to the house. Helen remembered her uncle: '...made a great deal of us, taking us on the river and to see his friends at Bisham and elsewhere.'

If Granny Ingles wasn't the fairy godmother the children had hoped for, her home, The Mount, was right out of a storybook, and they were given great freedom to explore it. The acres of gardens and orchards inspired Kenneth's descriptions in *The Golden Age* and its sequel *Dream Days* (1898) of crowding laurels, high-standing elm trees, lily ponds, orchards, raspberry canes and meadow grass thick with buttercups. The house's leaded windows, old Dutch tiles and heavy beams made of ship's wood ignited the young Kenneth's imagination and he later wrote about his secret den, The Gallery, in stories such as the autobiographical *The Roman Road*. The Gallery was a child's dream escape; under the eaves in the attic reached by a twisting staircase, Kenneth and his brothers and sister spent their days playing and reading books including R.M. Ballantyne's *The Dog Crusoe and His Master* and Aesop's *Fables*.

Without their proper equipment of parents, the four siblings became close as they learnt to cope with life as orphans. In *Pagan Papers*, Kenneth writes about a traumatised child who withdraws into his imagination:

Whenever a child is set down in a situation that is distasteful, out of harmony, jarring – and he is very easily jarred – that very moment he begins, without conscious effort, to throw out and to build up an environment really suitable to his soul, and to transport himself thereto... Of the herb called self-heal he has always a shred or two in his wallet.

In *The Golden Age*, a little boy escapes into nature to cope with his troubles: 'I slipped through the hedge out of the trodden highway, into the vacant meadow spaces. It was not that I was unsociable... but the passion and the call of the divine morning were high in my blood.'

Kenneth's core needs as a child were not being met and his way of coping was to retreat inside himself. He lacked an adequate measure of stability, love and nurture and this psychological damage would sadly follow him throughout his life. Yet in a way The Mount was Kenneth's own golden age. The quintessential English haven, set high above the Thames near Marlow, restored in him a sense of wonder, freedom and independence that he always remembered; photographs of him at around this time show him to look a serious, reserved little boy, with dark hair and pale skin. Little Kenneth escaped into his imagination as much as he escaped to the gardens and the river; he developed a love for the beauty of the countryside which soothed his young soul. He never forgot his early childhood, and described his eventual return to Berkshire as an adult: 'The queer thing is, I can remember everything I felt then, the part of my brain I used from four till about seven can never have altered. Coming back here wakens every recollection. After that time I don't remember anything particularly.' This homecoming came when he was a father as he repeated history by bringing his own 6-year-old son back to Berkshire. His childhood history became integrated with the present: 'I feel I should never be surprised to meet myself as I was when a little chap of five, suddenly coming round a corner...' The deep trauma he felt as a young boy made him cling to the idea of an idealistic rewriting of his own childhood. He was, in some sense, forever a vulnerable child.

Kenneth may have spent his days dreaming but neither Granny Ingles nor Uncle David could afford to. A curate at the local church, David was the youngest of her six children so it is hardly surprising the widow had little spare money for her grandchildren. Financial assistance came from another of her sons, John (a widower). As Helen acknowledged: 'our grandmother's income was a small one and if our uncle had not helped us I don't know what would have become of us.' Like his mother, Uncle John had left Scotland for England, and was employed as a parliamentary agent.

The odd little family rubbed along together for some eighteen months until they heard word from Cunningham Grahame; their father wanted the children to go back to Scotland and live with him. Granny Ingles duly sent them up north with their nurse. We don't know what happened during that summer of 1865 when the children were reunited with their father; they were all still under 11 years old, with Kenneth only 6. How different the lochs and the heather would have seemed compared with the gentle Thames and country garden they had become used to. How strange it would have been at first to get to know and trust their father over the course of a year. But, devastatingly, their trust was broken again. Still drinking, Cunningham realised too late that he just could not manage his four children despite Ferguson's help. He stood down from his job as sheriff-substitute and, effectively, resigned from fatherhood. He left Scotland for France and never spoke to his children again.

Kenneth could not forgive his father and when Cunningham eventually died some twenty years later in February 1887, Kenneth's reaction was extraordinary; he travelled to France for the funeral but refused a recent photograph of his father offered to him by the landlady and made just a cursory mention of the whole affair in his diary. Utterly devoid of emotion, Kenneth included only the facts of his father's death after a stroke in Normandy and that his grave was at Sainte-Adresse. The only slightly descriptive prose is that his father was buried 'on the heights overlooking the sea, near the lighthouses', making reference to water. Kenneth would never make mention again of his father.

A child will be profoundly affected after being detached from his parents; the Grahame children had now been rejected twice by their father. 'Grown-up people really ought to be more careful,' he would write decades later. 'Among themselves it may seem but a small thing to give their word and take back their word... But with those who are below them, whose little globe is swayed by them, who rush to build star-pointing alambres on their most casual word, they really ought to be more careful.'

Through it all, Ferguson held their little hands, but all Kenneth had to remember Scotland by was a tiny kilt that he cherished secretly for years. He clung to his toys for comfort: 'In moments of mental depression, nothing is quite so consoling as the honest smell of a painted animal,' he once wrote. As they took the train back down south, Granny Ingles yet again opened her door, although a few months later moved them all from The Mount after its constant maintenance became too much for her. Uncle David had married so she sold her beloved home and moved to nearby Cranbourne. Fernhill Cottage would be Kenneth's sixth home; leaving his secret Gallery and gardens of The Mount would be yet another crushing blow the poor boy had to face. 'The crude blank misery of a moment is apt to leave a dull bruise which is slow to depart, if it ever do so entirely,' he would later write.

It was at Fernhill that Kenneth became interested in literature. Alongside Helen and Willie, he took literacy and maths lessons with a tutor, and the local vicar taught him Latin. Helen remembers: 'It was at Cranbourne that Kenneth began to spout poetry, first Shakespeare, then Macaulay's *Lays*, then Tennyson.' The rest of their days were spent running through the pine trees playing soldiers, and dreaming of riding horses: '...a cream-coloured pony – it was always cream-coloured – with a long flowing tail (it always had a long flowing tail),' Kenneth would later write.

At only 7, Kenneth had learnt to mask unhappiness with politeness and became a favourite with adults, especially the domestic helpers at Fernhill. Kenneth's first biographer, Patrick Chalmers, was helped by Kenneth's wife Elsie to write *Life, Letters and Unpublished Work* in 1933, and recorded him as 'a little boy of grave and kindly courtesy, a courtesy beyond his years. He hated to give unnecessary trouble and to that end he was mindful to leave his bedroom tidy and to be as reasonable about his clothes and their neatness as could be expected.' Others remembered him as 'punctilious about brushing his teeth' and 'a reasonable boy in everything except his unbounded generosity'. Kenneth's cousin Agnes (Uncle John's daughter, whose siblings were Edward, Walter and Bessie) described Kenneth as 'a tall, good-looking boy of kind and charming disposition.' Kenneth's other cousin (Uncle Jack's boy), Reginald Ingles, writes: '[he] was the nice one, who was always kind, and who we were always delighted to see – and to go out with, who never ticked us off, and was always ready to help one in little things... Willie and Helen we did not like very much...'

He may have been a polite people-pleaser in public, yet in private Kenneth was desperately unhappy. He later wrote frankly and cathartically about his traumatic childhood: most bitterly in *Pagan Papers* and then more gently in *The Golden Age* and *Dream Days*, acknowledging the autobiographical origins of the stories. Kenneth believed his childhood was no different to 'most other boys of my own age and period, the mighty mid-Victorian'. Parents of the time were notoriously distant from their offspring, both physically and emotionally: 'I remember realising, in a quite impersonal and kindly way, the existence of that stupidity, and its tremendous influence in the world...' Kenneth reverses the idea of youth is wasted on the young: 'These elders, our betters by a trick of chance, commanded no respect, but only a certain blend of envy – of their good luck – and pity – for their inability to make use of it.' In *The Golden Age* he wrote of the anguish of childhood: 'A life... so rough... so full of pricks and jogs, and smartings.' Unfortunately for Kenneth, life was to get much, much rougher.

Chapter 3

Schooldays

'A small school-boy, new kicked out of his nest into the draughty, uncomfortable outer world, his unfledged skin still craving the feathers whereinto he was wont to nestle.'

The Fairy Wicket, essay by Kenneth Grahame

A quiet boy of 9 walked along the cobbles of the narrow New Inn Hall Street in Oxford, dressed in the St Edward's uniform of dark knickerbockers, matching jacket and single-breasted waistcoat buttoned to the neck. With dark hair smartly combed to the side and jammed under cap, intelligent eyes shyly lowered and pale cheeks flushed, Kenneth Grahame's apprehension of his first day at boarding school showed on his face.

It was at the start of the summer term in 1868 when Kenneth was sent with his brother Willie to St Edward's School in Oxford. They were two of five new boys that term. He adored his older brother, calling him 'a veritable god', and being with him on that first day at school would have helped his confidence. Three years before, *Alice's Adventures in Wonderland* had been written by the Oxford don Charles Dodgson (better known as Lewis Carroll); little did young Kenneth know as he entered the city for the first time that he, too, would become part of the great canon of children's literature. For now, he was in the thick of his own childhood and experiencing the raw emotion of being wrenched apart from the one adult who had been a constant in his young life so far: his nanny Ferguson. She was now employed with the Lidderdale family.

Kenneth was the 107th boy to be educated at 'Teddies', a school in Mackworth House, a two-storey stone-brick Queen Anne-style mansion, in the centre of Oxford. Leased by Brasenose College, the building was already 150 years old and falling apart – hence the competitive fees that allowed Uncle John to send his nephews there. Kenneth described his school as being nestled amongst 'a pleasant jumble' of buildings including a tavern, a Georgian vicarage and little two-storeyed white gabled houses. After Kenneth had been a pupil for five years, St Edward's reputation grew and numbers increased so the school moved to the larger and impressive red-brick premises in Summertown on Woodstock Road. Today it welcomes students – both female and male – with a memorial window in the chapel and a magnificent mural in the dining hall of their famous alumni Kenneth Grahame as a schoolboy, rowing on the river alongside animal characters. Kenneth was a success at school – he was head boy in his final year, a member of the debating society and in the first XV rugby team (as well as playing for the second XI cricket side). His friends remembered him as tall and good looking, a dandy dresser who was 'nobly simple' in his choice of phrase. One of his school friends shared the anecdote about when a contemporary asked Kenneth what he would wear for Gaudy Day and he replied: 'To-morrow I shall be superb.'

As for many of us, Kenneth's schooldays at St Edward's were formative in all sorts of ways; Oxford of the 1860s and 70s was under the influence of Matthew Arnold, William Morris and John Ruskin; their radical studies of nature, beauty and social order imbibed the young and impressed upon Kenneth the ideas he would grow up to believe. He famously hated trains, and always believed that nature must be preserved at all costs. Throughout his life, Kenneth wrote so little about himself that it is significant he chose his schooldays as a rare autobiographical subject. It was published after he died, in the magazine *Country Life*, and runs to more than 3,000 words, a colourful account of the city in which Kenneth spent seven years as a Victorian schoolboy. Despite decades away from it, Kenneth's indelible memory recalled every inch of St Edward's, from the 'rabbit-warrenish' dormitories to the flag-stoned floor of the pantry to the depressing gravel playground with its pathetic flower beds where the headmaster, Reverend Frederick Fryer, would hide pennies and halfpennies. The boys would have to find them in the dark: 'Pits were dug and filled with mud and water, and over them, and into them, the unsuspecting ones were lured.' Kenneth enjoyed all the high-jinks of a schoolboy, from having an illegal Guy Fawkes bonfire (which had the distinction of being stopped by both the fire service and police force) to playing cricket on Port Meadow amongst the cows. He preferred cricket to 'socker'. Unfortunately, caning was also par for the course. Rev. Fryer was succeeded by Reverend Algernon Simeon in 1870 who purchased the school outright. An immeasurable figure in the history of St Edward's, he would have been a great influence on Kenneth's life.

St Edward's boys were given considerable freedom to explore the streets of Oxford: 'before I was ten I knew all the stately buildings that clustered round the Radcliffe Library like my own pocket.' A naturalist even then, he adored sneaking into the college gardens to look at the flowers, other days exploring the atmospheric covered market, which remains today with its red gabled wooden ceiling. As an adult he wrote: 'It is still one of the pleasantest spots I know, and when I have half an hour to spare in Oxford, or when one of her too frequent showers sends me flying to cover, I love to roam its dusky and odorous corridors, gazing longingly at all the good things I am no longer permitted to eat.'

Characteristically, of his schooldays Kenneth remembered places rather than people: 'Misty recollections of friends – clear and distinct of desk, stair, cistern, room.' The one woman he did recall became a character in one of his stories: the school matron Mrs Reece would smuggle the younger boys into the kitchen to give them a sweet treat of bread and treacle (just like Martha in *The Golden Age*). Apparently she would hide a boy under a pile of dirty towels if he was at risk of being discovered by a master!

Kenneth joked that he had 'lack of care or respect for abstract schooling' and achieved only 'a painfully acquired ignorance of dead languages'. (The curriculum concentrated on Greek and Latin, with Homer, Horace, Virgil and Aurelius on the reading list.) He was, in fact, very bright and won the sixth form class prize as well as the divinity, Classics and Latin prizes that year and three other prizes during his time at the school. 'Whatever our individual gifts, a general dogged determination to shirk and to evade kept us all at much the same dead level – a level of ignorance tempered by subordination.' In hindsight, one of his teachers wrote that Kenneth showed 'no promise of the exquisite prose that was to be in later years the delight of thousands'. Yet, it was at St Edward's that Kenneth first felt the thrill of his writing in print. He wrote for the *Chronicle* school magazine – mostly anonymously, except for a prize-winning entry on competition, published in 1873: 'one of the most difficult things in the world is to feel kindly towards a rival.' As an adult he remembered his delight at being recognised for his writing: 'that far-away glow (mingled with self-satisfaction) which I used to feel when I won a prize at school.'

The River Cherwell running through Oxford left a lasting impression on Kenneth and he wrote a love letter to the city:

The two influences which most soaked into me there, and have remained with me ever since, were the good grey Gothic [architecture] on the one hand, and, on the other, the cool secluded reaches of the Thames – the 'Stripling Thames', remote and dragon-fly haunted, before it attains to the noise, ribbons and flannels of Folly Bridge... But these elements, the classics, the Gothic, the primeval Thames, fostered in me, perhaps, the pagan germ that would have mightily shocked the author of *The Sabbath*.

The author of that book was James Grahame, Kenneth's ancestor. The 'pagan germ' would eventually become his novel *Pagan Papers* and spread to the character of Pan in *The Wind in the Willows*.

In that gracious grey old city of our abiding, well-watered, of pleasant approach by bridge that bestrode the brimfull river or causeway through standing water lily-starred, grey straying side-streets looped or nestled all along the four noble thoroughfares rich in tower and steeple – the home of restless jackdaws forth-issuing day-long; the organ-mouth of bell-music vocal through daylight most passionately appealing at the quiet close of evening.

Kenneth saw the city from a boat, as he would canoe to Osney Lock amongst 'lush meadow-grass, wet orchards, warm, insect-haunted ponds... browsing cattle... haymaking, and... farm-buildings', describing the locks: 'let the old gates swing, work the groaning winches, and hear the water lap and suck and gurgle as it slowly sinks or rises.' In *The Wind in the Willows*, he describes the river as 'this sleek, sinuous, full-bodied animal, chasing and chuckling, gripping things with a gurgle and leaving them with a laugh... glints and gleams and sparkles, rustle and swirl, chatter and bubble.'

Kenneth's lifelong fascination with the circus was ignited at Oxford during his impressionable school years. It was in his second year that he experienced the fair: 'The first show of any importance that I ever attended – I was 10 years old at the time – was St Giles's Fair at Oxford, and I seem to recollect that giants, dwarfs, fat ladies, mermaids, six-legged calves and the distorted nature of every variety formed the background of the show,' he wrote. Kenneth didn't have enough money to see the sideshows close up but instead had to guess at the detail: he suggests that what he imagines is more powerful and satisfying than the truth of what was really behind the circus magic. Towards the end of his career, he wrote the introduction to the famous circus man George Sanger's autobiography *Seventy Years a Showman*.

Kenneth had a sad end to his schooldays in his penultimate year when his beloved elder brother Willie died from pneumonia (a weak chest was an unfortunate family affliction). Willie had left St Edward's in the Lent term of 1871 because of recurrent bronchitis, and in 1874 at Christmas went down with severe pneumonia. Kenneth was at home for the holidays and tragically witnessed his brother's demise; despite comprehensive medical intervention, the 16-year-old died on New Year's Eve and was laid to rest with his grandfather at Highgate Cemetery in London. Kenneth had now lost his mother, effectively his father, and now Willie. Even his nurse, Ferguson, had left the family.

The following year Kenneth turned 17; now a young man on the brink of leaving school, his ambition was to stay in Oxford and study at the university. He could not bear to leave the city, bewitched as he was by its beauty and rivers and inspired to become an academic. 'Take the Adventure, heed the call, now ere the irrevocable moment passes! 'Tis but a banging of the door behind you, a blithesome step forward, and you are out of the old life and into the new!' he would write in *The Wind in the Willows*. Yet, like both Rat and Mole, Kenneth's dreams were never realised. Uncle John refused to provide the funds for a university career. John was a partner in a firm of parliamentary agents, solicitors who were paid to draft, promote or oppose private bills. This prestigious position brought a regular income, so it is probable that Uncle John had the means of paying for Kenneth to go to university. Yet he refused out of principle, despite Kenneth's pleading. The Grahames were men who had always worked in conservative jobs as lawyers and accountants. What place was an academic in the family?

Kenneth's aspiration had been cruelly trodden on; his family had failed to validate his need to follow a career of his own choosing and not being given a chance to earn a degree would be something that would affect him for the rest of his life. Although he admitted he had no care or respect for abstract scholarship in itself... this was of some importance to me, as it turned out, because I had to depend on my wits for my living. But the consequence was, that I... had to go away with less of an education than we had a reasonable right to expect... never a year has passed since those far-off days – I might even say never a month – that I have not deeply and bitterly regretted it.

The piece he wrote about his first impression of the Oxford colleges as a schoolboy has more than a touch of *Jude the Obscure* about it, written by Kenneth's contemporary Thomas Hardy. As for Jude, those hallowed institutions of learning would forever remain closed to Kenneth, literally and figuratively: 'those great and lofty double gates, sternly barred and never open invitingly, what could they portend?' He emphasises the point: 'the barred windows, the massive, bolted and enormous gates, which every college had, which were never used or opened...' Although of Oxford's exclusivity he says he has 'nothing to complain of personally', it is evident he always felt disappointed not to have been included:

Among the blend of qualities that go to make up the charm of collegiate life, there was then more than a touch of (shall I say?) exclusiveness and arrogance. No one thought the worse of it on that account: still its presence was felt, and the gates stood to typify it. Of course, one would not dream of suggesting that the arrogance may still be there. But the gates remain.

With the taste of disappointment in his mouth and sorrow in his heart, Kenneth walked away from Oxford 'and the school that faces the Berkshire hills'. He left with nothing but a knotted string purse that he made for his sister Helen, who kept it for sixty years. Kenneth was bound for London, but he had little hope the streets were paved with gold.

Chapter 4

Forced Downstream

'Life may be said to be composed of things that come off and things
that don't come off.'

Dream Days

When he was just 17, two women changed the course of
Kenneth's life. Granny Ingles was powerless to influence
her son John over Kenneth's wish to go up to Oxford but
nevertheless did her best to give Kenneth the best start in the world of
work. She had remained in touch with Ferguson, the Grahames' nurse,
who had gone to work with the Lidderdale family. William Lidderdale,
Ferguson's new boss, was a director at the Bank of England. Granny
Ingles took it upon herself to put in a good word for Kenneth during one
of her visits to Ferguson, and it was arranged that Kenneth's name was
put on the two-year waiting list to take the entrance exam for gentleman
clerks at the Bank of England.

In the meantime, Uncle John organised for Kenneth to work for him in
a clerical role at his Westminster office. Another of Granny Ingles' sons,
Robert, offered Kenneth accommodation in London at Draycott Lodge
in Fulham; Uncle Robert was a merchant who worked in Manila.

And so it was that instead of starting as a student at Oxford, Kenneth
left his beloved rural Cranbourne and moved to London. 'All pasts are
hateful – one or two distinctly more hateful than others,' Kenneth wrote
in 1921. He aggressively described, as a metaphor, a funeral of his boyhood
aspirations, as they morph into corpses and are buried in front of him,
gone for good: 'Old hopes all of them, some pathetically deformed, others
of comelier build and hide and hue... I watch the vanguard pass, and
without a sigh; schoolboy hopes these, comically misshapen, tawdry and
crude in colour – let the pit receive them, and a good riddance!' Kenneth
reveals his internal dilemma over wanting to hold on to his dreams yet
being forced to let them go:

But those poor little corpses at their heel ... Who left these stout young fledglings to perish? Starvation and neglect are ugly words, in truth. Is it even now too late? With downcast faces the bearers pace on, and the chalk-pit engulfs their burdens one by one.

Let them go. Who cares?

He goes on to say such dreams would not have made a difference to his life: 'I should only have found myself where I am now,' he says. 'Achievement ever includes defeat: at best, and the grapes are sour; and the hopes are dead...' As the funeral comes to a close, he desperately attempts to hold on to one particularly precious wish: 'Not that one! Let me keep that just a little longer! Surely it cannot be dead? Only yesterday I nursed its failing little frame awhile. Take all the others, only leave me that! In vain. It will be easier, now that they are really buried all.'[1]

This powerful piece of writing reveals Kenneth's very real cycle of raw disappointment, short-lived attempt at anger and, ultimately, powerless acceptance. It was a cycle that would repeat itself throughout his life after other catastrophic events. By not having loving parents or caregivers to help him cope, he lacked the emotional strength to cope with the path his life was being forced down.

Thus Kenneth buried his hopes and moved to London; screwing up his courage he left familial comfort for the capital, becoming a 'paleface quilldriver' and joining the Victorian masses in his top hat, black silk suit, rolled-up newspaper and folded umbrella. He coped with becoming part of this new, strange world by retreating into his imagination. An early record of his initial impression of 'this great whirling London mill' with its 'clatter and roar' was to turn his eyes heavenward to escape from the urban. He wrote: 'Do but give a glance up, and you are whirled away from the roaring city as though it had never been.' His description of London through a picture being made by a chalk-painter is littered with references to water and nature, showing that while Kenneth's body was in the city, his heart and mind remained in the country. It is significant he sets the piece in early spring, his favourite season. Kenneth uses the image of mushroom spawn to describe the London Underground; elsewhere he notices the colour of the sky matches that of a hedge sparrow's egg. With relish he writes of how pigeons 'flash and circle, joyous as if they sped their morris over some remote little farmstead, lapped round by quiet hills; and as they stoop and tumble, the sunlight falls off their wings in glancing drops of opal sheen.'

Kenneth's nature-fantasy becomes confused with reality through the 'magician' chalk-painter as the city transfigures into an impressionist drawing: 'The golden afternoon wears on; and the London haze, by this time, enveloping, mellows every crudity and sharp edge with an illusion of its own. Through the park-railings one can catch, here and there, vistas of warm dim distance, broken by sparkle of water...' More water imagery is seen when Kenneth likens hansom cabs to great ocean liners.

The piece ends with the overriding sentiment that even an artist, permitted to follow the creative passion repressed in Kenneth, must make a living in London, as the chalk-painter 'cheerfully' inscribes his work with 'I do it for my daily bread'. There is a hint that alcohol helps to make life bearable: 'all that is artistic in him shall blossom and expand to the soothing smell of sawdust and of gin.' Kenneth was mindful that his place in London was to work to pay back Uncle John. He appreciated his was a situation familiar to many Londoners, and, like the screever, resolved to bear it cheerfully.[2] He worked as hard as he could for Uncle John, who admired his 'pluck and steadiness' – that is until his nephew became interested in the gentleman politics of Disraeli, began to learn shorthand and made noises about becoming a political journalist.

Yet again, John dissuaded poor Kenneth from following what he was really interested in, encouraging him instead to pursue more wholesome extracurriculars such as joining the London Scottish, a volunteer regiment of the British army. And yet again, Kenneth threw himself into what was asked of him, repressing his own desires to instead practise drills, boxing and fencing. Like many young people who move to a city, a hobby outside work brought rewards of a new social life and new friends, and he discovered he loved his regiment with its grey kilt, bonnet, pipes and drums. Characteristically, he worked as hard as he could to excel, becoming a first-class drill and was made a sergeant, finding himself on duty for Queen Victoria's Jubilee day (a decade or so later in 1887). On another occasion, while on exercise with the Scottish in a London park he was delighted to come across his old nurse Ferguson, who happened to be taking Evelyn Lidderdale and her sister out for a walk in the pram with another nanny. Kenneth ordered a complimentary charge to be made by his men, and the platoon flourished its muskets, cheered and leapt forward towards the excited little girls. Poor Ferguson was so shocked she cried out in horror that Kenneth had 'gone gyte' (lost his senses). 'Mighty me, I must save the young leddies,' she worried as the pram ('rickmatick') tipped over the low railing and the soldiers 'picked up its contents who were more enchanted than ever'.[3]

Kenneth became committed to voluntary work at the East End's newly opened Toynbee Hall in Stepney. As the world's first university settlement house, it was set up as a hub for social reform and research where students from Oxford and Cambridge could lodge and work as volunteers to properly understand poverty and explore ways to solve it. It was a cause Kenneth would be associated with for years, even when he gained literary fame; he fenced, boxed and played billiards with the locals, as well as organising sing-songs and leading the sentimental numbers – despite being a shy person. He was soon roped in to all sorts of charity events, from readings and talks to a guest lecture on literature for a class of underprivileged girls. Apparently the girls went wild for the bashful, handsome bachelor and stood on chairs and tables to kiss him and sing to him!

Kenneth's home life was happy during these early months in London. He lived with his Uncle Robert, his Aunt Georgina and their only child, Cousin Annie. She was about the same age as Kenneth and his first female friend (aside from his sister, Helen). He built a close relationship with her and they remained friends for the rest of their lives. She helped him settle into the great roaring capital, showing him walks along the Thames and the tourist hub of Hampton Court. They shared a love of literature and art, encouraged by Annie's mother, Georgina, the author of *In a Tuscan Garden* about a summer in Florence (which references Kenneth). Unlike Uncle John, who dissuaded Kenneth from becoming interested in the creative world, Annie and Aunt Georgina introduced him to the London arts scene, of William Blake, JMW Turner and William Powell Frith, and he basked in enjoyment of long afternoons at the National Gallery where he would gaze at a small painting of St Catherine by the Italian Renaissance master Pinturicchio, admitting it 'possessed my undivided affections'. The painting was hung very low so Kenneth would kneel on the floor before it to see it properly. He fell in love with the grand masters of Italy, such as Fra Angelico and Filippo Lippi. How wonderful it must have felt to finally be able to spend time doing something he was really interested in.

By the end of his first year in London, Kenneth had assimilated himself into city life. He loved dining in the exotic Italian eateries in Soho on his way home from work (weekly, when he could afford it), inspiring his lifelong love affair with Italy. Eating one evening in a restaurant, Kenneth could not help laughing at the joke of a fellow diner. The man introduced himself as Dr Frederick James Furnivall, and the die was cast for a friendship that would prove to be life-changing for both men. Kenneth, although steadfastly conventional, was always drawn to eccentric people. In his fifties, Furnivall was an extraordinary man. The instigator of the New English Dictionary and an expert in medieval literature, he was responsible for the revival in interest of Chaucer as well as Shakespeare. Passionate about social justice, he founded the Working Men's College in London and set up the National Amateur Rowing Association to make the sport accessible to women and working men. A vegetarian, he drank river water for health benefits (although never learnt to swim) and up until he died at age 85 would row 12.5 miles up the Thames every Sunday. Some believe that Kenneth based the character of Ratty in *The Wind in the Willows* on Furnivall. They both loved boating together along the Thames at Richmond, picnicking on cold gooseberry fool and singing the *Twickenham Ferry* song. Furnivall introduced Kenneth, and his cousin, Annie, to the New Shakespeare Society (which he had founded) in the summer of 1877. It is recorded in the June minutes of the meeting at University College that they are welcomed as new members. Literary figures of the day who belonged to the society included Robert Browning (the senior vice president) and Algernon Charles Swinburne.

Denied an academic education, Kenneth lapped up the literary nourishment. In fact, he was inspired to put his own thoughts down on paper. One of his early verses goes:

> Try we life-long, we can never
> Straighten out life's tangled skein,
> Why should we, in vain endeavour,
> Guess and guess and guess again?
> Life's a pudding full of plums,
> Care's a canker that benumbs.
> Wherefore waste our elocution

On impossible solution?
Life's a pleasant institution,
Let us take it as it comes![4]

It would prove to be wise words for what was to come; an opening had finally come up for Kenneth to take the entrance exam for the Bank of England.

Chapter 5

From Bank to Bank

'To know what you would like to do is one thing. To go out boldly and do it is another – and rarer.'

Kenneth Grahame

The thick yellow fog hung low in the heart of the city of London on the first day of 1879. Uniformed porters in frock coats held up their black iron lanterns to peer through the dense air outside the Bank of England on Threadneedle Street. It was the first day back at work after the festivities of the Christmas period, which, before the holidays, had seen gentlemen clerks get drunk at their desks, sing, and throw passbooks through the air for amusement.

A tall, well-dressed young man carefully made his way through the fog to arrive at ten o' clock; the weather had made the 3½-mile journey on foot take ninety minutes. 'You won't find anyone in yet,' sniffed one of the porters to Kenneth Grahame. 'The clerks get an extra hour in bed when it's foggy.' Undeterred, the 19-year-old walked purposefully through those famous doors; he was starting the new year with a new job at the most prestigious institution in the British Isles. His prospects were high because of his impressive 518 marks out of 640 in the notoriously challenging entrance exam.

Neatly recorded in ink for posterity in the Bank of England's archives is the first mention of its newest employee: 'Kenneth Grahame. Address: 3 York Street, Portman Square. Age 19. Will live with a friend. Religion: Church of England. Single. Educated at St Edward's School, Oxford, seven years. Left school in 1875. Employment for the past 2½ years.'

His mark for each discipline in the exam is recorded; handwriting 140 marks out of 200; orthography 95 out of 100; geography 60 out of 80. His marks for English were better than his arithmetic! English composition: 95 out of 100; arithmetic: 128 marks out of 160. His results found him noted as 'no.1 in place in election'.

Gentlemen clerks in Victorian times were not nearly as conservative as you might expect; many were wealthy and had no material need to work. Even the most well behaved had nicknames such as The Ghost or The Dead Horse, and would start late, have a long lunch at the local chop house followed by a nap at the desk or errands such as shopping. (It was perfectly acceptable to bring in meat from Billingsgate market, carcass and all.) There was even a Bank cat to entertain and stroke. The place was purely a boys' club; it would be another fifteen years before women began to work there.

Life at the Bank wasn't the academic career Kenneth had dreamed of leading, but he made the best of it, and remained committed to his work for almost thirty years. 'To know what you would like to do is one thing. To go out boldly and do it is another – and rarer,' he once wrote. Without a degree, many doors were closed. Kenneth's cousin Annie summed up Kenneth's dilemma when she said:

> We were very sorry for him as his work at the Bank was evidently uncongenial and unsuitable for him with his very decided taste for literature. I've always thought it splendid of him to stick to his work at the Bank as he did… and also manage to make a name for himself in literature which was his real vocation. And I often hold him up as an example of what can be done by sheer hard work and determination to overcome every obstacle.

Kenneth told Annie that 'any experience is worth having' and 'I would think it is worthwhile to go to Hell for the sake of the experience.'

Annie and Kenneth were growing closer; they began holidaying together when Uncle Robert and Aunt Georgina hired an idyllic house in Italy, overlooking Florence, with a stunning garden of fir and lemon trees, lilies, roses and jasmine. Twenty-something Kenneth was captivated by the Tuscan scenery and the romance of it all might have encouraged him to develop feelings for Annie. They strolled through the countryside together for a day, just the two of them, stopping to watch a village festival. Annie used the word 'beguiled' to describe how she felt as Kenneth told her fairy stories on the walk back to the farmhouse. Afterwards, he bought a souvenir to remember the enchanting moment, a plaque of the Virgin Mary with baby Jesus, which he hung on the outside wall of his London home when he eventually moved into his own place.

On paper, at least, Annie and Kenneth were a good match. A similar age, they began to travel regularly with each other, to Scotland as well as Italy, and they both loved poetry and literature. They spent hours discussing authors at the New Shakespeare Society. 'I had been reared on old Scotch ballads and stories and folk lore which appealed to Kenneth a lot and later on at any rate formed a bond of union between us,' recalled Annie in 1933. There has been speculation that she was Kenneth's first girlfriend; Annie never married, and it was clear they were close from her fond recollections of her cousin after his death. Perhaps Kenneth had a bond with her that he didn't have with his siblings, and Annie regarded him as a brother figure. Or perhaps it was something more. In 1892, shortly after Valentine's Day, he published a love poem in the *National Observer*, and the first verse runs:

> Cupid sounds the call to arms!
> And at once the Loves, upspringing,
> Hither running, hither winging,
> Snatching bow and catching quiver,
> Come a chattering, sparkling river,
> Like the hiving bee in swarms,
> All the merry call to arms!

Characteristically, Kenneth uses water imagery to evoke a host of cupids flowing downstream. The poem hints that he has fallen in love but his feelings aren't at first reciprocated. We can only speculate about whom it is written (if anyone at all). When in 1933 Annie wrote to Kenneth's widow Elsie to share her memories of Kenneth, she describes him as a man of few words: 'His work at the Bank can't have left him much time for society in the ordinary sense and I don't think he cared for it… I don't think Kenneth was talkative – but his talk was interesting.'

Annie and Kenneth's close friendship continued after he moved from her family home; he visited her and his aunt and uncle each month after he left Draycott Lodge for Bloomsbury Street, closer to the city, where he flat-shared with his younger brother Roland when he too started working at the Bank of England. Kenneth paid 25 shillings for a bedroom and sitting room (where Roland slept), receiving 'sumptuous' cooked meals from his landlady.[1] He would dutifully visit his other uncle, John, on Sundays, as recalled by his cousin Agnes, who was a little girl in those days. She described him as tall and kind to us children and nice to look at... we were always glad, all of us, to see his face at the door... it was a pleasure to see him come into the room, he looked so happy and pleasant. He was neither too talkative nor too reserved... I have never heard him talk about himself.

Kenneth's extreme politeness was a mask to hide from his own feelings and had become a personality trait that others noticed, including his boss's daughter, Evelyn Lidderdale. She remembered him as:

Very silent unless you got him to yourself and encouraged him to talk. Then he spoke most entertainingly and was a delightful and witty companion. He never spoke of himself but he was always so kind and so interested in writing and Kenneth was most helpful and encouraging and, I do believe, happier even than I was when an essay of mine gained first prize.

A logical, practical, sanguine man, he felt some degree of pride knowing that he was honouring his uncle, fulfilling duty and carrying out what was expected of him. After all, the world of finance was familiar to Kenneth (his ancestors back in Scotland had been bankers); for a stoic introvert who regarded himself as a 'spring not a pump', an alternative career as a scholar or writer was the luxury of a gentleman rather than a way for an honest man to make a living. As Kenneth once wrote: 'if all he was good for was to pay and take payments at least he recognised the fact, accepted it, boldly built thereon and went for it in its best shape.' This developed into an acceptance of his fate and even an embrace of it: 'If we are perfectly honest with ourselves we must admit that we always do the thing that we really like doing, for the sake of the doing itself.' After he retired, he was asked to write about his experiences at the Bank. 'Nothin' Doin' about B. of E. Much too dull a subject,' he wrote firmly in reply to his agent's request.

Kenneth's great friend, Arthur Quiller-Couch, explained Kenneth's stoicism:

[he] knew much of practical affairs and could judge them incisively if with amusement, while his own mind kept its loyalty to sweet thoughts, great manners, and a quiet disdain for anything meaner

than these. I must remember him as a 'classical' man, perfectly aware of himself as 'at best a noble plaything of the gods', whose will he seemed to understand through his gift of interpreting childhood.

Oxford remained always in Kenneth's thoughts, and as a young clerk he would spend his precious day off visiting his old school where his cousin, Reginald Ingles, had begun in 1877, shortly after Kenneth left. Reginald, a rugby player at school, recalls his older cousin very kindly:

> You know how pleased a boy is when some relation comes to see him at school – and very few ever came to see me? I was delighted to see K. and I thought him such a nice, kind sort to come and such a nice-looking chap. He played in a cricket match for a bit. I remember it quite well. He stood at the wicket with his bat up in the air – not on the ground (some cricketers did in those days) – and put up a good innings and hit some fine slogs. He was most awfully nice to me.

When Reginald left school at 16, he saw more of his cousin after he moved back to London with his parents. He'd spend the evening with his Kenneth and Roland in Bloomsbury Street:

> I remember their sitting-room well. Kenneth was always so kind when I went there. After dinner they smoked Honey Dew tobacco and nice briar pipes. And Kenneth made coffee. He was particular about coffee and he used to grind the beans and put the coffee in a brown earthenware coffee-pot with an earthenware strainer. It was good coffee that Kenneth made. Both he and Roland were very moderate drinkers, but sometimes we had a glass of hot whisky-and-water before I went home. Kenneth always treated me just as an equal though I know now that I was rather young and foolish. We used to talk a lot and discuss the ordinary topics that young fellows do discuss. And once Kenneth took me to dine at a small Italian restaurant in Soho and we had about ten courses for 1s. 6d. and drank Chianti out of a basket bottle and, afterwards, he took me to the Lyceum to see Faust. It was decent of him. And, once at Bloomsbury Street, I remember Kenneth lending me a long churchwarden clay pipe with red sealing-wax on the stem. It was one of his treasures

– that churchwarden. But I unfortunately broke the bowl off by tapping it on the fire-grate to knock the ash out. Kenneth, although he looked just slightly annoyed, was awfully nice about it and said that it did not matter a bit. But he was always like that.

As a young bachelor, Kenneth began retreating to the countryside at weekends, where he found nature a balm from his hectic city life, offering: 'peace, seclusion, a sweet-breathed wind, couch of bracken, swaying shelter of beechen green. Here might one lie and doze, and muse, and doze again, the most contented animal under the sun, the whole long, lazy afternoon,' he once wrote. Away from the polluted waters of the capital, the pull of the Thames attracted him; he would row with a single paddle between his former homes of Cookham Dean and Cranbourne, and even as far as Blewbury (near Didcot, where he would eventually live). Kenneth would make a weekend of it in Berkshire, staying the night in a rough-and-ready pub room, savouring his pipe and good dinner; the simple pleasures he always treasured. His banking friend Sidney Ward would sometimes join Kenneth, and here he describes one of their adventures:

A friend had lent him a fourteenth-century cottage in the main street [in Streatley], and we had a grand twenty-mile walk along the Ridgeway, the subject of his *Romance of the Road*. If we either of us said clever things that day they are forgotten, but we came home happy and tired, bought some chops and fetched a huge jug of beer from the pub. We cooked our dinner over the open wood fire, and how good the chops were! Then great chunks of cheese, new bread, great swills of beer, pipes, bed, and heavenly sleep!

Ward's description of these pleasures could have been lifted from *The Wind in the Willows*.

Essential for Kenneth's mental health, these weekends away also fuelled his creative side, and he got into the habit of recording his thoughts about nature and his life at the Bank. Brazenly, he did this in a small red ledger book from work, usually used to record checks and balances. Hastily writing in shorthand, he scribbled down quotes, anecdotes, prose and poetry; very sadly the book has since been lost, although Kenneth's first biographer Patrick Chalmers was fortunate enough to see it. Lacking in confidence at first, Kenneth carefully copied out the words of writers he admired; the first page was filled with a poem by Matthew Arnold:

> In the huge world, that roars hard by,
> Be others happy if they can!
> But in my helpless cradle I
> Was breathed on by the rural Pan!

'Life's a jumble and a maze/Where we trip and blunder ever', later lines profess. As Kenneth sorted out his jumbled thoughts, he began to jot down his own verses and observations and these bank ledger notes collectively formed a microcosm from which all of Kenneth's writing would follow – the major themes of his books and essays, his dry sense of humour, his unmistakable voice that at once drips with sad, tender poignancy and at other times is wryly, drily humorous. Much of what he wrote was about nature. More than once he sets his story on water and a particular theme is being contended after doing one's best. Another issue discussed is one that would become central to *The Wind in the Willows:* male friendship. He lays down the different sorts of friends we make through life, and asks whether those who pass away before us will always be made the saintliest sort of companions while familiarity breeds contempt. He thinks of his schoolmates: 'The friends of our youth, nearer then than brothers, one in sympathy... Because of the very height of the ideals we shared together, we cannot face them yet, while not one solid step has been made...'

To his colleagues, Kenneth Grahame was a quiet loner who worked dutifully at his desk and kept himself to himself. A former workmate who knew him throughout his career describes him: 'a shy, reserved man, with a fine presence and charm of manner, who did not fit in with my pre-conceived notions of a bank official.' The colleague recollects many small kindnesses Kenneth showed him, including advice on punctuation and the construction of sentences! Yet although he knew Kenneth for many years: 'I had no idea that he was then engaged in writing the books which would gain for him a world-wide reputation.'

In his own quiet, discreet way, Kenneth had begun to follow his dream of becoming a writer: 'To him who is destined to arrive, the fates never fail to afford, on the way, their small encouragements,' he wrote. And his literary talent was certainly about to be encouraged: Kenneth was to become a man of letters as well as numbers.

Chapter 6

The Familiar and the Friendly

'It was good to think he had this to come back to, this place which was all his own, these things which were so glad to see him again and could always be counted upon for the same simple welcome.'

The Wind in the Willows

Kenneth was put in mind of Lizard Lighthouse in Cornwall, as he climbed the winding staircase to the top-floor flat. He caught his breath as the estate agent turned the key in the front door. As he was ushered in, Kenneth's eyes were drawn to the window in the sitting room. As he gazed out on to the sinuous grey-blue Thames with the green of Battersea Park beyond, he knew he had found his own home at last.

Now in his early twenties and established at the Bank, Kenneth was blossoming into bachelorhood. He had grown a neat moustache, wore a flower in his buttonhole and took pride in dressing well (he always looked immaculate, even as an older man). Standing at more than 6 feet, he is described by a friend around this time as a 'fine looking young man… broad, and well proportioned – carried himself well – a good healthy complexion, large widely opened rather light grey eyes, always with a kindly expression in them.'[1] Kenneth carried himself with a young sort of dignity that was ready to become independent from his brother-come-housemate, Roland. Around 1882, he spread his wings away from Bloomsbury Street and found himself once more attracted to the Thames, moving into a single bachelor flat which was a compact rooftop apartment on Chelsea Embankment; 65 Chelsea Gardens would be a glorious experiment in freedom and independence and his home for more than a decade. It was geographically and culturally a world away from Threadneedle Street, as Chelsea was an enclave for the bohemian and the artistic. Kenneth had a delightful commute to work via ferry steamer and enjoyed getting up early for a morning stroll, describing how he 'got up at 6, and went a delightful walk by the river before breakfast.'

Home is important to us all but particularly so to an orphan. For the first time in his life, Kenneth had a private space to call his own in which to gather personal possessions. He would later write about the special significance of home in *The Wind in the Willows*: 'A certain little room very dear and familiar... a sense of snugness, of cushioned comfort, of home-coming... All was modest – O, so very modest! But all was my very own, and, what was more, everything in that room was exactly right.' Home is a recurring theme in the novel; Mole doesn't realise he misses home until he comes across it by accident, and later Rat is offered the chance to leave home but decides not to. Badger doesn't like being disturbed at home, and Toad takes his Hall for granted until it is overrun by weasels and his friends prove their loyalty by risking their lives to save it.

Children are comforted by familiar places and the toys that they know; for a boy who left Scotland with nothing but a tartan kilt and rubber ball, Kenneth cherished his small roof-top corner of London overlooking the river. With the help of Aunt Georgina and Cousin Annie, he enjoyed furnishing it with objects of beauty and significance, and began collecting toys – as an adult he would have many more than as a child. Annie said of her cousin: 'He had very good taste and a great appreciation of beautiful things.' His rooms were filled with books and pictures. Kenneth's favourite spot was by the sitting room window, where he positioned a gate-legged tea table. There he would linger, relishing the magnificent view of the Thames and Battersea Park.

Kenneth loved entertaining his friends, cousins and colleagues on the roof of Chelsea Gardens, and it wasn't long before he invited his sister Helen for tea. She brought her friend Mary: 'He opened the door and my first impression was of relief. For he was just as I would have had him be. He was fine looking... his grey eyes were rather widely open and his expression was one of the most kindly... The Scotch adjective "kenspeckle" [conspicuous] describes him better than any other, I think.' Kenneth delighted in sharing with the girls some of the knick-knacks he had collected, such as woodcuts, etchings and books from unusual shops. He had begun to travel to Cornwall and always brought home a hollow glass rolling pin that sailors gave to their sweethearts. 'He showed these to us, holding them very lovingly,' remembers Mary of the romantic tokens. Kenneth sounds just like Mole, when he finds himself modestly showing Rat his treasured domestic possessions:

Mole… related… somewhat shyly at first, but with more freedom as he warmed to his subject – how this was planned, and how that was thought out, and how this was got through a windfall from an aunt, and that was a wonderful find and a bargain, and this other thing was bought out of laborious savings and a certain amount of 'going without'.

Mary remembers:

He had a Chippendale bureau of which he was very proud. He had bought it as a bargain and it had, he said, belonged to the great Duke of Wellington. I said, 'What fun if you found a secret drawer in it containing dispositions and dispatches?' He beamed like a regular boy. 'What a jolly idea!' he said, and then his face fell and he added, 'Alas, if one may believe gossip, the drawer would be more likely to contain billets-doux and love-letters.' 'But, Mr. Grahame,' said I, 'possibly love-letters might be more interesting than dispatches?' 'Very likely,' said he, 'but neither I, nor I hope, anyone else, would think it right to read them.'

Kenneth had found the bureau on the Portobello Road and within it hid his treasures including seashells, miniature fishing nets, Maundy Money, the rules of roulette and a prayer card featuring the Old Testament tale of Tobias and the Angel. He later published a story about it, called *The Secret Drawer*.

Mary would never forget that tea party, and Kenneth left a lasting impression on her. She laughed when she remembered how his size was out of proportion with his surroundings: 'But, oh, he was altogether too big for his little flat!'[2] In 1894, Kenneth outgrew his Chelsea digs and went in search of a larger place with a housekeeper to cook and clean for him. For a man in his twenties, buying a property at the smart address of 5 Kensington Crescent was beyond his means so Kenneth 'went halves' with a friend, Tom Greg, a freelance writer for the *Pall Mall Gazette* and the *National Observer*. Greg brought with him his family housekeeper, Sarah Bath from Somerset (where else?), a capable, hardworking and charismatic woman who used to fend off the local Italians who performed religious devotions under the drawing room window (where Kenneth had affixed the souvenir he had bought with Annie from Tuscany, the blue and white plaque of the Madonna and child). Sarah Bath had been on holiday to Italy so she appreciated the religious significance but still refused alms to the performers! (Later, Kenneth included an Italian symbol in *The Wind in the Willows*, when outside Mole End its owner decorates the front garden with plaster statues.)

When Tom Greg married and left Kensington Crescent, a new male housemate moved in, Gregory Smith, who described Kenneth's home as 'very comfortable'. Sarah Bath stayed on with Kenneth. As an adult he had finally satisfied his core need for a stable home, which had been unmet during his peripatetic and tragic childhood. He wrote in *The Wind in the Willows* how Mole appreciates his burrow: 'He saw clearly... how much it all meant to him, and the special value of some such anchorage in one's existence ... this place which was all his own, these things which were so glad to see him again and could always be counted upon for the same simple welcome.'

As much as he loved his little corner of London, Kenneth adored travelling, especially to Cornwall. He first visited at the advice of a doctor, who said the fresh air would help him recover from being unwell. Kenneth's sister Helen, who had become a hospital nurse, accompanied him in 1884. It takes a special kind of person to become a nurse, and Helen had developed into a practical and capable young woman, who was nevertheless somewhat awkward, according to Kenneth. They stayed in a cottage on the Lizard peninsula, which belonged to their mutual friend Mary Richardson. Cornwall may be situated at the opposite end of the country from Scotland where Kenneth had first seen the sea, but the two places held many of the same charms for him – both dominated by water, they were largely unspoilt in those days without railways or a road network.

Cornwall changed Kenneth. From that very first visit he fell in love with 'the sea and the boats' and could not get them out of his head when he was back behind his desk in London. After that first holiday, little did Kenneth understand the extent of Cornwall's power over him: the place inspired some of his best writing, it was where he became engaged and married, and it was where he met two of his greatest male friends.

Chapter 7

A Man of Letters

'It's quite a long time since you did any poetry,' he [the Mole] remarked. 'You might have a try at it this evening – instead of, well, brooding over things so much. I've an idea that you'll feel a lot better when you've got something jotted down – if it's only just the rhymes.'

The Wind in the Willows

In 1887, Kenneth finally plucked up the courage to make something of the secret doodles in his red bank ledger, and took into his confidence Furnivall, his friend and literary expert. Furnivall was encouraging, asking to read Kenneth's prose as well as poetry, before advising him to concentrate on the former. It is ironic, really, that Kenneth should forever after have confined himself to prose when his writing has such a beautifully unique lyrical quality. Nevertheless, Kenneth began to submit to periodicals his short stories, essays and narrative features, admitting that he was unsuccessful at first: 'five out of six of my little meteorites came back to me,' he later reflected. In the Bodleian Library in Oxford, one of Kenneth's rejection letters of 1887 can be found:

Dear sir,
    Your little paper is too short & slight for the *Cornhill*, but the humour it exhibits has struck me as being exceptional, and leads me to hope that I may again hear from you.
                                    Yours sincerely
                                    James Payn

Encouraged by the editor's comment about his exceptional humour, Kenneth didn't give up. One of the rules of writing is to write about what you know, so it is probably unsurprising that Kenneth's first published piece is about a passion he had all his life: the Berkshire countryside. The 1,800-word essay about death and winter, *By a Northern Furrow,* was first seen in print in December 1888 in the London periodical the *St. James's Gazette*. His father had died the previous year. '...the old Pan still pipes to us at Mapledurham or in Hurley backwater,' he wrote. That symbol again, Pan: the demi-god of Greek mythology who protects wild nature – his name means 'to pasture' in ancient Greek. Pan was Kenneth's talisman, an idol who featured consistently in his thoughts; it is significant Kenneth referenced Pan in this, the first piece of writing he had published, and again in his last significant piece of prose twenty years later, *The Wind in the Willows*, which has a chapter devoted to the god.

Pan brought him luck and this first clipping was the encouragement Kenneth needed to kick-start his confidence; at around the same time, he wrote to the most famous editor of the time, William Ernest Henley, who sat at the helm of the weekly *National Observer*. Henley replied to Kenneth's submission of *The Rural Pan*, requesting a meeting at his office. Perhaps Kenneth, who grew up not far from the Berkshire waterside town of Henley, thought the editor's name was a fortunate coincidence.

Henley (1849–1903) was a poet most famous for his powerful verse *Invictus*, with its inspirational line: 'I am the master of my fate/I am the captain of my soul.' As a man who was powerless over his own destiny, this would have touched a raw nerve in Kenneth. Henley had written the poem after losing his leg to tuberculosis and became one of the most important editors of the day, nurturing the careers of Thomas Hardy, George Bernard Shaw, H.G. Wells, James Barrie, W.B. Yeats and Rudyard Kipling, as well as the artists James McNeill Whistler and Auguste Rodin. Known amongst his young writers for being a 'benevolent bully', he was a close friend of Robert Louis Stevenson who based his character Long John Silver in *Treasure Island* on him. (Stevenson was one of Kenneth's favourite childhood authors.)

Henley recognised Kenneth's enormous potential and admired his unique writing style – generally conservative and realist – and believed Kenneth could help strengthen his *National Observer*, a paper pitched as an alternative to the aesthetic movements of the period. When they met, the editor put up a powerful argument that Kenneth should give up the Bank of England and concentrate on writing full-time. It was an offer that, had Kenneth taken it, would have changed his life for ever. Yet he was resolved to stand by duty to his uncle and employer and refused to be persuaded by Henley's suggestion. Kenneth found writing emotionally exhausting and was nervous that he would not be able to sustain the exertion for commercial purposes. As a much older man, Kenneth gave a speech at Oxford about the art of letters (the irony of lecturing at the very university he had once hoped to study at surely would not have been lost on him). In a typically dry humorous allegory to underwear, Kenneth revealed that for him, as a very private man, writing was an agonising process that laid his soul bare:

> But you must please remember that a theme, a thesis, a subject, is in most cases little more than a sort of clothes-line on which one pegs a string of ideas, quotations, allusions and so on, one's mental under-garments of all shapes and sizes, some possibly fairly new, but most rather old and patched; they dance and sway in the breeze, they flap and flutter or hang limp and lifeless. And some are ordinary enough, and some are of a rather private and intimate shape and give the owner away, even show up his or her peculiarities. And, owing to the invisible clothes-line, they seem to have connexion and continuity. And when they are thoroughly aired, they are taken down and put away, and the clothes line is coiled up and disappears… my ideas, my illustrations, suggestions, my mental under-garments so to speak, have now been swaying and fluttering before you for the last forty minutes. My only hope is that some garment on my clothes-line may stimulate some train of thought hanging on the clothes-line in your adjacent garden, and that the result may be, some day, a little mental night-shirt, or at least the tiniest of chemises.

Kenneth may not have accepted Henley's offer of a full-time writing position, but nevertheless, the pair shook hands and Henley brought him into the fold, asking him to become a regular contributor. Kenneth would forever appreciate his editor and friend, one of the only people (after Furnivall) who had listened to, and validated, his passion for writing: 'Mr Henley was the first Editor who gave me a full and a frank and a free show, who took all I had and asked me for more; I should be a pig if I ever forgot him.' Kenneth wrote admiringly: 'Sick or sorry – and he was often both – he was always vivid. The memory of this, and of his constant quality of stimulation and encouragement, brings him best to my mind.'

Initiated into the famous 'Henley Regatta' group of writers (ironic, as Kenneth was a rower), Kenneth and his fellow gentlemen contributors would be invited on Friday evenings to dine at Verrey's Restaurant, a Victorian hotspot favoured by writers. An American journalist observed one such gathering, and noted Kenneth in particular:

> Among these leisure-hour gentlemen of the pen was a tall, well-knit man, who moved slowly and with dignity, and who preserved, amid violent discussions and altercations that enlivened the meetings of the group, a calm, comprehending demeanour accompanied by a ready smile. And yet this temperate, kindly looking man had also a startled air, such as a fawn might show... He seemed to be a man who had not yet become quite accustomed to the discovery that he was no longer a child, but grown-up and prosperous. Success did not atone for the loss of the child outlook. Every one of us has his adjective. His adjective was – startled.

Used to life as an anonymous banker, Kenneth probably was somewhat startled to find himself in the public eye surrounded by people who were very different from himself. Yet he embraced this new, creative world and began to write regularly for the *National Observer* and *St. James's Gazette*, steadily building up a body of some twenty literary essays. The first of his most well-known short stories, *The Olympians*, published anonymously in 1891, stands out as a powerful argument for parents to properly take into consideration the feelings of their children. He later acknowledged the autobiographical origins of the stories, which take a retrospective look at his early years with his three siblings as they grew up effectively orphans. As narrator he reveals his painful past through the eyes of four children – Edward, Selina, Charlotte and Harold – who make-believe their way through the long, loveless days. No mother or father are mentioned and the children live in a house visited by a string of 'hopeless and incapable' aunts, uncles and a governess – ironically nicknamed 'The Olympians' after the Greek gods for their careless dominance over young people whom they see as 'merely an animal'. The children are constantly at the mercy of adults: 'their butt, their martyr, their drudge'.

The narrative reads somewhat heavily today, yet when they were published Kenneth had hit upon a subject matter on which he was an expert; the misunderstanding between offspring, their parents and other carers was an issue he had been chewing over for years. His distinct voice as a child narrator comes through strongly, with his favoured satirical flavour, as he uses humour to make palatable a deeply elegiac message. The great sadness of the fleeting essence of childhood remains poignant for today's readers. Kenneth waited a year before publishing a further five instalments, equally stirring in their message and tone.

Henley could see the commercial potential of these stories beyond magazine and newspaper pages, and at the beginning of 1893, encouraged him to pitch these stories as a collection to the publisher John Lane at The Bodley Head. Perhaps because Kenneth had first published them without attaching his name, perhaps because the subject matter was so close to the bone, Kenneth was shy and nervous in his letter. But Lane accepted them, adding six further stories to make up a collection entitled *Pagan Papers*. (These further six stories were reprinted in Kenneth's second book, *The Golden Age*.) Kenneth was delighted with the commission, but kept a cool head and negotiated excellent royalties; Henley too, took a keen personal interest in the project.

Pagan Papers was illustrated by Aubrey Beardsley, one of the most fashionable painters of the day, whose erotic black and white style had illustrated Oscar Wilde's play *Salomé* with a piece called 'The Climax'. Kenneth's *Pagan Papers* was entirely wholesome (the *Pagan* title refers to his belief that children are closest to nature as the human connection is lost by adulthood) and yet the package was impossibly hip; the 'Beardsley Boom' of 1893 coincided with the release of the book and both Kenneth and Beardsley became two of the biggest names of the day.

'These *Pagan Papers* are by Mr. Kenneth Grahame; have you heard of him, gentle reader?' asked *The Pall Mall Gazette*: 'No? No more have we… his style is a delight, so high is its vitality, so cool its colours, so nimble and various its rhythms.'

A mysterious unknown sensation, Kenneth found himself in demand from a wide range of publications both at home and abroad, including America's prestigious *Scribner's Magazine* and the wonderfully named *The Chapbook*. He was constantly commissioned by editors who loved his style as well as his reliability and conscientiousness; when Henley moved to *The New Review* after his *National Observer* closed he took Kenneth with him. That same year saw a new magazine launch: the bohemian *The*

Yellow Book became one of the most influential quarterlies of the time. Although it only ran from 1894 to 1897, its list of contributors was a Who's Who of literary figures including Henry James. It came from the same publishing stable as *Pagan Papers* with the same illustrator, Aubrey Beardsley, who founded the magazine with the American editor Henry Harland. Through these connections it is unsurprising that Kenneth was asked to contribute, although his hearty style of writing wasn't a natural fit with the publication's ethereal tone. Nevertheless, Kenneth found himself part of *The Yellow Book* gang.

'It was a gay world then,' one of his fellow contributors vividly recalled. 'Piccadilly was charming, all the houses had flowers in window-boxes and striped awnings over balconies. And *The Yellow Book* set – it was gay too; very gay, very witty, very brilliant. It was like a flame flashing up and then going out – too brilliant to last, too unreal, too artificial. And in the set we all admired Kenneth tremendously and the appearance of one of his articles would be hailed as an event and discussed at length next Saturday night.'

Usually impeccably mannered, *The Yellow Book*'s bohemianism must have rubbed off on Kenneth one particular Saturday night, humorously recalled by one of his friends, Alan Lidderdale (son of the governor of the Bank of England):

Years ago Kenneth told me how late one night, after a very cheerful dinner, he, in full evening dress, walked out into Piccadilly, and seeing a vegetable cart making its way eastward, ran after it, and climbing up behind, made himself comfortable among the vegetables. He was then overcome by an 'exposition of sleep'. He woke in broad daylight. He was still in the cart, which, now empty, was moving down Piccadilly in the opposite direction… It was one of the regrets of Kenneth's life that he never knew what happened in the interval.

Kenneth wrote for eight of the thirteen volumes of *The Yellow Book*, and one of his most resonating is *Long Odds*, published in July 1895. Here, he writes about the comfort of re-reading children's books as an adult: 'For every honest reader there exist some half-dozen honest books, which he re-reads at regular intervals... as the years flit by... the number falls to three.'

While the general public was unaware that their beloved author held down a conservative job, Bank rumours began connecting the man in back office with the famous writer. It is a rare person who can turn his mind to both dragons and decimals, and Kenneth Grahame's success in these two opposing worlds indicates what a remarkable man he was. His friend Sidney Ward attested to his extraordinary capabilities:

In all the push and bustle of a great institution, the conflicting interests of different departments and the personal jealousies, sometimes, of the chiefs, Kenneth was just the man to hold the balance. Always there, always wise, never too busy to see anyone, a sound advisor of the Governor, never 'rattled' and universally respected – he was a far greater force than most men imagined at the time.

Chapter 8

Olympic Achievement

'It is the silent forces, not the noisy ones, which guide the world.'
Sidney Ward, of his friend Kenneth Grahame

The most famous of Kenneth's *The Yellow Book* stories were the continuation of his 'Olympians' tales, which marked him out as arguably literature's greatest authority on writing about childhood for adults. *The Roman Road* was the first of these; and this, together with eleven other Olympians stories, was compiled into a second collection of Kenneth's best work entitled *The Golden Age* and brought out in February 1895, a softer view of childhood than *Pagan Papers* but still a satirical one.

His cousin, Annie Grahame, has an anecdote about when Kenneth proudly sent a copy of *The Golden Age* to a relative

who returned it, saying that she could not have believed that any member of our family would write a book like this one, holding up to ridicule everything that she had been taught to respect... including aunts and uncles. I hope Kenneth heard of this as I think it would have pleased him very much.

Fortunately, the view held by this critic wasn't shared by most; *The Golden Age* lived up to its name and cemented Kenneth as a leading authority on childhood and beloved by fellow writers such as the poet Algernon Swinburne who called the work: 'well-nigh too praiseworthy for praise'.

Kenneth's work was well received in the United States and garnered him one particular fan whose family apparently read *The Golden Age* ten times: 'I am sure that no one to whom you could have sent those two volumes would appreciate them more than Mrs. Roosevelt and I. I think we could both pass competitive examinations in them – especially in the psychology of Harold!' wrote Theodore Roosevelt, the president of the United States, who personally invited Kenneth to the White House:

'Isn't there some chance of your coming over here?' On request, Kenneth had sent him an inscribed copy, with the words: 'To President Theodore Roosevelt with the highest respect and in grateful recognition of his courtesy, from Kenneth Grahame.'

The Golden Age was revolutionary; Kenneth wrote about what children are really like, destroying the sentimental, stylised view of the Victorian child. His deeply sympathetic view of young people was very different from what had been written previously, as he implored parents to come to understand their child. For example, a child's retreat into daydreaming is not rude behaviour but rather an extraordinary power to access the elusive 'fourth dimension' of the mind:

> At regular periods, the child steps deliberately out of the present tangibility into his property over the border; and again, when his time is up, steps just as deliberately back... the thing goes on with just the same regularity as that other routine of baths, bread-and-butter, lessons and bed; and is about as near a thing to a fourth dimension as can be found in actual working order.

Kenneth's psychological understanding suggests that kingdoms of the imagination exist alongside real life in the minds of children, what psychologists today call magical thinking. Kenneth believed in the power of imagination to heal past trauma: 'Cataclysmal periods arrive, and shake us, and pass, and the kingdom endures.' Retreat into thought is a comfort that should remain private: 'to reveal would be in some sort to break the spell; and this is his own treasure, his peculiar possession – perhaps the only thing he has got which is altogether and entirely his own.' Vitally, imagination is constant, unlike the disappointments and transience of childhood: 'the kingdom's chief charm lies in its constancy, in its abiding presence there at your elbow, the smiling gate wide open, whether fortune favour or frown... These kingdoms... are always close at hand, always attainable in case of need.'

Back in the kingdom of the Bank of England, Kenneth was bestowed with one of the highest appointments in the land. In 1898 aged just 39, he was officially awarded the position of secretary of the Bank of England – one of the top three jobs in the organisation. He was the youngest man ever to hold the position. Alongside his remarkable publishing success he had slowly and steadily been rising through the ranks, treading quietly but confidently as befitted his humble nature; in 1888 he had been promoted to the chief cashier's office, in 1889 he was elevated to the secretary's office and by 1894 he was acting secretary.

What is more astonishing, within a year of this prestigious promotion with all the responsibility and acumen it required, Kenneth published his third wildly celebrated collection of stories, *Dream Days,* in December 1898. A sequel to *The Golden Age,* it featured fan favourites Charlotte, Selina, Edward and Harold; most of the stories had been published in magazines over the past four years. In typical Kenneth style, behind the laughs lies a melancholic sorrow: the final story is called 'A Departure', about the sadness of the end of childhood as the children are told to give away their precious belongings to a local hospital: 'why, oh why did it never enter into any of our thick heads that the day would come when even Charlotte would be considered too matronly for toys?'

Kenneth's gentle genius had made him a household name and the impetus encouraged him to write more deeply about the stuff of childhood fantasy, including fairies and dragons. 'The Reluctant Dragon' is included in *Dream Days* as a new tale, telling of a young St George and the dragon, inverting the characters to glorious comedic effect. The dragon derides his fellow beasts 'always rampaging, and skirmishing, and scouring the desert sands, and pacing the margin of the sea, and chasing nights all over the place, and devouring damsels...' Kenneth's dragon likes to get his meals 'regular' and 'prop my back against a bit of rock and snooze a bit...' The story reads as one of his best, and was published as a separate volume shortly after *Dream Days.*

Like the dragon, Kenneth was considering the possibility of settling down. Hugely successful as both a banker and author, he was still a bachelor. Through his writing he was coming into contact with a very different sort of person than his daily hours at the Bank. Many of the men of *The Yellow Book* set were effeminate, some gay, such as Aubrey Beardsley, and the female contributors were the New Women of the age, almost the total opposite of the female family members modelled to him in childhood. Kenneth had grown up within a deeply conservative unit and his mother had very much played the part of a traditional Victorian wife; so far, his experience of independent women was limited to his cousin, Annie.

Women were certainly on Kenneth's mind around this time; in fact, the first piece he had had published in *The Yellow Book* is a satire about feminism, *The Headswoman*, which discusses the career option of a female executioner. His sensitivity as a writer, as well as his sense of humour, had made him a favourite amongst the female writers of *The Yellow Book*. One evening at a party, a young woman flirted with him about his accent: 'You have a Scotch name, Mr. Grahame. You are a banker and a journalist – both extremely Scotch things to be – but you have not a Scotch accent. Why?'

'I left it in Edinburgh when I came to London,' Kenneth told her.
'Oh, but can't you imitate it?'
'At school I was kicked for apeing.'
'Oh, but you look too big to be kicked.'
'No man,' said Kenneth, 'is too big to be kicked for imitating the
    Scotch accent."

Kenneth treasured his bachelordom, but his social life blossomed as his writing connections strengthened. Henry Harland, the editor of *The Yellow Book*, gave lively dinner parties at his rooms in Cromwell Road on Saturday nights, with singing around the piano and plenty of long, literary discussion, during which Kenneth would be much admired. He would be egged on (no pun intended) to make his famous omelette – being an Edwardian man who could cook only added to his sex appeal. With little competition from the 'affected' men in the group, Kenneth was not too handsome to be intimidating but good-looking enough with 'sensitive hands and mouth'. Through his kindliness and honesty peeped an irresistible vulnerability; one woman described him as being 'Distinctly reserved, until he trusted you – he seemed to me at times as if in his younger days he had been teased, and his boyish aspirations trodden on...'[1]

Netta Syrett, a fellow contributor, recalls Kenneth was often to be found in a corner: 'always a little conscious of his height... He never spoke much unless he had something to say,' she believed, 'instinctively I liked him... He answered my idea of a man... I should like to have known him better.' Netta described him as solid, both physically and morally, 'sane and normal' are the words she used. 'But he was shy and being shy myself then I found him difficult to talk to. I liked his sense of humour and his complete freedom from the affectations which so puzzled me in the other men of the set.' She highlights one of Kenneth's greatest personality traits, his kindness, when Harland read aloud and mocked a new manuscript that arrived in the post. 'I could see that his bad taste in so doing quite hurt K.G... he never said anything unkind about anybody, or to anybody, except through his inability to be insincere...' The pair found a mutual topic of conversation: 'he liked to talk of his work – if he knew you were not likely to gush about it. He was immensely pleased once when I had the cheek to say that I did not like his little girls, that they were not real, like his boys.'

Another contributor who became a great friend was Evelyn Sharp who knew Kenneth as a bit of a flirt. A decade his junior, she was extremely fond of him as 'the nicest kind of schoolboy'. She was first attracted to his fine taste in literature and the fact he made her laugh (and chuckled at her jokes): '[There was] not an ounce of humbug in him... He had a charming sense of humour and was a great tease.' Evelyn and Kenneth saw a great deal of each other over a period of five years, and their friendship is documented in letters. Evelyn regularly asked him to the theatre, to art galleries and out for tea, and although Kenneth mostly declined the invitations (his unfailing politeness always addressing her formally as Miss Sharp), his letters are warm and humorous. A mutual friend described Evelyn as 'coy and silent, whose huge black eyes yearned for the secretary of a bank'. Their editor, Harland, noticed the attraction and with his wife, Aline, attempted to matchmake the pair. They spent Christmas together in Brussels in 1895 and in Boulogne in 1896. They enjoyed summers journeying with the rest of *The Yellow Book* group to Dieppe. '[Kenneth] was the perfect traveller, and those two Christmas weekends stand out in my memory as perfect holidays,' remembered Evelyn. 'There was never any doubt about Kenneth Grahame being taken for an Englishman abroad because he was so very Scottish... [he] was, as a matter of fact, like nobody but himself.'

She wrote of those Saturday evenings at the Harlands, in Cromwell Road: 'I suppose we were as much interested in sex as young people are in all periods... we fell in and out of love with and without disaster...' Kenneth's emotional repression made him wary of getting too close to this smart, capable young woman: around Valentine's Day 1897 after their Christmas together, he curtly writes: 'I was very sorry about the theatre, but really you must not rush me in this sort of hysterical way.' This is an odd statement and indicates less about her personality than Kenneth's neuroses; in fact, Evelyn was as solid as they came. Through pluck and courage she had secured a commission from *The Yellow Book* to keep her afloat after arriving in London (at the disapproval of her parents) with just £10 in her pocket (£5 borrowed from her brother). She became a committed suffragette who was imprisoned twice for her cause as the founder of the United Suffragists movement and editor of *Votes for Women*.

Kenneth wasn't self-assured enough to confidently enter into a relationship, and Evelyn made him nervous. After *The Yellow Book*, she became a fearless newspaper journalist who witnessed starvation in post-war Germany, reported on the unrest in Ireland and trekked across the Siberian steppes in communist Russia. She herself didn't settle down until much later, marrying a fellow journalist in 1933 but always 'treasured' Kenneth's letters. She described him as delightful and 'a writer of stories about children after my own heart.'

It is one of the great tragedies of Kenneth's life that he wasn't ready to fall in love with Evelyn Sharp because she could have made him extremely happy; she perceptively understood him, loved to travel as he did and became a children's novelist. As it turned out, Kenneth's judgement of matters of the heart was woefully misguided and Evelyn was a remarkable missed opportunity.

Chapter 9

Elsie

'Save thy heart for me'

Elsie Thomson to
Kenneth Grahame in a love letter

A pair of huge deep brown eyes turned to Kenneth. An elegant face smiled, introducing herself as Elspeth Thomson, the hostess of that evening's society gathering. She was the epitome of the late Victorian beauty with her pale porcelain skin, soft chestnut hair swept into a wispy bun, an aristocratic nose and those oh-so-enormous eyes. As they talked, Elsie overflowed with girlish appeal; she was open, vulnerable and delicate. Kenneth discovered they were both published writers as well as from pedigree Edinburgh families; each had three siblings and both had lost a parent at a young age.

Elspeth (Elsie) Thomson was born on 3 January 1862, it is believed in Indonesia, as the second of four siblings. Her father was the brilliant Robert William Thomson who invented, amongst others, the pneumatic tyre and the fountain pen. His tyre changed the motor industry forever (although he failed to take out the patent on it – a certain J.B. Dunlop beat him to it). Robert married Clara (Hertz) in Java, Indonesia; she was a charming and highly sociable woman who passed on her literary and artistic leanings to her daughter.

Fluent in French and Flemish, Elsie was an accomplished Victorian with a touch of the bohemian about her. If she had been alive today, she might have been an 'It Girl'; she was a socialite who loved entertaining and writing. In her twenties, she published her story about a poor Londoner, *Amelia Jane's Ambition* (1888), as a penny novel under the pen name of Clarence Onslow (she lived at Onslow Square in London). She was a playwright and her verse was admired by Emma Hardy (wife of Thomas and a poet in her own right): 'I have read the poems with much interest,' Emma wrote to Elsie. 'There is a tender humour – shyness, if

I may say so – in them which is extremely rare in English poets of the other self.'

Elsie was educated at a French convent, and, as well as writing plays, novels and poetry, she loved line drawing, and chose children and animals as her subjects. Her pieces depict the rural and aristocratic ideal in a sentimental Victorian style, sweet domestic scenes with noted details such as particular toys and the soft down of children's hair. Elsie was part of one of the most successful families of her generation. Her brother, Courtauld (1865–1954), was a magnificent industrialist; it is said that their father told Elsie when Courtauld was just 4: 'Some day, baby will be a great man in business.' Distinguished for his development of the insurance industry, his philanthropic work and as director of the Red Cross, Courtauld was awarded a knighthood, taking the title Baron Courtauld-Thomson of Dorneywood in Buckingham.

Elsie's sister, Winifred Hope (1864–1944), became a respected musician and portrait artist, commissioned by the smartest members of society and whose work remains significant. There was a fourth Thomson, Harold, the eldest, of whom little is known.

The children grew up in Edinburgh's fashionable Moray Place, and had a very different sort of childhood from that of Kenneth and his brothers and sister; Elsie's grand home was presided over by a glamorous mother who regularly hosted the literati of the day. The story goes that Mark Twain turned up unexpectedly one afternoon while Elsie's parents were away. The girl was confident enough to offer him tea; when he told her he preferred whisky, Elsie asked the butler to fill a teapot with the stuff! Another anecdote tells how when she was only 10 her mother introduced her to the poet Tennyson, and her charm made such an impression that the pair became firm friends for years, despite their age difference. Elsie had met Tennyson in Switzerland, where her mother had taken the children to recover after her husband died of a horrible illness called locomotor ataxia, which damages the brain. The trauma of losing her father affected Elsie so greatly that she never properly matured into womanhood; Robert had been of such genius and joie de vivre that no man could ever live up to him in Elsie's mind. Like Kenneth, she would forever remain a child; unlike Kenneth, she outwardly craved love and affection rather than masking it with crippling politeness.

Clara remarried three years later, and as a young teenager Elsie was asked to accept a new stepfather, John Fletcher Moulton, and stepbrother, Hugh. Moulton was a charismatic, well-connected yet impecunious barrister who would eventually sit in the House of Lords. Fortunately for him, Clara's business sense had secured financial safety for the family and they moved to the smart Onslow Square in London. Moulton became a Liberal MP and the power couple's combination of glamour, creativity and politics transformed their house into a magnet for friends Oscar Wilde, Algernon Swinburne, Robert Browning and Frank Dicksee (who painted a portrait of Elsie when she was 19).

Yet more tragedy was to come for the young Elsie; Clara died when Elsie was just 26. Despite her grief, Elsie kept her duty to her stepfather and took over the running of the large house, managing Moulton's relentless schedule of entertaining the great and good of the day, from the Asquith family to the eminent politician Henry Campbell-Bannerman (later British prime minister from 1905–8). One particular visitor to the house would change Elsie's life forever. It is believed that Kenneth came on business to see Moulton and was first received by Elsie, who was now 35. A household name, Kenneth was an eminent man – upright (literally and figuratively), a kind, empathetic and sensitive creature with a steady job who loved children and the idea of childhood. It was a winning combination to a motherless woman desperate to be cared for and loved. If eyes were the window to her soul, Elsie laid her enormous brown ones bare in front of Kenneth.

Alison Prince (*An Innocent in the Wild Wood*)[1] was Kenneth Grahame's first female biographer and the first to analyse in detail and without bias his love affair with Elsie Thomson. Prince pieced together evidence to suggest Elsie was a somewhat muddled person who found the world confusing. Lacking in analytical intelligence Elsie fumbled along disconnectedly, gradually losing her confidence as an unmarried and undistinguished member of the family while her siblings were successful, independent and happy. Tired of the drudge of being the ever-cheerful hostess for her political stepfather, Elsie yearned for a man to take care of her and deliver her from a lifetime of spinsterhood. More desperate than devious and a hopeless Brontë romantic, she recognised Kenneth could be her last chance. A quote from a fragment of a letter in the Bodleian Library says she feels 'every Jack has got his Jill & even more than one', indicating she was acutely aware that many of her contemporaries were settling down.

He may have been a highly eligible bachelor, yet Kenneth was clueless about matters of the heart. Having lost his most important primary attachment when his mother died, Kenneth had lacked the role model of a female figure for his entire life. Granny Ingles, Nurse Ferguson and, more recently, sister Helen had organised the practical matters of his physical care, but they had not prepared his heart and mind for finding a wife. Quite simply, Kenneth had not been taught how to love. Around the time he met Elsie, Kenneth was showing signs of wanting to settle down. He was approaching 40, and had recently become an uncle after his younger brother Roland married a widow with two sons. By becoming an uncle to Anthony and Keith, Kenneth was reintroduced to real childhood and could not help but imagine having a son of his own. Rather than merely writing about being a child, he was more than old enough to try for one of his own.

And yet. One of the adjectives repeatedly used to describe Kenneth's facial expression is startled, and startled he was when Elsie fell in love with him at full force. Alison Prince astutely notes that Kenneth's greatest personality trait – his kindness – prevented him from rejecting Elsie's advances; a dangerous cocktail of love and pity meant that by the time he realised what he had got himself in to, it was too late. After he met Elsie, rather than being inspired by the joy of being in love, he wrote little and was ill often; was his endless stream of colds and flu the result of romantic lovesickness or the abject terror of a confirmed bachelor becoming unwittingly committed to a worrisome woman? Perhaps it was just that he was under serious pressure at work as he stepped up to his new promotion as secretary in 1898.

Whatever the emotions of the couple in question, the love affair between Kenneth and Elsie is strange and most unsettling. One of the best examinations of their relationship is not to be found in a biography but in a play; *The Killing of Mr Toad* was written by David Gooderson in 1982 and has been broadcast on the BBC as well as performed across the country. Gooderson cleverly mixes real human characters with the fictional animals from *The Wind in the Willows* to produce a powerful, poignant and little-told story about the dysfunctional relationship.

No diaries survive to detail the couple's relationship; we don't know how soon it was before they met again after their first introduction in 1897 during their two-year 'courtship'. The only facts we can gather are those revealed in Kenneth's letters to Elsie; undated, written in smudgy pencil, in an odd West Country-come-Cockney dialect. They make for extremely uncomfortable and difficult reading, painfully obvious that both were pitifully inexperienced in the physical and emotional aspects of love and forever stuck in child-mode personas. Kenneth either didn't keep Elsie's replies or she chose to throw them away. A single reply from her survives from this time, written in her creatively loopy handwriting – signed not in her name but one that is undecipherable, beginning with M:

Zur

Plaze to vorgive that I make so bold as to write-ee. Sithee wen I parted from 'ee – all i' the garden green – 'ee spook kine to mee – so thought I – sure and certain-sure, will he send me some writin – kine (like the words he spoke i' the gardin) to say may-be he wanted me back there where the flowers grow and the birds sing cheery – or that he's think o' me like he thinks o' the flow'rs and the green things i' th' gardin.

But now 'ee don't think o' me do 'ee? Happen 'ee forgets the gardin and all that stood in't now 'ee are back i' th' town and the streets, and among gay folks. Happen 'ee has one mind for t'country, and t'other for th'town. Happen some dame with diamonds – dimunds that shine more than the dew drops has caught thy notice. And then the Playhouses and the Singing-places, and gran' sights and the fine meat and drink – what chanst has the gardin – and what chanst have I? But 'ee spook kine, and the trees heard 'ee, and I remember – an' sithee! – 'ee may look at the Theatre-ladies – 'ee may listen to the singing-ones – 'ee may may do what 'ee will so thee save thy heart for me – will 'ee? 'Ee hast no need of it in London-town from what folks say, and I need it sore, for mine goes but halting.

Zur, I am too simple to know how 'ee should be wrote to. I would never have been so bold to write to 'ee now, but that 'ee onct spook kine to me in t'gardin – for kine 'ee spook.

Zur, if so be as 'ee will pardon my venture and write me kine – do and remember to save thy heart for me –

Thy little

M

Subsequent letters would be addressed to her by Kenneth as Minkie; his pet name was Dino. Here, Elsie sets herself up with this first letter almost as a Thomas Hardy-esque innocent country heroine, as if Tess of the d'Urbervilles was trapped in the sinful garden of Adam and Eve. Elsie was, of course, inverting her real status as a wealthy London socialite.

Valentine cards were Elsie's speciality – both sending and receiving. Now, she wrote her first valentine to Kenneth, maintaining the exaggerated milkmaid persona. It is found in the Bodleian Library and is signed with fourteen kisses for 14 February. One of the verses runs:

> But if you've got anuther flame
> Why never mind 'tis all the same
> For I'm not one to sulk nor pout
> Becos a feller won't walk-out –

Her sentiments echo those of her letter – don't forget me, save your heart for me, don't throw me over for a glamorous young thing. The first reply from Kenneth to Elsie that survives was written at Easter in 1889, making reference to a serious chest infection he was battling. Elsie was ill as well (perhaps in sympathy?) and sent him a book (likely *Moby-Dick*, as Kenneth jokes it is very long and about a whale) to cheer him up. Elsie was always incredibly thoughtful with her gifts to him and, indeed, to all her family and friends; she never forgot a birthday and present-giving was one of her greatest pleasures.

It is somewhat of a shock to read Kenneth's reply; one of the most eloquent writers of childhood reduced to communicating in childish nonsense. Kenneth's letter reads:

Darlin' Minkie, Ope youre makin steddy progress & beginning ter think of oppin outer your nest & facin a short fly round. I ad nuther good nite & avnt ardly corfd torl terday – but it aint so nice a day, & doesn't tempt one out... Feel orfle slack still but am wearin down the cold grajily. Wish the sun wood cum out fer a bit, im very dull & bored ere. Spose youre a bit dull'n bored were you are, aint you? But you've got a maid, & a poodle, (tho they're bicyclin most of the time) & your friends do drop in sumtimes. Easter is always detestable. Your whale-books a rippin good book, wif lots of readin in it, &

it sor me froo Good Friday triumphantly. Spose you've got a sort o mudie box spread out on your quilt.

This aint much uv a letter my deer but aint got no spirits and don't take no interest nor no notice just yet. But im wishing you elth & appiness my deer & a speedy recuvry & peece and quiet. Goodbye darlin from your own luvin Dino.

After the letter was written, Kenneth's health rapidly deteriorated and he was sent to hospital with pneumonia and emphysema, and his ribs were operated on. It is possible that he fractured at least one rib through repeated coughing. When he finally came home he was cared for by his housekeeper, Sarah Bath, along with his sister, nurse Helen, who moved in temporarily. The women were protective over their patient, not allowing him to see anyone nor informing him that friends had been to visit – including Elsie, who must have been hugely disappointed to be turned away. She showered Kenneth with carnations and grapes, and even persuaded her stepfather to send gifts of wine and the use of his carriage. But still she wasn't allowed in. Did Helen and Sarah know that Elsie was in love with Kenneth? Eventually the patient secretly wrote to her, describing his life frankly as a 'bad two months':

Darling Minkie, This is just a smuggled line – for I'm not supposed to sit up writing letters yet – to say I've begun coming down in the afternoon and seeing my friends. I did not even know you had not gone away for the holiday, till this morning – and indeed while I was in quod I was told nothing about anybody. The surgeon has done with me – says I've made a famous recovery as far as his share of the thing goes – but says I must go away the moment I can – in a very few days if possible – & for a long time, so as to get through the winter without a breakdown. My dearest I mustn't write any more – but I wonder if I shall see you? It's been a bad two months. Your loving Dino

Shockingly for the time, he sneaked an illicit reunion with Elsie, 'Come when you can, tomorrow afternoon – I rather think my sister's going out about 3.30 or so, for the rest of the afternoon...' Kenneth is frightened of his domineering nurse-sister and behaves like a furtive child rather than asserting his rights as a grown man to be attracted to a fellow grown woman. What he suggested was somewhat extreme: Victorian social rules would never allow an unchaperoned woman to be alone with a man unless there was a strong romantic attachment between them: Kenneth had all but given Elsie a promise of engagement.

What happened during that fateful afternoon? No one will ever know – except, perhaps, for the housekeeper Sarah Bath. She would for ever dislike Elsie. No record survives of how Kenneth really felt about Elsie; he didn't write a diary nor any love poetry around this time. Either way, the reunion was just in the nick of time as the next day Helen bundled Kenneth out of the house for four months down to the west of England. Helen must have felt relieved to escape from London and away from Elsie, whom she didn't like. She was a practical woman and thought Elsie silly and not good enough for her clever brother. Helen was a spinster (she never married), and when Kenneth tried to discuss matters of the heart with her she wasn't interested. 'No object in talking things over with my sister now,' he confided to a female friend, 'Irresponsive is not the word.' He described his sister as 'awkward' in a letter to Elsie, noting when she had been in a better mood 'sister as bin distinckly more amiable'.

Once spirited away to deepest Devon, Kenneth wrote to Elsie in secret as soon as he could, describing the delights of the countryside: 'Goodbye darlin pet & I wish you were here we wood go cros the bay in the little steem ferry bote & not cum back – there is poppies t'other side. Your lovin Dino.'

But Helen discovered their correspondence as Elsie wrote so regularly. We cannot know exactly what Elsie wrote, but we can guess from Kenneth's replies she was trying to be protective of her sweetheart, by suggesting certain foods or sending local friends to visit him. He rejects it all: 'Don't bovver to let loose enny muvverly large people on me I don't want to be muvvered just now'

'I eets wot I chooses & wot I dont & I don't care a dam wot they does in Berlin thank gord I'm British.'

In another letter he jokes that he should push her into the sea: 'I could play at frowin you over – over the cliff I mean...' and teases that she might find another man 'you cood play at bandonin me artlessly for nuther – but you wouldn't no that...'

But he writes a racy follow-up:

Chambermaid don't share your views – ses she aint paid to old
'ands orl nite – & she'd lose 'er karacter besides – she 'ad on a nice
wite gown wif pink spots this mornin, wot 'stood out' wif starch
and virtue. Praps if you starcht your gowns you woodnt tork so
lightly bout spendin orl nite wif Dinos – but praps you'd better not
starch 'em!

Kenneth imagines his love in a dressing gown and bare feet; Elsie in
practical mode sends him an extra stamp and paper so he can write to her
in secret. She writes of the Brontës and *Wuthering Heights* – giving a clue
to her wild, passionate, exaggerated and unrealistic views of what love
should be like. He writes back that he 'never took no stock in Brontës'!
He sometimes writes formally to 'My dearest Elsie' and at other times
teases her with nicknames such as 'Sweetie', 'love-child' and 'nannie'.
Elsewhere he confuses her by accusing her of preferring a single bed to
a double one. The ultimate lead-on is when he asks Elsie if she would
like to live with her father during the week and 'cum away wif me' for
the weekends. It is a wild fantasy and a desperate attempt at getting out
of something he was too deeply into – Kenneth had never done anything
remotely unconventional in his life!

In his letters, Kenneth describes getting about with a stick, and
complains of being bored of Helen's taking him on horse-carriage rides
for 'a nice drive' when he would rather be walking 'arm in arm' with Elsie
looking at the 'beautiful' pink and blue flowers. Ever practical, Helen
organised a change of scene and in 1899 took him to the Cornish seaside
beauty spot of Fowey, with which he instantly fell in love, igniting a
passion for the place that would last his lifetime. '[I] never want to leave
it,' he wrote to Elsie. On the west shore of the estuary of the River Fowey,
there is a deep sea harbour, port and ferry which Kenneth loved to gaze
out over from his seat on the Town Quay: 'The sea has all the blues in the
world and a few over.' There he quietly observed the town's characters,
from the fishermen hawking baskets of 'blue-black squiggly lobsters' to
the men going for a drink in The Ship Pub. He called it the place where
time stands still.

The allure of Fowey, its fresh air and his colourful new friends bolstered
Kenneth tremendously and he began to feel better. It was the sea that
strengthened him the most and, after gazing longingly at the boats for

weeks – 'the schooner won't let me alone, she's just tacked across – like a minx' – Helen finally allowed him to go out for a gentle row. She helped him do exercises to inflate his lung before removing the dressings from his operation.

Kenneth had survived an extremely serious illness: pneumonia was the leading cause of death in the late 1800s. Imagine what a relief the good news must have been for his sweetheart, Elsie, as she waited anxiously for him in London after months of being apart.

Chapter 10

A Cornish Affair

'It's a rather serious thing, settling down...'
Kenneth Grahame, *The Reluctant Dragon*

By early summer, Kenneth's mind as well as body began to be refreshed, his senses gradually awakened as he wrote of colour, the scent of flowers and the taste of local Cornish food. He was inspired by the exotic flora growing in the warm climate to romantically ponder: 'In the lanes, they are pink and yellow and blue like the boats.' He recalled:

There's valerian in masses of pink which sets off the blue of the sky as the Judas trees do in Italy – by the way I saw a Judas tree in blossom just lately at Torquay – and there's pink campion and cranesbill and blue speedwell and white stitchwort thrown in and yellow wild-mustard – and here and there a scarlet poppy, not many, but big ones.

Kenneth's appetite returned as he indulged in Cornish delicacies including star gazy pie (fish pie with pilchards pointing upwards through flaky pastry), thunder and lightning (warm bread spread with cream and treacle), splits (fresh rolls spread with Cornish cream) and licky pasties (pasties made with leeks and wrapped in a hot flannel). Kenneth always loved food and became overweight in later life; comfort eating is a sign of emotional need, and craving nursery food can suggest a longing for childhood. Food, as in many children's books, is celebrated in *The Wind in the Willows*: who can forget Rat's fat wicker luncheon basket and the description of his picnic:

'Coldtonguecoldhamcoldbeefpicklegherkinsaladfrenchrollscresss andwichespottedmeatgingerbeerlemonadeandsodawater'.

Extending his recuperation vacation, Kenneth embraced Cornish life, going out fishing with local crews, dressing and eating as they did: 'very glad... to feel the fresh breeze and the sea-spray in my face once more.' In Fowey, Kenneth learnt how to catch fish and eels, sometimes staying all night with friends such as Captain James in a boat loaned by an old fisherman Tom Roberts. Kenneth's transformation was finally complete when, walking up the quayside dressed in a blue jersey and hat, he was mistaken for a fisherman by an Oxford academic (Dr Boyd, the principal of Hertford College). Kenneth writes: 'He came up and asked had I had good luck with the fish? 'The best, sir,' said I and touched my cap. Presently, after a few more remarks, he went away. But, in a minute, he was back again and begging my pardon for his mistake. 'Sir,' said I, 'I have never been more flattered in my life."

Roberts' daughter was Mary Ellen and she recalled Kenneth's enthusiasm for the water as well as his kindness to children:

I remember young Mr Kenneth, he was very fond of my father and was always very nice to us and to my family. He used to love going out fishing all night with father. They used to set a boulter and they would catch very big fish, cod-fish and ling, which people used to salt and dry for the winter... I think the first time I remember Mr Kenneth was in 1887. He had been out with father fishing that day and he called in on his way back. I happened to be out getting something and when I came in he was sitting in his sea-boots with my two little girls in their nightgowns one on each knee. They had heard someone come in and come creeping down for a peep who it was and he had taken them up. I can still see the three of them now.

Kenneth would eventually pen a tribute to Fowey in *The Wind in the Willows* when the Sea Rat talks of 'the little grey sea town that clings along one side of the harbour'. It was at Fowey that Kenneth began to cultivate the security of the male friendships he had surrounded himself with in London. His sister Helen introduced him to Sir Arthur Quiller-Couch, nicknamed Q, a novelist, essayist and critic who was four years Kenneth's junior (in 1912 he became Professor of Literature at Cambridge). Q had worked in London as a journalist before moving to Fowey to try to live off the proceeds of his books (three at the time). A cheerful fellow, he spent his days boating and writing and lived in a wonderful home overlooking the harbour, The Haven, with his wife and two children. Q invited Kenneth to his wife's family home, Fowey Hall, which some say was the inspiration for Toad Hall. (Today it is a hotel with eight of the bedrooms named after the animals in the book.) Q was great friends with 'Atky' (Edward Atkinson), the first commodore of the Royal Fowey Yacht Club. A confirmed bachelor in his sixties, Atky was somewhat eccentric; he owned thirty boats, was an art collector and his home was stuffed with toys. Rose Bank, his house in Mixtow, apparently had a rope ladder instead of stairs, which would have delighted Kenneth. Perhaps he saw Atky as the character of the Sea Rat, lean and keen-featured, and somewhat bowed at the shoulders with 'eyes much wrinkled at the corners... His knitted jersey was of faded blue...'

Q described Kenneth as 'eminently a "man's man" and keen on all manly sports', and with their common interests of sailing, travelling, literature and eating well, the trio enjoyed a lifetime of friendship, which was immortalised in print when Q wrote his novel *The Mayor of Troy*. Set in Fowey, Q dedicated it to: 'My friend Kenneth Grahame and the rest of the crew of the *Richard and Emily*' (the name of the skiff in which they sailed together). Kenneth was delighted to be 'officially connected' to the Cornish town, under the spell as he was of 'the call of the South' – of the south of England (Cornwall) and also the south of Europe (Italy): 'Its songs, its hues, its radiant air!... one passionate touch of the real southern sun, one waft of the authentic odour...' he would later write in *The Wind in the Willows*. Kenneth called Fowey 'the best place in the world' and always dreamed of retiring there. In fact, his sister, Helen, settled at the Lizard after her career in nursing (she would live there until her death in 1940) and other members of the Grahame family made Penzance their home. Fowey represented a paradise for Kenneth, an accumulation of all that he loved the most – the open water, fine weather, male company – and everything he would eventually write about in *The Wind in the Willows*. He described the halcyon days: 'The skies so blue, the sun so golden, and the moon so silver. Picnics with the Qs, long sails in their yacht, the Vida, over the Bay... Rowing with the Qs in their red boat, the Picotee...' Over the years, he became close to Q's two children – his son Bevil and fair-haired daughter Foy Felicia, who would beg: 'I am going to live with the Grahames.'

Kenneth endeared himself to children and becoming a father was on his mind as he wrote to Elsie to tell her of his Cornish adventures. But she was sniffily disinterested in his new friends and watery hobbies despite his encouragement that he wanted them to be 'two boats sharing the same wave' and 'you mustn't fink I'd ever frow you over for boats.' Kenneth soothed her Elsie by sharing his vision of them together at last: 'I play at your bein' 'ere, honeymoonin' and call it our poppy-moon, 'cos it's a dream moon. I only 'ope the real one'll be as nice. Come and be stroked, my sweet…' He asked Elsie to visit him while Helen was away at the Lizard: 'you & me wd be free, my deer'. Elsie, instead, suggested eloping.

On 22 June, after weeks of being apart, Kenneth fulfilled his unspoken promise to Elsie and wrote to her stepfather to ask for her hand in marriage. But Fletcher Moulton refused.

Perhaps Moulton wasn't as liberal as his politics when it came to a match for Elsie, maybe he was affronted at Kenneth's suggestion of a quiet, quick Cornish wedding rather than a society celebration in London. Or he might have objected to the thought of having to organise his busy social calendar himself if his stepdaughter left home. Whatever the reason, he refused to support a union.

Yet so strong were Elsie's feelings for Kenneth, she persuaded her stepfather to change his mind and within a week Moulton wrote to Kenneth who confirmed to Elsie: 'Me deer Ive ad an streemly kind & nice letter from your farver' but, tellingly, wants to talk no more about it all: '& now I mus leave the matter ntirely in your fare ands & I will say nuffin till you tells me to, cos we gets no further with discushins – on paper.'

For a beautiful aristocrat and a famous author, it is surprising that a large celebration wasn't planned. Maybe because Kenneth was embarrassed at fussy nuptials at their age, or perhaps Elsie was worried he would change his mind, the couple made it clear they wanted to marry as quickly as possible. They decided on a date in just a month's time, and joked about a 'wemmick-marriage' (a reference to *Great Expectations*). Previous biographers have painted a picture of Elsie greedily ensnaring Kenneth, desperate to lure him into her clutches, but to be fair to her, she stayed in London to prepare herself properly and coolly arrived shortly before the wedding.

Returning from the Lizard, Helen first heard the news of the engagement in the newspaper on 1 July – and wasn't very happy about it, as Kenneth reported to his new fiancée: 'She's just sed she'd seen it, & that was abslootly orl. There must be sumfin at the bottom of er sullen sort o silence wot I aint got at yet.'

Helen confronted her brother and asked him if he really intended to go ahead with the wedding: 'I suppose so; I suppose so', he is believed to have spluttered nervously. Helen realised that Kenneth's kindness had got him into a situation that he was entirely unsuited for. Like her brother, she was principled, and simply could not, in good conscience, support his decision to marry a woman she viewed as utterly mismatched. She left Fowey just days later. The siblings never recovered from this falling out and remained estranged until Kenneth's death.

Kenneth, still likely to not be in full health, moved in with Q and his family, who helped him organise the wedding – finding a local vicar and assisting with the honeymoon, flowers, organists and bell-ringers. Kenneth also made preparations for his future in London with Elsie and took out a lease on a fine family home at 16 Durham Villas in Campden Hill, Kensington (now Phillimore Place, boasting a blue plaque with Kenneth's name). It would be the Grahames' home from 1901 to 1908; close to Kensington Gardens, the handsome and elegant house remains one of the smartest addresses in London. To complete the new household, Kenneth had asked his housekeeper, Sarah Bath, to move in with them, but she refused (like Helen, she didn't like his new bride).

Kenneth wrote to an anxious Elsie to reassure her that everything was under control ahead of their big day and sent her a romantic wedding present, a pretty pendant: 'as you've got your dino on a string you mays well wear is pendant remind you ee's a angin very near your art,' he soppily professed. As the wedding drew closer he called her 'my darlin Nannie Elsie of Fowey'. He writes: 'I'm agoin' ter be pashnt my pet & go on a dreemin a you till youre a solid reality to the arms of im oo the world corls your luvin Dino.' He imagines happy-go-lucky days at the beach together:

Darlin, its getting on tern ex wee aint it – & then we'll fink o nuffin for a bit, but you & me – & you'll let me paddle in pools wich ave bin left by tide, cos they gets as ot in the sun as a warm barf, an I'll let you tadpole – wifin reesnable limits.

Curiously, Elsie refused to wear the engagement ring Kenneth chose for her. Always fancying herself as a bohemian, it is possible Elsie didn't want to appear bourgeoisie. In return, Kenneth did the most extraordinary thing; he sent it to his closest female friend, Miss Bradley, writing:

> Elsie refuses to have anything to do with an engagement ring of any sort. And I respect unconventionality of any kind too much to even protest ... But I do feel strongly that there ought to be a ring in the business somewhere – to appease the gods – and circumstances seem to mark you out for it clearly. So I hope you will not refuse the one I am sending along with this. It is of no value, unless it will sometimes remind you of a friendly action – and if you do friendly things you must be put up with being reminded of them.

Was this a sweet gesture of genuine friendship or a last-ditch attempt for what might have been a conventional marriage to a sensible, loyal, steady woman as the daughter of the Dean of Westminster? Miss Bradley had been Kenneth's friend for several years and he knew her father well. Their relationship was purely platonic as her letters to him are always sensible and objective. It is clear Kenneth thought highly of Miss Bradley as he wrote to her in parallel with Elsie during his convalescence in the West Country, confiding to her his secret relationship with Elsie; later, she was one of the first people he shared the news of his first-born son.

Kenneth was a shy man, although greatly endeared himself to women such as Miss Bradley with whom he stayed in touch for many years. The physical distance of letter-writing helped him relax into friendships with the opposite sex, and he wrote to other women just as warmly and wittily, such as Helen Dunham whom he reassured he would never grow up. Forever man-child he may have been, yet Kenneth never wrote to these women in the baby language he shared with Minkie.

Helen and Miss Bradley were 'safe' friends that he held at arm's length; he was confident there was no possibility of them falling in love with him, unlike other women such as Evelyn Sharp who had made that mistake. As Evelyn wrote years later, Kenneth looked 'as if he thought you might be going to bite if he wasn't very careful!' Almost 40, he was still a virgin and his deep-rooted insecurity about a physical relationship indicates he might have been confused about his sexuality. As his wedding night drew near, he wrote to a friend about asexuality: 'My beastly virtue has been my enemy through life, but once married I will try & be frankly depraved, and then all will be well.' His last words to his new bride before she arrived in Fowey was a nervous, teasing note to break the ice after months of not seeing each other and a hint at their mutual lack of sexual experience: 'Goodbye sweetie and don't sorst yourself cos it's a long journey down & I want ter do the sorstin of you wen you gets here.'

Did Kenneth love Elsie? He found her interesting and entertaining, certainly; a friend had told him he would never be bored with her. She validated his core need to be a writer, something that his family had always been suspicious of. Why did he marry her? Characteristically, he felt obligated to fulfil his moral duty to a woman his kindness prevented him from hurting. First his career had been dictated by an obligation to his uncle, and now his love life and even his happiness was being ruled by an overwhelming sense of duty. Had duty become a sort of Olympian that Kenneth was powerless against? Like the heroes of classical literature that he had studied at school, Kenneth believed that he had no choice but to follow what the fates had planned for him. No matter how much he adored bachelorhood, Kenneth was conventional to his core and felt his only respectable option as a Victorian gentleman was to take a wife and start a family.

Elsie arrived in Cornwall the night before the big day, and stayed at the Fowey Hotel with her sister Winifred and two brothers Courtauld and Harold, along with her pet poodle and maid. A wedding organised in remote Cornwall hurriedly scrambled together in a matter of weeks with just a handful of guests probably wasn't the fairy-tale day Elsie had dreamed of. Arising early the next morning, she prepared for what was to come by taking a walk. Just like a romantic heroine from one of her beloved Brontë novels, she wore a white muslin frock and looked to the elements for reassurance about how her life was about to change. While her mind raced ahead to thoughts of a lifetime with a fellow she had spent barely an hour alone with, her hands whimsically made a daisy chain.

Kenneth, too, is likely to have gone walking or maybe even swimming that morning; an organ grinder had awoken him early – a joke played by his best man and cousin, the novelist Anthony Hope Hawkins (better known as Anthony Hope), who organised a sort of morning stag party high-jinx.

As Elsie walked back to the Fowey Hotel, she decided that she would not allow her maid to dress her in the wedding gown she had carefully chosen and brought down from London in its fine box. Maybe it was her last stab at unconventionality, a wildly romantic gesture. Perhaps it was her way of making her mark on a wedding that had been organised by Kenneth in a place entirely unfamiliar to her. Despite, it is likely, protests from her smartly dressed stepfather, prettily attired sister and sensible brothers, Elsie was determined not to change for the wedding service and simply wear her white muslin dress. She kept the daisy chain around her neck for good luck.

Elsie took a deep breath as she stepped into St Fimbarrus on 22 July 1899 on the arm of her stepfather. Q's 8-year-old son, Bevil, was the pageboy, dressed in a white sailor suit with roses in his buttonhole. Q was a witness.

As Elsie caught a first glimpse of her betrothed standing at the altar, greying, tall, upright and bearing a nervous smile, her daisy necklace was already beginning to wither, echoing the words of one of her poems: 'No lasting chain is made of flowers.'

Chapter 11

Marrying the Princess

'Then there is the Princess... She is sympathetic, appreciative, and companionable... And yet – an embarrassing person somewhat at times.'

Kenneth Grahame, '*The Reluctant Dragon*'

After a week's honeymoon in St Ives, Kenneth helped Elsie over the threshold of their marital home at Durham Villas in London, returning to the capital for the first time in almost four months. As a new bride, Elsie would have felt excited about her future; she was independent at last from her family, with a famous husband and a lovely home. Perhaps a small part of her felt smug about being married: she had been the least successful of her siblings, now she had achieved something they had not (neither Winifred nor Courtauld would marry and instead lived together as housemates for forty years). But a growing sense of unease was already creeping over her; the honeymoon had been an anti-climax, as Kenneth spent much of it boating with his (male) friends and their wedding night had been spoilt by his nerves. She had longed for a handsome hero to sweep her off her feet, just as her mother had been by her brilliant, sociable first husband and penniless but loving second. Elsie had lost both her parents at a young age leaving her ill-equipped to deal with her need to be loved. How could Kenneth, repressed, shy, a virgin, live up to his new wife's wildly romantic expectations? He was a man's man who had lived so as a happy bachelor for close on twenty years. He may have been a sensitive writer but a sensitive lover he was not. The truth was that Kenneth and Elsie had known each other only through letters before they married, spending just an hour alone together unchaperoned – a situation almost unthinkable today in Western society. Neither had witnessed at close quarters a happy, functional marriage – after all, Kenneth had effectively lost both his parents and was brought up by an austere grandmother. Now even his spinster sister had abandoned him. For Elsie, first her father and then her mother had died. She knew the familial love of her two close-knit siblings yet they too had little experience of romance.

Now they were in London as Mr and Mrs, Kenneth and Elsie were thrown into reality to conduct their lives as grown-ups. Kenneth's solution was to return to work immediately: perhaps not entirely his choice, he had been absent for such an extended period, it is likely the Bank of England was calling him back as soon as he could get to the office. Not long promoted to secretary, it was a job that kept him employed for long hours.

On that first Monday morning back in London at the very start of her married life, Elsie felt alone as she gazed about the surroundings that would be her home for the next six years. Number 16 Durham Villas was geographically close to her stepfather at Onslow Square but a world away from it. There she had been in charge of organising her stepfather's perpetually busy diary, preparing for and entertaining endless dignitaries and guests. Her marital home was silent: Kenneth preferred the company of a few male friends. Now living in his house, Elsie was uneasily learning more about her husband. The home was filled with toys; he was a collector and hoarder of childhood treasures. One of Elsie's poems expresses the protagonist's wish that she'd met her lover as a child of 4 rather than as an adult. It reveals an odd state of mind, as these selected verses (somewhat clumsily composed) show:

> In knowing you, I've one regret
> (That is not much one might have more)
> I wish that you and I had met
> Some time ago, when I was four!
>
> Of course you'd be too old for toys
> Like tops, or marbles blue and red,
> They're only fit for silly boys –
> I'd let you play with me instead
>
> For you should pinch my cheeks, and take
> Me in your arms, or on your knee
> Like some big doll, that would not break
> Think what a plaything that would be

This role of passive woman and dominant male would be both carried out and subverted during the course of Kenneth and Elsie's unusual relationship.

Previous biographers have damned Elsie for being a wickedly scheming spinster who trapped an unsuspecting Kenneth into marriage: in 1959, Peter Green (*Kenneth Grahame – A Biography*) was vicious in his accusations of her as being a doggedly ruthless, dominant obsessive. More recently, in 2018, Matthew Dennison (*Eternal Boy*) interpreted Elsie's falling in love with Kenneth as: 'Her pursuit was single-minded and unwavering, by turns assertive and submissive, pathetic, frustrated, loving.' It could be argued that Elsie was an irrepressible romantic who fell head over heels for Kenneth and remained devoted to him throughout her life. Elsie wasn't aware that, for her, the idea of falling in love was greater than love itself. Unlike Kenneth who would write nothing for seven years, Elsie poured her heart out into poetry during the early years of their marriage. They are entitled with names such as 'Ah Stay Love Stay', 'I Wonder When You Said Goodbye', 'Illusion' and 'A Conceit'. The recurrent theme is rejection, misery and anger:

> Rejected
>
> Ah love, I dare ask but the slenderest boon
> For I know thou art cold as the half risen moon
> Yet thou surely wilt grant me so trivial a part
> Of the bliss I once dreamt might illuminate my heart

Kenneth was disinterested in his new wife and failed to notice Elsie's dissatisfaction with him carrying on as if he were still a single man. If he wasn't curious about the sexual side of marriage, neither did he view a husband's role as being best friend to his wife. Elsie wasn't the sort of woman he had come across before and she made him nervous; she was altogether more emotional and fragile – less a powerful princess and more elfin pixie. It was a case of intellectual introvert meets under-educated extrovert as he relished solitary time with little conversation and she was used to an endless stream of company; Kenneth had academic leanings, his wife had only a rudimentary education.

Elsie's sorrow grew into frustration; Kenneth had promised faithfully in church to love and cherish her yet only weeks later acted as if she simply didn't exist:

> When I go out, you stay at home,
> No sooner am I in,
> Than you desire at once to roam,
> I vow it is a sin!
>
> Oh! It really is unbearable
> And would provoke a saint!
> By all oaths that are swearable,
> There's reason for complaint!

As early as August, just a month after they wed, Elsie desperately sought the counsel of an older, experienced friend. A friend who happened to have been married for twenty-five years to a writer famed for his intensely romantic novels but who was undemonstrative as a husband; Emma Hardy once wrote that her husband Thomas 'understands only the women he invents – the others not at all.' (It has been suggested that the Hardys' marriage was never consummated.) 'There is ever a desire to give but little in return for our devotion and affection,' said Emma, who believed that it was simply not in men's nature to give their wives 'proper and enduring' love.

'It is really too "early days" with you to be benefited by advice,' Emma sensibly replied to Elsie's begging for counsel. Emma asks for specific details about Elsie's frets and offers a pessimistic and sweeping view of a husband's attitude towards his wife, describing it as: 'being akin to children's – a sort of easy affectionateness and at first, a man's feelings too often take a new course altogether. Eastern ideas of matrimony secretly pervade his thoughts and he wearies of the most perfect and imitable wife chosen in his earlier life. Of course he gets over it usually somehow, or hides it or is a martyr...'

Emma later writes more cheerfully (assuming Elsie could bear to keep reading through her crushing disappointment), inviting the couple to visit, and encouraging them to look to God for help.

I must qualify all this by saying that occasionally marriage undoubtedly is the happy state (with Christians always if both are) which it was intended to be. There must, of necessity, be great purity in the mind of the man, joined with magnanimity and justice... Similarity of taste is not to be depended on, though it goes some way...

Emma cites fear and jealousy as the downfall of a relationship. She ends her letter with good wishes to Elsie ('though I rather congratulate a man in these cases') and, as a Cornishwoman, praises the couple on their choice of honeymoon destination (although cannot resist putting her last pennyworth in): 'but best in winter'!

Frustratingly, Elsie's letters to Emma have been lost or destroyed (perhaps by Elsie herself) so we can only guess at what she wrote in reply. It is possible she admitted the couple was no longer sharing a bed as Emma wrote: 'Keeping separate is a good idea and a wise plan in crises – and being both free – and expecting little gratitude nor attentions, love not justice nor anything you may set your heart on – love interest, adoration and all that kind of thing is usually a failure.' Mrs Hardy bitterly concludes with a warning: 'if he belongs to the public in any way, years of devotion count for nothing...' In a third letter, the older woman grimly writes:

Hundreds of wives go through a phase of disillusion – it is really a pity to have any ideals in the first place... This is grievesome, horrid, you will say – and perhaps Mr Grahame is looking over the bride's shoulder as bridegrooms often do. But you have asked me and someday we may talk further of these matters – there is so much to say – and to compare. Everyone's experience is different.

What a ghastly blow for a romantic, whimsical young bride.

Elsie was bitterly disappointed and deeply hurt by her husband's rejection of her, which caused her great mental anguish. Yet she bravely attempted to make the best of her hollow marriage. Through her family, Elsie was connected with the finest of society and, to keep her confidence up, gamely attempted to recreate the famous dinner parties that she had hosted with her stepfather in Onslow Square. Their now mutual friend,

Miss Bradley, was a frequent visitor: 'the easy informal hospitality at the Grahames' house on Campden Hill will be remembered with peculiar pleasure by many of their intimate circle,' she wrote. She continued:

> Kenneth's mind was not ruled by the ordinary conventions. He made little attempt at small-talk but his silences were curiously companionable; & presently the thought would flow... He was a good – sympathetic – conversationalist because he was genuinely interested in the person he was talking to & in the latter's views as his own – he was entirely without pretensions or affectations of any description. Never a great talker in mixed company, he would sometimes give utterance to his least conventional sentiments with genial but unhesitating conviction.

Kenneth preferred a small group of friends, while Elsie was used to a constant flow of people through the house: 'Oddly enough (for he was a most attractive man),' wrote their mutual friend Graham Robertson, 'Kenneth had few friends. He simply didn't want them. He would say rather wonderingly to his wife: "You *like* people. They interest you. But I am interested in *places*!"'

Elsie was a popular, lively personality and a consummate hostess; as a friend and sister, her kindness, thoughtfulness and loyalty were unmatched; she was a prolific letter writer and never forgot a birthday, always choosing the perfect present. She loved introducing her friends to each other and was a skilled networker. They say you can tell a great deal about someone through their friends and Elsie's were extraordinary; the huge and diverse collection of letters held at the Bodleian Library indicates her eclectic wide circle, including both men and women, from many countries, different classes and corners of society, spanning a 60-year age difference. Her letters reveal a likeable personality, at odds with the one previously portrayed, and collectively document Elsie growing up from a somewhat light and frothy young lady to a woman of substance. Elsie was a charismatic correspondent, her scrawled handwriting is full of snippets about the arts, parties and nature although, rarely, about her husband. How hard it must have been for her, desperate to be loved, to have all the admirers in the world except the one she really wanted.

Characteristically, she made the best of the situation and threw her energies into her friends.

During the 1900s, one of the most prominent families in Great Britain were the Asquiths, and Elsie knew them well, receiving letters from Margot Asquith at 10 Downing Street (she was the prime minister's second wife), who wrote, amongst other things, for advice about her son Anthony's education: 'I am writing you a line to thank you more than I can say for your letter about the school,' effused Margot. (Anthony grew up to become one of the finest film directors of his generation.) Of all the Asquiths, Elsie was closest to Margot's daughter-in-law Cynthia, who was a diarist, novelist and biographer. Elsie proves in her letters that she was a loyal and thoughtful companion; twenty-five years Cynthia's senior, she helped mentor the young woman. It is worth noting that letters also exist between Elsie and H.H. Asquith's predecessor, Henry Campbell-Bannerman; she was on first-name terms with him and his wife Charlotte.

The Bodleian letters reveal Elsie had plenty of male friends too, and wasn't short of admirers – from a Frenchman in Paris who flirts with his 'petite amie', to her correspondence with the artist John Tenniel over a period of fifteen years. Tenniel (1820–1914) was an illustrator most famous for his work in Lewis Carroll's *Alice's Adventures in Wonderland* and was knighted for his unparalleled artistic skill. Unfortunately, just like the Emma Hardy correspondence, only Tenniel's replies survive; Elsie's letters to him have been lost. More than forty years Elsie's senior, they started writing to each other when he was 72 and corresponded between 1892 and 1907 – about the time when he was the principal cartoonist at *Punch* (where he worked until he was 80). Blind in his right eye, Tenniel lived a solitary life after his wife died just two years into their marriage. Witty, warm, sentimental and lonely, Tenniel clearly enjoyed a little harmless flirting with Elsie. He always signed off 'very sincerely yours' – sometimes with a heart underneath, with the letters E and J intertwined. He would come along to Elsie's parties and shared a warm affection for the younger woman, as they exchanged Christmas wishes and birthday gifts; she wrote him poems, made sketches and gave him gifts such as a cigar-cutter that he described as 'simply perfect' and a statuette of an old gentleman, which he proudly displayed on the mantelpiece. Neither missed a year of sending each other valentine verse, despite his crippling rheumatism and even after she was married, with Tenniel always professing to be her faithful valentine. One leap year he teased her about proposing marriage to him. His final letter is from 1907, and signed 'Your old true Valentinest'.

Another admirer of Elsie's was Henry Lucy (1842–1924), a prominent political journalist who was so beloved by the public, the explorer Shackleton named a mountain after him in Antarctica. For whatever reason, he didn't capture Elsie's heart, but that didn't stop him writing to her about 'loving looks' and butterflies and 'thinking of my valentine'.

No valentine letters from Kenneth to Elsie survive. When it came to sex, Kenneth was underwhelmed by losing his virginity. He found the whole business distasteful and wished never to think of it: 'Clean of the clash of sex' and 'free of sex', was how he proudly introduced his most famous manuscript *The Wind in the Willows* in 1908. Because he had not fallen passionately in love with his wife on their wedding night, Kenneth again raised a question in his mind that forced him to confront his sexuality.

Chapter 12

From Minkie to Pinkie

'The eternal boy, keenly alive to the beauty and wonder of the world around him, yet shy of giving expression to the strange happiness that bubbles up within him...'
   W. Graham Robertson, about his close friend Kenneth Grahame

Writing is a complex, creative process and it can be inaccurate to extrapolate biography from fiction. However, it would be remiss to ignore the possibility that Kenneth was asexual or homosexual. His attitude towards sex and marriage was far from enthusiastic. Kenneth never felt entirely comfortable with women and only ever properly relaxed in the company of men. *The Wind in the Willows* is a powerful celebration of the unbreakable bonds of male companionship, highlighting man's greatest strengths – loyalty, bravery, strength, determination and sacrifice. Throughout the book, females make only shadowy appearances; the four principal characters are male.

One particular friend who might have known the truth of Kenneth's sexuality was his neighbour, the stage and costume designer, playwright and artist W. (Walford) Graham Robertson (1866–1948). The two men met in the 1890s; Kenneth was living at Durham Villas and Robertson moved into a house around the corner (possibly to be near Kenneth), and they remained dear to each other for the rest of their lives. They became lifelong friends, professional collaborators and, possibly, lovers.

Robertson was a tall, slim, handsome dandy (he dressed beautifully) with porcelain skin, six years Kenneth's junior. Like Kenneth, he came from a Scottish family; unlike Kenneth, his was wealthy and he was very close to his mother. Robertson became famous at about the same time as the pair met. A gentleman artist, he knew everyone there was to know at the turn of the century, from William Morris to Robert Browning (who apparently ran across the road at Hyde Park Corner to give him an umbrella). Robertson had lived in Paris and as a child spent hours in the dressing room of famous actresses, coming to know and love theatre's finest, and was introduced to Oscar Wilde in 1887 when he was 21. They became lovers. The day before the premiere of *Lady Windermere's Fan*, Wilde asked Robertson (among others) to order a dyed green carnation buttonhole: 'I want a good many men to wear them to-morrow – it will annoy the public.' The flower came to symbolise Wilde and his group.[1]

Kenneth was attracted to Robertson's effervescent personality and their mutual love of the theatre. Outrageously, Kenneth had made an uncharacteristic appearance on the London stage in 1886 in front of Wilde and George Bernard Shaw in Shelley's *The Cenci*, scandalously about incest. Perhaps Robertson had been in the audience and his attention captured by the handsome, well-spoken new actor. The performance had been staged by Kenneth's friend Furnivall's Shelley Society at the Grand Theatre in Islington and was a rare sighting of Kenneth treading the boards – perhaps yet another artistic expression that was frustrated in him.

Kenneth and Robertson both became subjects for John Singer Sargent, who depicted gay men and lesbians amongst his other many works of art. (Sargent's portrait of Kenneth is on this book's jacket.) At 28, Robertson by accident became the subject for one of Sargent's most well-known paintings, after he commissioned the artist to paint his mother. Robertson visited the studio with his toothless poodle, Mouton, who 'was always allowed one bite by Sargent whom he unaccountably disliked, before work began,' wrote Robertson. '"He has bitten me now," Sargent would remark mildly, "so we can go ahead."'

Sargent asked Robertson to sit for him, wearing a very long black winter coat, under which he was naked.

Robertson lived in Argyll Road, a couple of minutes' walk from Kenneth and Elsie's home. On his way back from work, Kenneth would drop in, preferring to sit in companiable silence with Robertson rather than go home to his wife. 'The Rat let him rest unquestioned, understanding something that was in his thoughts; knowing, too, the value all animals attach at times to mere silent companionship, when the weary muscles slacken and the mind marks time,' he later wrote in *The Wind in the Willows*. The men initially found something in common through their love of William Blake's literature and art; Robertson was a collector and had a watercolour over his mantelpiece that Kenneth adored called *The River of Life*, showing a mother swimming with a child in each hand.

Although initially devastated by her husband's emotional coldness, Elsie came to understand, accept and even embrace the men's close friendship. 'I cared for him very deeply,' wrote Robertson to Elsie in the 1930s after Kenneth had died; Elsie replied that she knew the feeling was mutual – any jealousy she may felt at the time long since dissolved. A long and detailed recollection by Robertson of his friend is held at the Bodleian Library, as well as letters between the two men (frustratingly, not always synchronous). These documents provide clues as to the great admiration they felt for each other and are worth reproducing here. Written in retrospect after Kenneth's death, Robertson's artistic account could be read as sentimental nostalgia with more than a touch of emotional flourish, but there is also genuine feeling and thoughtfulness in his words. He writes perceptively:

When I first met Kenneth Grahame in the nineties, he was living in London where he looked all wrong – that is to say, as wrong as so magnificent a man could look anywhere. As he strode along the pavements one felt to him as towards a huge St Bernard or Newfoundland dog, a longing to take him away into the open country where he could be let off the lead and allowed to range at will. He appeared happy enough and made the best of everything, as do the dogs, but he was too big for London and it hardly seemed kind to keep him there.

He goes on to describe how close the pair became:

A two minutes' walk lay between us and the path soon became well worn. As we were such near neighbours, he would happen in casually to dinner or later in the evening, and though we often spoke hardly more than did the somnolent dogs crouched at our feet, yet memory seems to give me back hours spent in long and intimate conversation... As his house was full of toys so mine full of dogs, and we each found the other's surroundings quite normal and satisfactory...

He had a marvellous gift of silence. We all know the old rustic who said, 'Sometimes I sets and thinks and sometimes I just sets.' Kenneth Grahame had reduced 'just setting' to a fine art. He would

Kenneth on his first day at school, aged 9. (*St Edward's School*)

...neth, centre, with his schoolmates in 1870, looking unenthusiastic with head resting on hand. He ...at the feet of Reverend Algernon Simeon, St Edward's charismatic headmaster. (*St Edward's School*)

Inside the Bank of England where Kenneth was employed as 'a paleface quilldriver'. (*The Bank England Archive*)

The magnificent Frederick James Furnivall, who taught Kenneth how to row on the Thames. (*Mary Evans*)

Kenneth's favourite holiday destination of Fowey in Cornwall, where he visited all his life. (*Mark Camp*)

WE Henley, the editor who gave Kenneth his big break. "I should be a pig if I ever forgot him," said Kenneth. (*Mary Evans*)

Evelyn Sharp (holding placard), editor of *Votes for Women* and Kenneth's early love interest. (*Mary Evans*

Elspeth Grahame aged 19. Many men fell for her beauty and charm including Mark Twain and Alfred, Lord Tennyson. (© *National Trust Images*)

"I wonder when you said goodbye" [89]

I wonder when you said goodbye
So lightly - almost with a smile
If you remembered love how I
Should miss you all the weary while

For every hour has seemed a day
Each day at least a hundred years
Ah love how can you stay away
And smile in spite of all my tears

For days to you like hours seem
The hours as moments only
And so you neither think nor dream
Of me so sad and lonely

I wonder when we meet again
If you'll come gaily with a smile
As if forgetful of the pain
I have suffered all the weary while

This poem of Elsie's shows her heartbreak at Kenneth's coldness at the start of their marriage. (© *Bodleian Library, University of Oxford*)

...ndyish portrait of W Graham Robertson aged 28
John Singer Sargent: he was naked under the coat
...make him appear slimmer. (© *Tate*)

Mouse as a young child. Kenneth joked about his "hyacinthine locks". (*The Dorneywood Trust*)

Mouse by the windmill at Littlehampton, aged seven. This picture was discovered in an old ph album discarded behind the squash court at Dorneywood. (*Private collection*)

oodhall Spa in Lincolnshire, where Elsie tried numerous times to recover from depression. (*Woodhall* *Cottage Museum, taken from Nicholas M Duke Cox's book Taking the Waters at Woodhall Spa*)

GREEN BANK HOTEL.
FALMOUTH.
10th May 1907.

My darling Mouse

    This is a birth-day letter, to wish you very many happy returns of the day. I wish we could have been all together, but we shall meet again soon, & then we will have treats. I have sent you two picture-books, one about Brer Rabbit, from Daddy, & one about some other animals, from Mummy. And we have sent you a boat,

painted red, with mast & sails, to sail in the round pond by the windmill — & mummy has sent you a boat-hook to catch it when it comes to shore. Also mummy has sent you some sand-toys to play in the sand with, and a card-game.

    Have you heard about the Toad? He was never taken prisoner by brigands at all. It was all a horrid low trick of his. He wrote that letter himself — the letter saying that a hundred pounds must be put in the hollow tree. And he got out of the window early one morning, & went off to a town called Buggleton & went to the Red Lion Hotel & there he found a party that had just motored down from London, & while they were having breakfast he

"Have you heard about the Toad?" The first letter Kenneth wrote to his son about the story that became *The Wind in the Willows*.
(© *Bodleian Library, University of Oxford*)

DEAR DADD
WE RECEI
ED THE TOAD
LETTER

Mayfield, where Kenneth wrote *The Wind in the Willows* from the study to the upper right of the front door. (*With thanks to Herries School*)

The willows are as beautiful as ever on the Thames at Pangbourne where illustrator EH Shepard spent an afternoon on the riverbank to inspire him for his *The Wind in the Willows* commission.

The River Lerryn in Cornwall. Could this stretch of water be the one in Kenneth's most famous book – rather than the Thames? (*Mark Camp*)

NO MORE "SHOTS IN THE LOCKER."

Suggestions for Precautionary Measures at the Bank of England.

["EASY ACCESS.—We confess to some surprise at the ease with which a wandering lunatic, without apparently stating any very defini[te] business, can obtain access to high officials at the Bank."—*Pall Mall Gazette.*]

The day Kenneth was shot at whilst at work made for an amusing cartoon in Punch. (*Mary Evans*)

t Fimbarrus Church in Fowey where Kenneth married Elsie in her white muslin day dress.
Barbara Woodward)

EH Shepard's iconic illustrations have endeared readers of *The Wind in the Willows* for all time. But he made a mistake in this image, depicting Rat rowing instead of Mole.

'Coldtonguecoldhamcoldbeefpickle gherkinsaladfrenchrollscress sandwichespottedmeatgingerbeer lemonadeandsodawater'.

The ineffable Constance Smedley, original champion of *The Wind in the Willows*. (*Mary Evans*)

HE WHITE HOUSE
WASHINGTON

Personal.   January 17, 1909.

My dear Mr. Grahame:

     My mind moves in ruts, as I suppose most minds do,
and at first I could not reconcile myself to the change
from the ever delightful Harold and his associates, and
so for some time I could not accept the toad, the mole,
the water-rat and the badger as substitutes. But after
a while Mrs. Roosevelt and two of the boys, Kermit and
Ted, all quite independently, got hold of "The Wind Among
the Willows" and took such delight in it that I began to
feel that I might have to revise my judgment. Then Mrs.
Roosevelt read it aloud to the younger children, and I
listened now and then. Now I have read it and reread
it, and have come to accept the characters as old friends;
and I am almost more fond of it than of your previous
books. Indeed, I feel about going to Africa very much
as the seafaring rat did when he almost made the water-

rat wish to forsake everything and start wandering!

     I felt I must give myself the pleasure of telling
you how much we had all enjoyed your book.

          With all good wishes,

               Sincerely yours,

               Theodore Roosevelt

Mr. Kenneth Grahame,
     16 Durham Villas,
          Kensington W.,
               London, England.

have never read anything of yours yet that I haven't enjoyed to the full,' wrote President Roosevelt. *Bodleian Library, University of Oxford*)

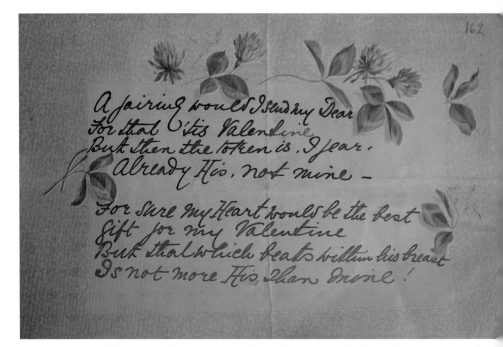

A fairing would I send my Dear
For that 'tis Valentine,
But then the token is, I fear,
Already His, not mine –

For sure my Heart would be the best
Gift for my Valentine
But that which beats within his breast
Is not more His, than Mine!

A true romantic, Elsie wrote valentine cards each year but never received one from the one she loved the most, Kenneth. (© *Bodleian Library, University of Oxford*)

Boham's, the Grahames' beloved farmhouse in the English countryside.

Mouse as an undergraduate of Christ Church College, Oxford. It was the university his father had always longed for.

Kenneth walks with a cane in 1921. He is recovering from his son's untimely death. (© *National Portrait Gallery*)

Above: Elspeth in her late sixties, after a lifetime of anxiety and depression. (*The Dorneywood Trust*)

Left: Kenneth, on his retirement from the Bank of England: his relaxed pose hides the drama of his resignation. (*Mary Evans*)

Pretty Church Cottage in Pangbourne, Kenneth's final home, which is within walking distance of the Thames.

slowly become part of the landscape and a word from him could come as unexpectedly as a sudden remark from an oak or a beech. He could not have been thinking, because a silent thinker is, socially speaking, quite as disturbing to serenity as a motor cyclist. No, he was 'just setting' – in other words he was on the threshold of Nirvana, his brain was receptive but at rest, a great peace was with him and about him and his companion was drawn into it.

It is a lovely description which could only have been written by one who knew (and cared for) Kenneth deeply.

Robertson was a great lover of dogs, he kept them all his life, and became closer to Kenneth because of them: 'Animals loved him. They felt safe with him, and indeed his presence even bought a sense of security, like the shelter of a hill on the shadow of a great tree. His quiet strength soothed and sustained.' Kenneth used Robertson's dog, Portly, for the character of the baby otter in *The Wind in the Willows*. Robertson recalls the moment he asked him: '"I hope you don't mind," said Kenneth Grahame in his courteous, deliberate way as he showed me the MSS. "You see, I must call him Portly because – well, because it is his name. What else am I to call him?"'

Both took homes in the countryside (Kenneth to Cookham Dean in Berkshire, Robertson to Sandhills in Surrey) but it suited them to have a London base to work from so they kept their homes near each other in the city. While this practice wasn't unusual among married working professionals of the day, there is a possibility the arrangement afforded the men an opportunity to develop a relationship. Robertson was creative, fanciful and a romantic, the total opposite of outdoorsy, wholesome Q and Atky. Quite seriously, both men believed in fairies and would talk at length about this imaginary world: 'We would discuss the points of view, proclivities and antecedents of its inhabitants with all the passionate earnestness displayed by really sensible people when speaking of latest quotations, lunch scores or cup finals,' wrote Robertson, who went on to publish the children's story *Pinkie and the Fairies* in 1909.

When Robertson staged *Pinkie* at the prestigious His Majesty's Theatre in the West End, Kenneth came for the dress rehearsal. 'I was naturally much wrought up by his presence at the performance and enormously relieved when he expressed appreciation and I really think he enjoyed himself – anyhow, he said less than ever afterwards, which I knew to be a good sign,' wrote Robertson. He reveals their friendship had been almost exclusively private, when he hints the evening was the first time they had seen each other in public: 'I had hardly even, before then, met Kenneth Grahame amongst a crowd, we had nearly always been alone together,' writes Robertson vividly: 'I remember, as he came towards me through the press, realising how distinct he was from the people around him.' The description could read as a love scene from a film; the crowds part and Robertson's hero appears:

> There was something not abnormal, but super-normal in his presence – he was the slightest bit over life size (any painter will know what that means) – there was a splendour about him that was both of the body and the spirit. He was a being of a different race, or perhaps a throwback to what our race may have been before it became stunted... It was the impression of a moment but I never forgot it.

A sentimental memory or painful romantic recollection? We will never know. But it is plain Robertson was attracted to Kenneth:

> His good looks I had thither to take as a matter of course – it seemed natural that the writer of such books should look like that – but, as I then saw him, towering above his fellows, his beauty took on a new significance, showing him as the lost Arcadian, the wanderer from the country of the young, one who had looked into the eyes of Pan and listened to the Piper at the Gates of Dawn.

This reference to the seventh chapter in *The Wind in Willows* reminds the reader of Kenneth's somewhat sensual description of Pan in the book: 'the rippling muscles on the arm that lay across the broad chest, the long supple hand still holding the pan pipes only just fallen away from the parted lips; saw the splendid curves of the shaggy limbs disposed in majestic ease on the sward...'

Kenneth and Robertson's meeting at the theatre is given further significance by being the subject of a rare and emotionally charged note between the pair. Robertson doesn't address it formally 'To Kenneth

Grahame' as he does in his other letters, but rather jumps straight into what has been troubling him with a flash of passion: 'It was maddening only to get that brief glimpse of you yesterday.' He goes on to explain: 'But I was wanted on the stage & had to plunge in at once to try to patch up the many ragged places which you must have noticed in the performance.'

He finishes: 'It was kind of you to come… I wish you had not vanished away so completely but I know – one in the country – how difficult it is to leave it.'

Was Kenneth embarrassed to be seen in public with Robertson, paranoid that he would become connected with the gay community? Robertson was Oscar Wilde's former lover, a figure whom Kenneth had been careful never to be associated with; he had immediately stopped writing for *The Yellow Book* when it became connected with Wilde, who was reported to be holding a copy when he was arrested for gross indecency in 1895. It was, in fact, a different publication in Wilde's hand but the magazine became forever linked with him (even though he thought it 'dull and loathsome').

Another letter from Robertson is undated but possibly written during the record-breaking heatwave summer of 1906 as Robertson refers to his house as being extremely hot. It is impossible to be absolutely sure to what the letter refers, but the delicacy of the emotion running through it is unmistakable. From piecing together the information, Robertson seems to be replying to Kenneth's request that they put some distance between each other, since after they had taken the lease at Mayfield, Cookham Dean, it appears Kenneth and Elsie sub-let their London home to someone for a short period. The letter begins: 'No – I am not angry, only hurt. In fact there are moments when I almost regret the terrible inconvenience which I have caused you by coming into the neighbourhood.' He goes on to refer to the new occupant of Durham Villas and makes a self-deprecating joke about giving the fellow a discount: 'I hope you mentioned my mean presence to your incoming tenant & reduced his rent in consequence.' Robertson continues, characteristically polite: 'But I hope that Mrs Grahame is really better – in fact, all right again – and enjoying herself in the country and the cool.' The last sentence could explain one of the reasons (or at least Kenneth's guise) for his backing off. Elsie, like her husband, was frequently ill. Had she encouraged Kenneth to move permanently to the countryside out of jealousy and neurosis? Robertson ends the letter with a jaunty reference to a sailor friend: 'This house is like a little Hell above – but luckily I like that, and a sailor man from Africa who is staying with me is much delighted, as he finds the weather unpleasantly chilly.'

Writing years later, Robertson nostalgically explains away the change in circumstances, confirming the pair stayed in touch and that they still cared deeply for one another:

> Soon afterwards he retired wholly into the country and our frequent meetings were at an end, but a chain of happy memories still held us together. Many years later I spent a day with him at Blewbury and found all unchanged between us.
>
> As we strolled together down the lane to 'Boham's' [Kenneth's home from 1910] we might have been dodging busses in Kensington High Street; time had stood still with us and with our friendship.

A link of the 'chain of happy memories' is that Robertson was one of the very first people Kenneth showed his manuscript of *The Wind in the Willows*. He had written ten of the original bedtime stories to his son at Durham Villas, so perhaps Robertson had been part of the writing process. He wanted Robertson to illustrate it, but the artist turned down the commission, claiming it was because he didn't have the time nor skill to paint animals. Robertson agreed to the frontispiece instead, which became his fondest piece of work and the only image in the first edition: 'I am inflated to bursting point with pride,' he wrote to Kenneth, who returned with: 'It's as windy and willowy as they make 'em, and we are critics of willows down here, and of wind too.'

The letters that remain between Robertson and Kenneth confine themselves to wholesome subjects of holidays, the beauty of the changing seasons, nature and polite enquiries about the health of the other's family.

If Robertson and Kenneth did enjoy a love affair, anything physical was likely to have brought to a swift end after Kenneth permanently left London for the country in 1908; the Bodleian collection only references one or two letters that suggest the pair met up in the years following Kenneth's resignation from the Bank ('can't you get over here at some point?'). Kenneth eventually found it in himself to see Robertson again but not until many years later as an older man. And, oddly, the correspondence abruptly switches from between Kenneth and Robertson to between Elsie and Robertson. Robertson admits as much to Elsie when she writes to him after Kenneth's death, asking for recollections: 'I received very few letters from him – you and I did most of the correspondence, I think – but I always felt that I had his friendship and it was very precious to me.' Elsie characteristically stayed in touch by sending Robertson birthday and Christmas gifts, and they exchanged notes on gardening tips.

After Kenneth died, Elsie asked Robertson if he would write about his old friend. But Robertson refused on the grounds that he 'entered so little into his life' and that others were more capable of reviewing his work:

All I have of my very own is our few short years – or was it months? – of intimacy, and of that there is so little to be said, though so much to be cherished and remembered. I cared for him very deeply and when you say that he cared for me you give me great joy – though I think I knew it at the time. His portrait hangs here behind me in my study – & I remember seeing mine on his desk at Boham's.

The fact that both men always had a picture of the other indicates the secret depth of feeling they shared. 'In those long ago days when we saw much of each other, I always felt that, with all the frankness and jollity of his boyishness, there was also, beyond the boy, a man known by few, remote, but very much to be reckoned with,' Robertson wrote. Was he one of the few who knew the man beyond the boy?

What we do know is that Robertson wasn't the only friend of Kenneth who was homosexual. Kenneth was friends with Frederick W. Rolfe, otherwise known as the flamboyant and openly gay Baron Corvo, and the two wrote frequently. It is also worth noting here the private life of Kenneth's agent, the wonderfully named Constance Smedley, who persuaded him to publish *The Wind in the Willows*. A year after the book came out, she married Maxwell Armfield, a gay artist. The newlyweds socialised regularly with Kenneth and Elsie; perhaps they were a support for each other's lavender marriage. The outspoken feminist Constance would not usually have been the type of person Kenneth befriended (although Elsie might have), indicating there could have been a stronger reason for their lifetime of staying in touch.

At the risk of stereotyping, it could be significant that Kenneth loved clothes and always dressed well, even as an older man. He was on first-name terms with tailors in Oxford and loved the fashion of the city:

> Before leaving the High, where fashion used to sun itself, I should record that there was still a good deal of dressiness in Oxford. It was a sad falling off when I found myself, a generation or so later, discussing with Mr. Hall, in his shop in High Street, the decadence of the times, and the good old days when one ne'er appeared in the High except in some sort of toilette – and sometimes a good deal of toilette! And as we talked, there would enter to us a semblance of a Man, with hatless and tousled head, wearing a shabby Norfolk jacket with belt flying loose.

He bantered with Evelyn Sharp about putting 'gold braid put on the collar of his frock-coat and round his silk hat', when she congratulated him on a promotion at work which meant he could ride in the Lord Mayor's Show. 'I feel sure this was not the Kenneth Grahame known to his colleagues at the Bank of England,' she wryly commented on this hidden flamboyancy.

Kenneth was a man who lived a double life; the straight-laced conservative banker with a society wife versus the creative writer who preferred male company and yearned for exotic climes. A divided conscience is something that was clearly on his mind when he wrote *The Wind in the Willows*. Having just left London (and his companion Robertson) permanently for the country, a recurring theme in the novel is the dilemma of heeding the call of nature as three of the main characters grapple with obligation over temptation. Kenneth ensures that Toad ends up back home safely and well fed after his spell in prison, and Mole is kept within the safe boundaries of the riverbank when Rat deters him from the unknown Wide World. The roles are reversed when Ratty is tempted by the Sea Rat to escape the confines of the countryside:

> Restlessly the Rat wandered off once more, climbed the slope that rose gently from the north bank of the river, and lay lookout out towards the great ring of Downs that barres his vision further southwards – his simple horizon… his limit behind which lay nothing

he had cared to see or know... to-day, the unseen was everything, the unknown the only real fact of life...

Kenneth writes of the Rat's 'inner eye' seeing clearly ahead: 'What seas lay beyond, green, leaping and crested! What sun-bathed coasts, along which the white villas glittered against the olive woods! What quiet harbours thronged with gallant shipping bound for purple islands of wine and spice...'

Ultimately, each animal denounces adventure and follows the status-quo, mirroring Kenneth's decision to commit to Elsie and start a family rather than follow a different way of life. Imagine what he might have been capable of writing had he been allowed to follow his own particular call of the south. The freedom to pursue the academic and creative career he had always wanted whilst being able to love whom he chose might have led to an entirely different literary output.

When *The Wind in the Willows* is read with the possibility of Kenneth's homosexuality in mind, the story takes on new meaning. 'The Piper at the Gates of Dawn' hints with bridal references of veiled and forbidden joy that must all be forgotten by the end of the chapter when Mole and Rat's minds are wiped clean of the dream:

In midmost of the stream, embraced in the weir's shimmering arms spread, a small island lay anchored, fringed close with willow and silver birch and alder. Reserved, shy, but full of significance, it hid whatever it might hold behind a veil, keeping it till the hour should come, and, with the hour, those who were called and chosen... Then suddenly the Mole felt a great Awe fall upon him... he felt wonderfully at peace and happy...

Later: 'Trembling, he obeyed and raised his humble head; and then, in that utter clearness of the imminent dawn, while Nature, flushed with fullness of incredible colour, seemed to hold her breath for the event.'

In 1990, Alan Bennett recognised gay connotations in the novel and wrote a play version of *The Wind in the Willows* staged at the National Theatre to critical acclaim. 'Bachelordom is a status that had more respect (and fewer undertones) in Grahame's day than it has now and certainly he seems to have regarded it as the ideal state from which he had disastrously fallen,' writes Bennett in his introduction to the play.

Bennett ends his production with Toad being kissed by the gaoler's daughter. Toad, at once, wants Rat to try it too. 'Rat, of course, is reluctant, but finds to his surprise there may be something in this kissing business after all, and generous animal that he is, wants Mole initiated, too,' writes Bennett. 'So the play ends with a hint of new horizons. It is a large departure from the text, of course, where all four of our heroes are left in bachelor bliss, but this alteration is not entirely without justification, echoing as it does the course of Grahame's own life. Courtship and marriage were late joys for him too, and not such joys either, but that's another story and not one... that I managed to tell.' He writes of the risk of rethinking a children's classic: 'To fans of the book, even to discuss these well-loved characters in such terms might seem, if not sacrilege, at any rate silly. But an adapter has to ask questions and speculate about the characters in order to make the play work.'

Yet whatever Kenneth's sexual orientation, there was no question of his leaving Elsie. Edwardian convention mixed with his self-confessed 'beastly virtue' held a powerful rein. The couple went on to have more than thirty years of marriage, and although there is evidence to suggest that the marriage was unhappy, the pair proved to be devoted to each other in their own way. One significant example occurred early on in their marriage when a family drama erupted that would not have ended as it did without Kenneth's careful and dedicated intervention. It was discovered that Elsie (and her sister Winifred) were not being given the full amount of the allowance promised by their late mother in her will. John Fletcher Moulton, Elsie's stepfather, refused to allow Elsie and Winnie access to the £600 a year from his late wife's estate. When their brother, Courtauld, confronted him about it, Moulton denied any foul play. Courtauld, living in the same house as his stepfather, challenged him and took him to court; Moulton argued over the meaning of trustee and disagreed with the amount of money released for the girls.

Courtauld asked for Kenneth's help with the matter, and both men pragmatically committed themselves to a long and arduous process. Courtauld represented the family in court and Kenneth put his economic knowledge to good use in preparing their defence. Although he could have paid someone to go through the paperwork, Kenneth patiently corresponded with his father-in-law and painstakingly wrote nineteen letters over the two-year period, devoting a significant amount of his time to working through complicated financial details. Despite being denied a university education, Kenneth demonstrated he had a well-informed mind and conducted himself with intelligence and integrity.

This would have meant the world to Elsie; as a young woman she had loved and supported her stepfather, encouraging his career in politics and entertaining his wide circle of friends. Now, as her only surviving parent and the final link to her mother, he had betrayed her. That her husband Kenneth was fighting for her corner must have been a great comfort and without his help, and the help of her brother, she would have lost thousands of pounds and been beholden to a deceitful stepfather. Kenneth also proved himself to be an emotional brick; the trauma of what her stepfather did to her caused Elsie to become mentally ill for months from shock, but Kenneth steadfastly stood by her, taking her away to the seaside on doctors' orders for weeks at a time to recuperate. When it became impossible for him to take any more time off from the Bank of England, he arranged for her to be treated at a health spa on two separate occasions, so concerned was he that the condition could become chronic. He was careful that Elsie be shielded from worrying about the court case in order for her to recover properly; she had developed a painful condition of the neck, which may have been entirely physical in nature or possibly psychosomatic in relation to overwhelming mental stress. Nevertheless, the couple was determined to appear in court when called: 'E is fully resolved to go through with it,' wrote Kenneth.

Being apart from one another may have strengthened their bond; Kenneth certainly knew his wife's mind well, but it must have been a trying time for their marriage ('we are all agreed in wanting it over, & the sooner the better.'). Kenneth never failed to stand up for Elsie, defending her inability to appear in court and diligently meeting with the Lord Justice presiding over the case.

Elsie eventually recovered sufficiently to bravely stand up and tell her side of the story to the judge, which was a sad and shocking admission that the family had to borrow from their butler and cook to cope with lack of money. She and Winnie were awarded compensation of £8,250. (Kenneth had previously calculated each sister was owed approximately

£11,000 in back payment.) They also had to pay legal costs. It was a disappointing result, and Elsie relapsed into depression.

Peter Green's biography damns the Grahames' marriage as wholly unhappy. But a family friend, a professor at the University of Birmingham, objected to this opinion:

> I do not know what is meant by the statement that 'his marriage was not a success'. At all events the marriage lasted for over thirty years until Kenneth Grahame's death... [Elsie's] gift of imagination and intelligent sympathy enabled her to follow her husband's mind and give him throughout his life an ideal companionship.

In any event, the Grahames' companionship was to enter into a new dimension when Elsie discovered she was expecting their first child.

Chapter 13

Mouse

'He did not heed the dull Olympian patter
But turned a wiser ear
Toward the river where the water's chatter
Told of what he would hear'

Anonymous tribute to Kenneth Grahame,
possibly written by Elsie

A lastair Grahame was born on 12 May 1900, at home in Campden Hill. Elsie, who had been anxious about the birth, unexpectedly delivered a few weeks early. Kenneth nicknamed him Mouse because of his large, pink ears; no middle moniker was given as Kenneth believed one name 'is enough for any man'.

Very unfortunately, little Mouse was blind in his right eye because of a congenital cataract, and his left eye had a pronounced squint. He was examined carefully by the family's physician, Dr Heath: 'we must be anxious of course for some days yet,' wrote a concerned Kenneth to his friend, Miss Bradley, one of the first people with whom he shared the news of his firstborn. The day after the birth, Kenneth told her:

I know you will be relieved and glad to hear that Elsie had a small son yesterday, and that both are doing very well. It was rather unexpected but it all came right, and now it's a blessing to think she has been spared some weeks more worry... The boy is a big fellow, and very good.

Auntie Bradley delightedly sent her congratulations and the gift of a hairbrush, most fitting for a lad whose chief physical characteristic was thick curly hair. The next day Kenneth passed on his thanks, slightly more relaxed as he joked:

Elsie tasks me to write and thank you very much indeed for your beautiful present to master. It seems that a brush was the very thing that he wanted, as his hyacinthine locks were getting quite beyond control. And it was his first present – and Elsie was glad that it should have come from you… The boy has taken possession of Mrs Exley [his nurse] and swears like a trooper if she leaves him for a moment to go to his mother.

When Kenneth introduced Mouse to his close friend Arthur Quiller Couch, his friend exclaimed in his typically witty way: 'Never be afraid for a boy with a head shaped like this.'

In addition to his son's wellbeing, the health of his wife was on Kenneth's mind; as was customary for the middle classes of the time he arranged for her support in the form of the 'excellent' Mrs Exley and a 'brick' of a housekeeper. Although there is no formal record of Elsie's physical or mental state immediately following the birth, it seems reasonable to assume she found the experience deeply traumatic. Throughout Mouse's childhood she suffered with depression and muscular pain, which may have been related to her mental illness. In 1900, medical knowledge of mental health in relation to childbirth was in its infancy (pardon the pun) and it is highly possible she suffered from prolonged and debilitating postnatal depression. There were days when all she could manage was to lie on a duvet and sip hot water.

Alison Prince, in *An Innocent in the Wild Wood*, suggested that sexual relations between the Grahames came to an end with the birth of Mouse because Elsie was terrified of falling pregnant again. Prince perceptively cites a poem of Elsie's that indicates a huge shift in her mood:

> Dear, leave me for a while,
> Endeavour to forget
> Dance with the rest and smile
> You may be happy yet
>
> But I have fought with fate
> And fallen in the strife,
> Your love dear comes desolate
> Leave me to live my life

I cannot keep your love
I may not give you mine
Take up your flowers and glove
Let others see no sign

Forget your grief and me
But I'll remember you
Your tender sympathy
So innocent and true.

Although undated and copied out in pencil, the tearful, fearful verse is very unlike the angry poetry she wrote out of frustration when she furiously protested against Kenneth's close friendship with Graham Robertson. However, another piece of evidence to be examined later suggests the couple had at least one further sexual encounter.

During Mouse's young childhood, Elsie began to spend long periods away from home at Woodhall Spa in an effort to get better; the town in Lincolnshire was famous for the therapeutic properties of the mineral-rich waters of its bathhouse. Like Kenneth, she sought out water to heal her. Treatments such as 'fango' or mud baths might have helped Elsie's muscular complaints, and the mud and mineral-rich water were used to help promote feelings of relaxation and revitalisation. Elsie's Woodhall physician, the respected Dr Gwyn, refers in letters to her 'melancholia'. Elsie might have taken heat treatments such as an electric light bath or Dowsing luminous heath baths to encourage wellbeing.

Elsie found it hard to be apart from her son and wrote to Kenneth as many as three times a day, desperate for news from home. Kenneth always replied (although not as regularly as she wrote) in his baby-language way about his adventurous 'larks' with Mouse in Kensington Gardens playing 'yumpy-yums' outside the Albert Hall. The pair would eat bread and butter under the trees while the little boy begged for stories all afternoon.

Back at home, Elsie attempted to make the best of her situation and at times was able to find the strength to cherish her new baby, carefully noting her beloved son's small accomplishments, little anecdotes and sweet memories. Elsie's notebook, small, well-thumbed and written in pencil, reveals her most private thoughts. It is kept in the Bodleian; half of the book is about her husband (from the first page until the middle page) and the second half is about Alastair (turned upside down and starting from the back page). It captures many of her happy memories, such as when she, Kenneth and Mouse were taken by the Dean of Westminster (their friend Miss Bradley's father) to see King Edward's coronation robes. Her remembrances of her young son are very sweet: 'from his infancy he certainly was no conveyer of kisses, and greatly objected to being kissed'; he liked the 'growling' of thunderstorms and wished someone happy birthday by saying 'Happy turn to the day'.

Such tender reminiscences are made all the more poignant knowing that by 18 months of age little Mouse had less than half his vision; because his left eye was over-compensating for the right, he was diagnosed as oversighted by an ophthalmologist before he was 2 years old. Elsie refused to acknowledge her son's affliction – she would gaze into his unseeing eyes and pronounce that they shined like jewels. He grew into a confident boy, as family friend Anstey Guthrie remembers, telling the story of when Mouse was taken on a railway journey at 3 years old, his nanny kept asking him to look at the lambs and countryside out of the window and the pretty ships in the sea. 'Oh Nannie, do leave the boats in the water, they look very well there,' Alastair told her firmly. When he was 4 he was asked if he had been good: 'Yes, but there was a good deal of vulgar eating and arms on the table,' he cheekily replied.

As a young child, Alastair was difficult to handle, perhaps explaining Elsie's nervous mental state. He once tried to break down the bathroom door while his father was having a bath, and would regularly kick his governess, Dutchy (his European nanny), who explained how the park-keeper at Kensington Gardens made an official complaint about Mouse after he kicked and smacked some little girls, digging his fingernails into them. Kenneth seemed unconcerned about the episode, making light of it in his letters to Elsie: 'I perceive serious difficulties between 'im and the German forces – larst I sor of him he sullenly [sic] retiring in good order before enemy...'

Mouse's bad behaviour was overlooked by his parents who concentrated on encouraging his writing. The boy inherited his father's love of letters ('born with vocabulary'). Elsie kept his earliest letter: 'Dear Mum, I have been thinking. A Grahame'. 'A dramatist at 5 yrs old,' Elsie proudly noted; Alastair made up plays and dictated them to his governess to write down, and at 7 he requested to read Spenser's *Faerie Queene*. His nanny remembers Mouse's extraordinary command of the English language:

He had, as a child, a vocabulary beyond his years and his speaking voice was one of noticeable beauty. Of the former a girl, much older than he, said to him once, 'You are only a baby who has swallowed a dictionary.' He was never at a loss for a story or a rhyme.

Elsie remembers how he came up with a three-act play called *Beauty Born* and dictated it to his nanny 'with all the Acts, Scenes, Characters and other instructions'. Later, in a letter he told his parents 'I have made a vow that i will run away to the Stage!!! As soon as i can!!! help!' When he went on holiday with his governess to Littlehampton, he loved hearing the music hall performances and entered a children's singing competition.

As her son grew, Elsie was a somewhat overbearing mother who encouraged Mouse to live in a world of his own imagination rather than equip him for life outside the nursery. As an older child, Mouse wrote very well and 'edited' his own magazine, *The Merry Thought*, with a friend's daughter (whose father was an illustrator). One of Mouse's contributions was an allegorical poem about women's struggle to be given the vote. Called 'Hunting Song', it depicts a policeman chasing rabbits just as policemen were hunting suffragettes:

> Ye red-faced policemen
> Ye suffragette pursue,
> Ye magistrate says 'fourteen days',
> Ye suffragette says 'Booh!'

Impressive work for a 9-year-old. (One wonders if Kenneth mentioned to his son the close friendship of his youth with Evelyn Sharp, the prominent feminist.) 'Published' ad hoc, Mouse only made one copy at a time of *The Merry Thought* to read with the family at home, and it continued to run until he was sent off to school. Of course, he roped in his father to contribute and one such feature was *Bertie's Escapade*, the true story about the day the family's black pig escaped from their Cookham farmhouse (pigs were Kenneth's favourite animals). Mouse was fascinated about how such a large creature could have got out of his sty, and so his father wrote it up in his attractive, distinct handwriting, and submitted it to the editor. The names of the animals were the real names of the Grahames' farm creatures who got up to all sorts of adventures, culminating in the safety of the farmhouse and a slap-up picnic. As well as Bertie the pig, the story includes a mole and rabbits who speak as humans and even Kenneth himself as the adult who wakes up in the night hearing noises. Elsie wrote years later: 'The whole thing is really a sort of rehearsal for *The Wind in the Willows*, though I think quite unintentional and therefore the more striking.' (Without Elsie's foresight, *Bertie's Escapade* may have been lost: she helped it to publication after Kenneth's death.)

Mouse's second governess, Naomi Stott, took over from Dutchy when Mouse was 5 years old, and knew him until he died. She describes him as highly strung, quick-minded with a keen sense of justice, unselfish and a child who didn't hold a grudge:

> He was a gay and a happy little boy, always laughing and playing. He loved to put his hand against a running tap and see the water squirt. He lived a great deal in an imaginary land of his own making. He called it 'Puppyland where it is never silly to be silly'. In that land lived his band of brigands and his dog Kaa… He loved animals and would never want to catch crabs, shrimps or butterflies. He loved flowers but did not want to pick them.

When asked how she best remembered Mouse, she said:

> I have so many memories. But perhaps as clearly as any I see him as a young schoolboy. It was Christmas Eve and there was a party for the village… Mouse had been put up to sing and he stood on a table, under a storm-lantern from the lambing-fold, swung to a rafter. He was a tall young thing and if I say that he was beautiful, you won't misunderstand me? He stood in the light, round him in the shadow sat the party, Newgate fringes and gaiters, shepherds, gamekeepers and carters, men and women of the down country. Mouse piped [sang] as sweetly as a thrush. I think I remember that best of all.

Naomi, who arguably knew him better than his parents, hinted at a darker side to the young boy:

> He was a bit of a mystic too, a strange thing in so young a child. On one of my early days with him he saw a picture of Our Lord in a Holland Street shop. Mouse pointed it out to me, 'That is my

Friend,' he said, 'the Carpenter. When I was ill (he had appendicitis) He came to see me and sometimes I go and talk to Him.'

More disturbingly:

On another day he said to me, 'Death is a promotion.' I told his father what Mouse had said for I thought it possible that the child (Mouse could not then read) might have heard him say something of the kind. But Mr. Grahame assured me that neither he nor Mrs. Grahame had ever spoken to Mouse about death.

Tellingly, Naomi describes Mouse as rarely making a fuss: 'I was often to notice afterwards how reasonable he was and, in sickness and health, how entirely fearless under all circumstances. He never shirked anything however disagreeable it might be to a child of his imaginative and highly strung nature.' This paints a different picture from the scratching boy at the park, but like his father, Mouse learnt at an early age not to complain and instead hide his emotions – an unhealthy coping mechanism which would eventually prove fatal. 'He was always an unusual boy,' confirmed Arthur Quiller Couch, who described him as 'gentle'.

Mouse categorised adults as Goods and No Goods, just as his father had done with the Olympians, and there were many similarities between father and son. They were both water-loving creatures who adored the circus and mechanical toys, and were utterly enchanted with Christmas. Each year, Mouse was allowed to choose the family's Christmas tree and where to put it in the house, and one year he decorated it with pink, red and yellow pop guns as well as animals from his Noah's ark, monkeys, horses and jockeys.

Unfortunately Mouse also inherited his father's poor health, regularly suffering from colds and flu throughout his childhood. A violent illness befell the little boy when he was 4 and the family almost lost him. He was suddenly taken seriously ill with peritonitis (inflammation of the membranes of the abdomen) while on holiday at Broadstairs with his nanny: 'The poor little fellow has suffered a great deal of acute pain, but his pluck and cheerfulness have been wonderful,' wrote Kenneth. He had rushed to his son's bedside from the Pyrenees, where he was holidaying en route to Spain.

Elsie was ill herself, and staying at Woodhall Spa for a neck problem and her recurrent depression. She left as quickly as she could. 'It is a bad set-back for her,' wrote a concerned Kenneth. 'She had to cut short her cure just when she was getting most benefit from it, and the anxiety and strain have been very great.' By July, her neck was better: 'a great success', writes Dr Gwyn from Woodhall's Tasburgh Lodge. More significantly, the doctor writes that Elsie's depression is improving and that she is beginning to look like her old self again with 'the suspicion of a wicked twinkle in the eyes not often seen in those of the melancholy'. One of Elsie's poems called 'Constancy' indicates her stronger state of mind around this time:

> There is no force that can divide
> Your soul from mine for they are one
> Nothing so vast or deep or wide
> As can oppose what we have done

Elsie is reassured that Kenneth will remain by her side, no matter his emotional coldness, giving her the confidence to resume her responsibilities as a mother to Mouse once more.

But in November of the same year, Elsie returned to Woodhall for a much more serious medical issue. It is not entirely clear but evidence suggests she may have been pregnant and possibly suffered a miscarriage or stillbirth. The facts we can deduce from the letters from her trusted doctor, Dr Gwyn, is that she had a painful and enlarged uterus, which Dr Gwyn explains cannot be operated on because of her 'weakened state'. One of the causes of an enlarged uterus is pregnancy, and Dr Gwyn refers to a 'little chap' in his letter. Could he be referring to the fact that Elsie had delivered a stillborn baby boy? Dr Gwyn's letters are deeply sympathetic, indicating Elsie had suffered a significant trauma. The only medical assistance he can offer at Woodhall is a douche or *Mutterlauge* (a concentrated form of the spa water), unlikely to provide her with significant pain relief. An enlarged uterus, of course, can be a symptom of other conditions. At the very least, we can be sure that Elsie was in considerable physical discomfort after suffering a concerning gynaecological complaint.

Alone at Woodhall without her husband beside her, Elsie thought carefully about her future and wrote to a woman called Muriel Bure for some advice about birth control. She could not help with Elsie's request for a 'prescription' of some sort, but gently shares family planning information including the address to buy a quinine pessary, and also recommends a special sponge, chemically cleaned, small, soft and soaked in antiseptic. Her letter doesn't indicate she was a medical professional as the advice is anecdotal: 'It does not hurt and neither the man nor the woman feels it… A friend of mine and also my sister has used this for several years and found it beneficial.'

Mrs Bure may have been an acquaintance ('thanking you for your kindness to me') but it indicates the depth of Elsie's debilitating embarrassment about sex that she was unable to ask for help from her trusted Dr Gwyn or any other medical professional at Woodhall Spa to discuss her deeply distressing fears about falling pregnant again. These were the very concerns likely to have been causing her mental illness.

If only Elsie had known that she was part of the new generation of women using birth control – by 1900 the birth rate had declined by almost a third because of the first commercial suppository as Elsie is advised to use. 'I shall only be too glad to help,' writes Mrs Bure kindly. 'If you are not feeling too tired, I should be so glad if you will write and let me know how you are.' No further letters between the women can be found.

Eventually Elsie returned home to London to be with Kenneth. If they had lost a baby boy, their unhappiness would have been acute. He would have been a brother for Mouse, a companion for the little boy who grew up to be so unhappy. Perhaps with a close ally at his side, Mouse's life would have turned out completely differently.

Elsie dealt with her disappointment by overcompensating as a parent, aggressively seeking perfection and aggrandising her son, encouraging their friends to do the same, including Anstey Guthrie who was introduced to Mouse aged 7: 'I have never met a boy with such natural distinction, or a more fascinating personality. It was rather like being presented to a young prince,' he gushed. 'He was a handsome little boy, tall for his age, with rather long brown hair, a singularly clear and beautiful voice, a subtle smile and an air of complete self-possession.' As an only child, Mouse spent more time with adults than other children might have: 'From our first meeting I had been struck by a certain maturity, not in the least priggish, in his choice of words, and a delicate sense of humour which was far beyond his years…. "Kensington Gardens!" he said disdainfully, "simply starchy with perambulators!"'

Guthrie later wrote:

> In addition to a charming and lovable nature, Mouse had the ability and originality that in all probability would develop into genius. I know now that as he grew up, he never lost his charm, and as a boy and a young man, was fearless, generous, kindly and gracious to all he met, while there were already indications that he would eventually be among those who leave literature the richer for their existence. I myself believe that he would have been a very great writer.

What Elsie and Kenneth lacked in love for each other, they poured into their affection for their only son, resulting in unhealthy expectations and an astonishing lack of boundaries. If they had lost a second child, their emotional confusion would have been even more acute. Kenneth had always felt disappointed with his own education and was determined that his son should enjoy the opportunities he was denied. He and Elsie were resolved that Mouse would be given the very best schooling – a decision that would change the course of his life for ever.

Chapter 14

Moving Upstream

'Darlin M – Just a line to tell you not to be alarmed at any rumours or statements on posters re. There was a lunatic in here this morning "shooting free" with a revolver but *nobody* got hurt at all except the lunatic who was secured after some trouble. Yrs....'

Kenneth to Elsie on 24 November 1903

Even the most dangerous, life-threatening emergency could not shake Kenneth Grahame's outward stoic calmness. Just after 11 am on 24 November 1903, a stranger walked into the Bank of England asking to see Sir Augustus Prevost, the governor. Sir Prevost (who was at that time no longer the governor but rather one of the directors of the Bank) was out of town. The stranger, in his early thirties and smartly dressed, offered his card with the name of G.G. Robinson, saying he had business to attend to. The man was shown into the governor's apartment, and the card taken to the secretary, Kenneth Grahame. 'I suppose you are in charge,' Robinson demanded, giving him a scroll to read. Kenneth asked him to briefly state his business, to which Robinson replied: 'If you won't...' and produced a six-chambered revolver. As Robinson fired two or three shots, Kenneth rushed out of the room into the Director's Corridor shouting for help. Robinson fired again in the corridor before being locked in the Director's Library by the head doorkeeper as senior members of the Bank debated what to do before the police arrived. The Library was a long, narrow room with just one door into the corridor. Several volunteers went silently into the room to see Robinson at the end with his revolver now covered. The volunteers then aimed the fire hose at the man from behind, which caused him to fall over still firing his revolver until it was empty, when he threw it aside. When police arrived they strapped him down and took him to Cloak Lane station. There he gave his name as George Frederick Robinson, an unemployed mining engineer living in Westbourne Street in Sloane Square.

He was charged on account of 'wandering, deemed to be a lunate', before being detained for observation at Bow infirmary. Later at the Old Bailey, he explained that the documents he had presented Kenneth with were tied with white ribbon at one end, and black ribbon at the other; because Kenneth had chosen the black end, he had therefore chosen his own fate. Robinson was found guilty but insane and sent to Broadmoor. Later it was discovered that the only live cartridges in the gun had been fired at Kenneth.[1]

The ordeal had only taken about an hour, but it was an hour of his life from which Kenneth would understandably never properly recover, despite his typically understated note to Elsie to reassure her he was unharmed and that '*nobody* got hurt at all.'

The incident made headline news, with a cartoon in *Punch* captioned: 'Mr Kenneth Grahame is wondering what is the meaning of the expression "As safe as the Bank of England".'

An entire archive at the Bank of England's library is devoted to the volume of letters and telegrams that Kenneth (and Elsie) received following the incident, each offering good wishes and support from peers, friends and strangers alike from across the country and the world, indicating the high esteem in which Kenneth was held. Kenneth probably read some of them when he was recuperating at Littlehampton. Apparently, even his barber commented that he'd seen his picture in the newspaper. When Kenneth asked him what he thought about it, the barber replied: 'I thought you wanted a hair-cut pretty badly, sir.'

Returning to work after the event must have been deeply traumatic for Kenneth, and signalled the beginning of his lack of interest in the Bank of England. Perhaps he felt unsupported by the institution after the awful experience – as far as we know, he was offered little or no counselling or therapy to help him recover.

A happier highlight occurred a few years after the shooting, when in 1907 four special visitors came to the Bank; the royal children of the Prince of Wales (the future George V): Edward, Albert, Mary and Henry. It was an impromptu outing, and the best man for the job was obvious: Kenneth knew exactly what would interest children – royal or otherwise – and ordered a magnificent tea for them while showing them the Bank's treasures and allowing them to see (and sign) a £1,000 note.

Kenneth was a hit and received a sweetly handwritten thank you note from the children the very same day.

But delights such as this were few and far between. On 15 June 1908 he decided it was time to leave the Bank and wrote his resignation letter:

To The Governor, Bank of England

Dear Sir

For some time past I have been forced to realise that the constant strain entailed upon me by a post of much responsibility is telling on me in a way that makes me very anxious, both as to my ability to continue rendering proper and efficient service, and as to the wisdom of facing further deterioration of brain and nerve; and I feel strongly that even at heavy cost I ought to seek relief from the burden, I'm asking that the Court will allow me to place my resignation in their hands. I am conscious how much I am relinquishing – most of all the kind consideration and full and pleasant confidence which I believe the Governors and Directors have always displayed towards me, which I have been very proud to possess, and without which my task for the last fourteen years would have been difficult indeed. But I believe that in taking this step, which I am driven to do by considerations of health, I also serve the interests of the Bank, which call for a more efficient and unimpaired performance of duties than I can now give; and I venture to hope that I may count on the consideration of the Directors in regard to a past service much of which has been rendered under circumstances of special strain and which amounts in all to close upon thirty years.

I am,
Dear Sir,
Your obedient servant

Kenneth Grahame
Secretary

His departure was a sudden, abrupt and mysterious. Kenneth was only 49. Although his personal physician diagnosed arteriosclerosis with symptoms of insomnia, constant headache, amnesia, depression and nervous breakdown, when examined by the Bank's doctor a few weeks later, Dr Davies recorded he: 'saw nothing to lead him to think there was mental deterioration or loss of memory... his colleagues would certainly have noticed such deterioration if they existed.'

The directors offered Kenneth a year's holiday on full pay, but he refused and instead walked away with just half the amount of pension due to him, despite thirty years of service; he was entitled to an early retirement pension of £791 drawn from his salary of £1,700 per year.

'The retirement was very sudden, as I believe Mr Grahame did not appear at the Bank again after the day the incident happened,' wrote the Bank's historian and archivist W. Marston Acres, who had been employed at the same time as Kenneth. 'Evidently his remark was immediately reported to the Governors, and he was probably told to absent himself from the Bank until the Court had considered the matter, when he was retired and granted the not very liberal pension of £400 per annum,' says Acres, also recording:.

> All that I can be aware about is that his retirement had nothing to do with ill-health but to his resentment of the bullying nature of a Director with whom he was discussing some official business, when he was provoked into saying: 'You're no gentleman, sir!' I believe the Director concerned in this episode was Walter Cunliffe (afterwards Lord Cunliffe) whose over-bearing manner made him the terror of high officials in later years when he was Governor..

There is a theory that Kenneth found Cunliffe so unpleasant that in his mind he turned him into a toad: some believe that the character of Mr Toad in *The Wind in the Willows* is based on him. Kenneth and his colleagues were used to a relaxed way of working – Kenneth had managed to write three books in the offices of Threadneedle Street. He took regular holidays, was frequently ill and had four months off work for his wedding and honeymoon. He was regularly seen leaving work shortly before four o'clock, working hours that Cunliffe's shrewd management style would not have taken kindly to. There is a chance, too, that Kenneth's private life had been discovered; any hint of perceived sexual impropriety would not have gone down well at the Bank of England. It would be another sixty years before homosexuality was decriminalised. For her part, Elsie stuck to her husband's story: 'The responsibility was a great strain & was telling on his health,' she told a friend about his resignation.

The exact reason why Kenneth permanently traded the fiscal bank for the river bank before his fiftieth birthday remains a mystery. Everyone seems to have been surprised at his resignation, not least the Bank's Library and Literary Association, of which he was president. 'We can only hope that your health will soon be comfortably returned, and that …[it] will result in further… works from your pen,' wrote the Association regretfully. No other letter is recorded in the Bank of England archives expressing thanks or admiration for Kenneth's lifetime of service. Yet had Kenneth continued to work in London until usual retirement age, one of the greatest stories in English literature might never have been realised.

Chapter 15

From Your Affectionate Daddy

'There was a story in which a mole, a beever a badjer & a water rat
was characters...'

Kenneth Grahame in a letter to Elsie

Two years before Kenneth took early retirement, life had come
full circle. His happiest childhood memories had always been at
Granny Ingles' cottage, The Mount, in Cookham Dean. In 1906,
he finally followed the Thames upstream from London to Berkshire taking
a lease on Mayfield, a countryside idyll just around the corner from where
he grew up. It is a large, pretty white house with bay windows framed in
black with a contrasting red roof and chimneys. It must have given Kenneth
a special thrill when he found out about the house's connection with the
sea; it is partly built with timbers salvaged from Elizabethan ships.

Mayfield's façade has changed little since the Grahames' time, although
then it was hidden behind a high stone wall shrouded in thick shrubs. It
sits high above the stretch of the Thames running below Winter Hill
near four crossroads, with one lane rising to the uplands, another through
a deep forest (Quarry Wood, possibly an inspiration for the Wild Wood),
and another road swooping down to the valley. It was the landscape
Kenneth had immortalised in *The Golden Age* and *Dream Days*, all twiggy
hedges, meandering lanes and earthy smells.

The Grahames lived at Mayfield for four years until 1910, on and
off at first – Kenneth was still working, and Elsie stayed there alone
without him and even without Mouse. It is not until 26 July 1908 that she
confirms to her friend Betsey Purves:

We've disposed of the lease on the London house... Mouse is quite
charmed with this place (he's been here since Xmas) he has no end
of friends in all classes of life – plays chess & is busy all day. He has
2 rabbits & there is a robin that eats out of our hands & lips.

Kenneth, Mouse and Elsie loved Mayfield's lush grounds, in which they kept a small farm. Mouse had a cat and a pony as pets and wasn't a bit afraid of large farm beasts despite growing up in London. He would say to his nanny: 'Come on, never mind the cows, and if there's a bull, haven't I got a stick?' Just like Kenneth, he had a deep respect for nature. A towering Wellingtonia (Giant Redwood) still stands proudly on the hill in the garden, facing the house – the tree mentioned in Kenneth's story *Bertie's Escapade*. In the 1940s, the house became a preparatory school, Herries, and today the school remains proud of its literary connections, with a huge, colourful mural of *The Wind in the Willows* painted on the nursery classroom wall. It seems appropriate that Kenneth's former home is now filled with happy children who read (and perform) his most famous book.

Since Mouse had been 3 years old, Kenneth had been spinning him a long-running bedtime story saga about a mole, beaver and a water rat, as recorded in a letter to Elsie (in their shared baby-talk language):

There was a story in which a mole, a beever a badjer & a water rat was characters & I got them terribly mixed up as I went along but 'ee always straitened them out & remembered wich was wich… I 'erd im telling [the nanny] arterwards "and do you no… the mole saved up all his money and went and bought a motor car!"… You will perceive by this that Mr. Mole has been goin' the pace since he first went his simple boatin spedition wif the water rat.

Mouse absolutely loved the stories and would not let a night go by without being told the next instalment; Kenneth joked to Elsie on the rare days when he managed to escape bedtime, the determined little boy would bother their housekeeper, Mrs Blunt, to tell the tales. Kenneth wryly reported that she was 'pale and exhausted' after the experience.

As Kenneth wove ever deeper his tales of the riverbank, so father and son became more closely bound together in an atypical Edwardian relationship. Romping about on the floor with a son was pretty unusual in those days, yet Kenneth and Mouse would have a grand old time turning the sitting room into a river, complete with a boat (the sofa) for fishing. When they were not together, Mouse would write of his 'travels'.

'I am very glad to hear that you have been having some boating, and sea trips to America & other distant lands,' wrote back Kenneth. Mouse loved rowing for real on the stretch of the river at Cookham below Winter Hill, and on holiday one year enjoyed a rare treat of a motor boat. So much of Kenneth's psyche had been preoccupied with thinking about his own disappointing childhood; now he had the chance to make a happier life for his son. Although he had not written for children before, Kenneth's consummate understanding of them meant he knew exactly what Mouse would be interested in and how best to tell him the tales; Kenneth was the only one who could soothe his son to sleep after a nightmare: 'He had a bad crying fit… and I had to tell him stories about moles, giraffes and water-rats (he selected these as subjects) till after 12.' Elsie remembered how Kenneth made them late for a dinner party one evening because he could not bear to cut the bedtime tale short. The story goes that one May evening Elsie asked her maid where her husband was: 'Up in the night [nursery] telling Master Mouse some ditty or another about a Toad,' she replied. The family's beloved housekeeper Mrs Blunt also enjoyed eavesdropping: 'I listen to your stories and know how real they are to Master Alastair,' she recalled.

Over the summer of 1907 (and again in 1908) Mouse was separated from his parents. He was taken to his favourite spot, Littlehampton, by his governess Miss Stott, while Kenneth and Elsie returned to Cornwall for the first time since their honeymoon. It may sound odd for a family to holiday alone, but it wasn't so strange in Edwardian times. Kenneth didn't like Littlehampton and called it 'a horrid little place'. He wrote to a friend to explain: 'I wish our taste in places were similar, so that we could be together; but in any case E. can't take her bad eye to the sea yet, on account of the glare.' Elsie was suffering with an inflamed optic nerve in one eye but that didn't stop them from returning to Fowey (also by the sea). Mouse was upset that they would not be together and at first refused to go to Littlehampton with Nanny Naomi. Even the draw of watching his son learn to fish and row wasn't enough to get Kenneth there – quite extraordinary, really, considering they were two of his favourite passions.

But if Kenneth and Mouse had not been separated that summer, *The Wind in the Willows* might never have been written. Father promised son that, in lieu of their aural bedtime stories, he would send him written instalments of the tales of the Toad, and thus began the early skeleton for the novel. The letters are beautifully written in ink, in Kenneth's distinctive handwriting. Some are written on hotel notepaper, others are on the blue headed paper of the Grahames' London address at Durham Villas. He almost never made a mistake or crossing-out. He punctuated the writing with words in all capitals to emphasise particular points and included tiny illustrations whenever Toad falls into the river with the word 'splosh!!' The letters are almost grammatically perfect, and the last ones were hardly edited at all before being published.

We know this from the painstaking work carried out by David Gooderson, the author of *My Dearest Mouse*, who published for the first time the original letters in their entirety and analysed their association with the final text.[1]

The first two letters are from the Green Bank Hotel in Falmouth, and then from 28 May the couple returned to the Fowey Hotel where he wrote three more. It was a hotel close to Kenneth's heart, the place where he proposed to Elsie in a letter, and where they spent their wedding night. The later ten letters are written from the London house and sent to Cookham Dean once Mouse had come home from holiday.

Kenneth was still spending a considerable amount of time apart from his family – he stayed at Durham Villas from mid-June until at least mid-September, coming to Cookham Dean sometimes at weekends. It is likely he saw plenty of Graham Robertson during this time and it is not beyond the realms of possibility that Robertson had some sort of input into the stories in the letters. We remember that Kenneth named one of his characters, the baby otter, after Robertson's dog Portly. Elsie wasn't happy with Kenneth's absenteeism; in fact, she told his first biographer, Patrick Chalmers, that her husband wrote all his letters to Mouse during the seven weeks their son was on holiday and then returned to live at Mayfield for the summer. Maybe it made for a better story about how the novel was composed, maybe she was ashamed of her husband's bachelor lifestyle.

Nurse Stott read the letters to Mouse each night while at Littlehampton; the first was written on 10 May 1907 for Mouse's seventh birthday: 'I wish we could have been together', Kenneth writes, and lists the presents he has sent him. And then those immortal words: 'Have you heard about the Toad?… He got out of the window early one morning and went off to a town called Buggleton & went to the Red Lion Hotel & there he found a party that had just motored down from London…'

Mouse wrote back on Friday 13: 'Dear Daddy. We have received the Toad letter on a Friday and it was such a fine day that everybody forgot that it was unlucky. From your affectionate Mouse.'

The letters show great affection between father and son, not least because Kenneth refers to himself as 'daddy' rather than the more formal 'father'.

Kenneth's childish relish for adventure mixed with the delights of rowing and picnicking form the basis of the letters, which mostly centre on Toad's outrageous wrongdoings. The language is surprisingly sophisticated for its 7-year-old audience, with Kenneth using vocabulary such as 'valiantly' and 'conceited', and phrases including 'yelling for vengeance'.

The descriptions too, are often rather graphic with the warning of an attack by 'hundred bloodthirsty badgers, armed with rifles', 'rats, with pistols and cutlasses' and 'Die-hards, or the Death-or-Glory Toads'. Kenneth's final letter ends as the book does, with the Toad sitting amongst friends and appreciatively, albeit smugly, looking around at his restored home '& this gave him the greatest satisfaction.'

On 21 June, Kenneth and Elsie returned home from their holiday in Cornwall – he to London, she to Berkshire. This proved too much for Mouse who was still in Littlehampton and he began to resent his parents for spending time apart from him. He begged for them to come and see him: 'Could you come down here for the week end please do!' When his wish went unheeded, Mouse called himself 'Thine Bad Boy' and by the sixth letter begins referring to his father as Robinson – the man who had shot Kenneth at the Bank four years before. Mouse made up the excuse that Robinson was a better name than his own but attempting to shock his father concealed the boy's deep hurt and confusion over whether he had done something wrong for his mother and father to choose not to visit.

Very sadly, the special bond between father and son began to show signs of damage. David Gooderson, in his book, *Dearest Mouse*, perceptively examines the breakdown of the relationship between Mouse and his parents. Kenneth's letters grew less frequent and served solely as instalments of the animal's adventures with no chatty exchange of news. He never again addresses his letters tenderly to 'my dearest Mouse' nor signs off sweetly 'ever your affectionate daddy'. At one point, the tale becomes pointedly moral; when Toad sings a boastful song about how even the Queen admires him, the narrator warns: 'But his pride was soon to have a fall. Let it be a lesson to us, not to be so puffed up & conceited as the proud Toad.' This line is clearly meant for Mouse and didn't make it into the final book.

The sadness of the cracks in the relationship between father and son is made all the more poignant when reflected against Kenneth's desperately unhappy childhood, spent without either of his parents. Kenneth and Mouse had, just for a brief moment, sparked something incredibly special and rare. But it was gone, never to be properly rekindled. Yet although the spell between father and son had been put out, the magic of the letters would be preserved for ever. According to Elsie in her short biography of Kenneth, *First Whisper of The Wind in the Willows*, at the end of the holiday in Littlehampton, Nurse Naomi saved all fifteen of the letters and posted them to her. This is probably not strictly true although it makes for a good story – Naomi's foresight may have rescued some of the letters but many of them were received by Elsie herself when she was back at Mayfield with Mouse. Either way, it was these two women who preserved the bones of a story that otherwise may well have been lost: 'if restored to the author, they would merely be consigned to the waste-paper basket,' Elsie wrote in *Whisper*.

Unbeknownst to Kenneth and Mouse, the letters would eventually come to represent the wonder and magic of childhood for generations of families, although it would take the literary brilliance of another woman to make it so.

Chapter 16

The Women Behind The Willows

'He was a genuine river devotee; only those who belong to the Thames know the intensive character of that devotion...'

Constance Smedley of Kenneth Grahame

Enter one Constance Smedley. Charismatic and well connected, she was the European agent for an American magazine called *Everybody's*. The publication was successful in the US with well-paid contributors including Rudyard Kipling and George Bernard Shaw but it was almost unknown in the UK. The editor, John O'Hara Cosgrave, had his sights set on signing Kenneth Grahame and believed Constance was the person who could persuade Kenneth to break almost a decade of writing silence.

A feminist and suffragist, Constance was a freelance journalist, illustrator, novelist, playwright and stage designer who would publish forty books during her lifetime. The year she met Kenneth, she had written an early feminist manifesto called *Woman: A Few Shrieks!* and reported on suffrage for the *Daily Mail*. A socialist, she dedicated her life to campaigning for everyone to have access to the arts, no matter their background, and for women to be able to compete on a level playing field against men. She founded the Lyceum Club for Women Artists and Writers when she was just 28; it is still going strong around the world more than a century later.

Kenneth had read and admired her novel *An April Princess* (1903). Set in Cookham, it was about the dilemmas facing modern young women. So when Constance wrote asking to meet him, to her surprised delight he immediately wrote back in agreement. She lost no time in hopping in her car – for she was only 5 miles away, having spent the summer at the River Club in nearby Bray. In 1907 it would have been a rare sight for a woman to be humming through the countryside in a motor vehicle: 'the mists of early autumn were invading hedge and lane,' wrote Constance rather romantically in her autobiography, *Crusaders*.[1]

When she knocked on the door of Mayfield, she introduced herself with characteristic flair as a relation of Mrs Smedley, the governess in *The Golden Age*. Kenneth didn't appreciate the joke: 'Mr Grahame seemed as remote and shadowy as the countryside,' Constance wrote of her first impression: 'about him was that peculiar English aroma of dogs, ploughed fields and fire-lit libraries.' At first he was prickly about why Constance had come: 'he was encased in the defensiveness which dreads coercion... Mr Grahame refused all entreaties to dig nuggets for Mr Cosgrave. He hated writing; it was physical torture. Why should he undergo it?' But Constance wasn't about to give up: she was under significant pressure to fulfil her editor's brief: 'The panegyrics on *Everybody's* elicited the promise that if he ever wrote again he would write for them,' she wrote, 'but his admission that there was a store of memories he had access to did not carry with it much conviction of his intention of opening it for public consumption. As Secretary of the Bank of England his days were full and his river home meant peace and quiet among the books he loved and the lonely country-side.'

Yet Constance's famous charm slowly began to soften Kenneth, and he relaxed a little when she asked him about his favoured subject: 'We spoke of the country and the curious way in which the ground heaved up above the lanes, and the rushing moving growing feeling of the air. "We are very high up," said Mr Grahame, "and this is the Berkshire Downs, the skies are very high here."' Constance's sensibilities touched upon a tender nerve:

> Further conversation elicited the fact that he was a genuine river devotee; only those who belong to the Thames know the intensive character of that devotion, the curiously rigid river laws whether in its boating or fishing worlds. It came out also that this was the country where he had been brought up and that he had just come back to the district after many years.

Constance's gift for conversation and her genuine enthusiasm for his work won over Kenneth, and deeply interested Elsie. The women had plenty in common – both were lively, literary and, like Kenneth, saw the wonder in life. Later, Constance set up the Cotswold Players to give underprivileged communities access to art, and the theatrical group still performs. Elsie was fascinated with her bubbly new acquaintance, whose nicknames were Princess (because of her benevolence and wild imagination) and Peter (for her wish for the same freedoms as men). Constance's zest for life encouraged Elsie to look on the brighter side again and she was inspired to resume her poetry. Constance showed the verse to her contact Thomas Hardy in the autumn of 1907 and it gave Elsie a real boost when he described the verse as 'charming'. Constance's achievements impressed Elsie and inspired her to make more of her own life, especially as her new friend had recently been confined to a wheelchair after using crutches since she was a teenager. She suffered from an undefined disability, possibly of the hips. Typically, Constance doesn't dwell on the issue in *Crusaders*, just briefly mentioning the fact: 'When I was 2 years old a nurse let me fall down a flight of stairs and from that time, although my parents very wisely arranged as far as possible a normal life for me, I was shut off from all forms of physical exercise except driving.'

The women's friendship 'quickly ripened' according to Constance. 'I used to go over there to dinner from the River Club, and then at their house in town.' When she was organising a Fairy-tale Dinner at her Lyceum Club in Piccadilly, it was Kenneth and Elsie to whom Constance turned for advice. She also roped in the artist Maxwell Armfield, who designed and made the evening's elaborate table decorations: 'I discovered that he and I had exactly the same subtle point of view as to what as worthwhile in the realm of imagination and what was artificial, ugly and silly,' wrote Constance. 'The Kenneth Grahames knew too and they were my chief coadjutors in getting up the dinner.' (Kenneth, we remember, believed in fairies and enjoyed discussing them at length with Graham Robertson.)

Constance described the premise of the evening as not a 'foolish fairy world' but 'the fairy-lore of Grimm and Andersen [which] has much more common sense... Opportunity exists forever and for the poorest and most handicapped, provided he be sufficiently high-hearted,' she wrote, conscious of the limitations of her disability. Kenneth was put in charge of the catering, the eccentricity of the evening appealing to his senses as he suggested goldfish and rowan wine (a version of his favourite sloe gin) among other delicacies. He also thought male guests should wear velvet hoods as the dress code. The extraordinary evening was a success, reported *The Times*.

Two years after Constance met the Grahames, she married Maxwell; yet for all her romanticism, Constance's mention of her husband in her biography is purely practical, describing him as: 'the sternest and most unbending Crusader I had met, one who shared all my tastes, varied as they were...' The fact was, Maxwell was a homosexual and the Armfields' relationship was a lavender marriage. It was nevertheless a rewarding one: the couple spent a lifetime together, successfully and happily collaborating on art and theatre projects including seven years in the United States. Perhaps their unconventional relationship helped forge a deeper connection with the Grahames; if the theory is true that Kenneth Grahame was gay, then Elsie may have found support and sympathy in Constance, as the shared experience between the two women afforded them mutual understanding. Kenneth wrote to Constance very warmly to congratulate her on her engagement, on 3 January 1909, showing his quirky sense of humour and love of word play. Marriage, whatever form his took, may not have been his cup of tea but it didn't stop him wishing his friend well:

My dear Princess

Well and truly done! Very hearty congratulations to you and Mr Armfield! I drink to you both in foaming tankards of mulled ale laced with sloe gin – a favourite beverage of Queen Elizabeth. OF COURSE you will live in Gloucestershire – in the heart of the Cotswold country – the only possible place. At least, there is only one more possible county, and that is Double-Gloucestershire – if you can find the way there.

Of course you know there are sort of 'astral' counties, much nicer than the real ones. Cheshirecatshire is another delightful one: and Yorkshirepuddingshire and Devonshirecreamshire are first-rate to live in. Lie-in-bedfordshire is warm and sheltered, and an excellent county for a prolonged stay. Ten-to-forfarshire is chiefly inhabited by retired government officials: you would not care for that. But Hunt-theslipperingdonshire has lively society, and several packs meet in the neighbourhood.

Still, you can't beat Gloucester, double or single...

...This will be a happy New Year for you indeed – I need not send you 'wishes'. But I do ask you to believe that as far as we can we are taking a part in your happiness and looking forward to a more real share in all that is yet to come.

Yours most truly
Kenneth Grahame

Kenneth hints in his letter that the wedding is to be a secret; no details of the ceremony are shared in *Crusaders*, although Constance notes that her Lyceum friends gave her a pony as a wedding present. It is possible that Constance and Maxwell eloped, or, at least, had a much lower-key wedding than would have been expected of such a high-profile couple. We remember too, that Kenneth and Elsie's wedding day was an equally humble affair.

'Wonder is mixed up with, and found in, all sorts of apparently commonplace relationships,' wrote Constance, yet later letters between Kenneth and Constance were quite formal, indicating they didn't know each other that well – although this seems unlikely, considering their regular socialising and professional collaborations. Could it be that their rather stiff letters masked a secret connection of her knowing he was homosexual? Perhaps the two families made a pact to keep correspondence from becoming too familiar to make sure no one ever found out.

Either way, Constance seems to have shared Kenneth's view about keeping sex out of life. When she described the fairyland that she organised for the Lyceum Club dinner, she wrote about her vision for a utopian Arts and Crafts-inspired society: 'It is the world of William Morris without its cruelty, savage passions and fighting and its somewhat heavy sexuality.'

Constance was a children's writer but was never to have a family of her own. So she was delighted when she met the third member of the Grahame family: 'I made friends with Mouse. He was an unusually attractive child, with very beautiful thick dark hair cut straight across his forehead and bright calm eyes. He had about him something of his father's remoteness and was perpetually playing games with himself,' wrote Constance perceptively. 'He had a land of imaginary men whom he captained, and he crawled about beneath the table which was a mountain pass, or mounted the chairs in desperate adventures.' It was when Mouse was put to bed that something magical happened; Constance happened to overhear Kenneth telling his son their precious bedtime tale: 'an unending story, dealing with the adventures of the little animals whom they met in their river journeys.' It was 'a bedtime visit of extreme secrecy', so she only heard the briefest of snippets before she got in the car to drive back to Bray, but it was enough to excite her interest.

Every other agent and literary editor around the world had failed to entice Kenneth from his literary silence, yet Constance succeeded in sparking new inspiration, and she and Elsie worked together to develop a new writing project for him. In *First Whisper of The Wind in the Willows*, Elsie claims she had the idea for using Kenneth's letters to Mouse to make up a children's book: 'I bethought me of the bedtime stories more or less in manuscript form,' Elsie attests. Constance was less sure of the details (*Crusaders* was published before Kenneth passed away and fifteen years before *First Whisper*):

I do not remember when the idea came of Mr Grahame writing Mouse's story: I know when it was broached Mouse was thrilled; he was the only person who could have persuaded Mr Grahame into so hated a task. But he did: and the adventures of Rat and Mole and Badger slowly became chronicled.

Now a third woman was engaged to help with Project River Bank: Naomi Stott, the governess without whose foresight the letters might have been lost forever. She was asked to help Kenneth flesh out the written words by recalling all those countless bedtime stories she had borne witness to, along with Mouse, and write down anything and everything they could remember. Stott's account of the stories were:

The mole and the water rat go to Badger Hall in the Wild Wood. On their way it comes on to storm and rain, and they get lost. The mole falls over something hard that hurts him and finds it is a door scraper, then they find a door and Mr Water Rat's housekeeper says 'What do you mean? You must go to the front door.' She grumbles but at last lets them in at the back door and Mr Badger gives them clothes and supper, and they all have a good time and the next day they go off.

Naomi begged Kenneth: 'If you could tell me any leading questions, I might casually be able to extract more.' These recollections, however, were enough to help Kenneth write chapter four, although the grumpy housekeeper (a female) didn't make it into the book.

Without the significant effort of these three women, *The Wind in the Willows* may well not have been published. It is ironic, then, that the novel is dominated by male characters and there is no mention of females at all until halfway through the plot. Yet although women appear only briefly, they serve as important catalysts, working together with the male characters rather than clashing with them (at least at first) to help Toad. Kenneth cannot resist having a dig at his sister Helen and other female nurses who cared for him (probably rather bossily) during his frequent bouts of illness: "'And no more weeks in hospital, being ordered about by female nurses, Toad," added the Mole...' But after this jokey reference to females, the gaoler's daughter is introduced as being good-hearted, wise and – most importantly – fond of animals and doesn't confuse them as pets (Kenneth's highest compliment). She is crucial to the action as she helps Toad escape by engaging a second woman (her aunt) to help Toad cross-dress in her clothing to slip out of prison. Kenneth hints somewhat wistfully that females have an easier time of it when he writes of Toad's experience of drag:

> [he] was soon agreeably surprised to find how easy everything was made for him, and a little humbled at the thought that his popularity, and the sex that seemed to inspire it, were really another's. The washerwoman's squat figure in its familiar cotton print seemed a passport for every barred door and grim gateway...

A third female is essential to Toad's success when he meets the barge woman and gender is used for farce, as the two 'women' converse before she helps Toad towards the final leg of his journey. Interestingly, it is only Toad who is helped by women – he may be nouveau riche but he is adaptable and cunning, surviving against great odds – Rat and Mole have absolutely no dealings with anyone female; they must solve their (much smaller) problems on their own.

Constance was a constant during the project. She regularly visited Mayfield: 'The Kenneth Grahames' environment was conducive to the imagination and I delighted in my visits there,' she recalls.

> I remember the sloe gin poured into tiny cordial glasses, a stirrup-cup before the long drives home: the ceremony of the salad, served in a great basket with herbs and flasks of condiments and solemnly prepared by Mr Grahame; the rows of tear-bottles of Bristol glass, the peasant toys from all countries, the wonderful collections of old glass and china used, not only looked at. One night I remember being greatly intrigued. Some very tall glasses with a curious convoluted edge were before us through which one saw everything as through the wrong end of an opera glass. They were most fascinating to drink out of: Mr and Mrs Grahame appeared like animated toys miles away across a miniature dinner-table. When I left, the housekeeper was waiting in the hall with one of these glasses most beautifully packed up and tied. 'It is the custom,' said Mr Grahame, 'to give your guest the cup he has drunk from.' At every turn and corner one encountered some magical possession full of memories and suggestions.
>
> Best of all was Mouse, with his ardent gravity, his bright keen pleasure in the world of his imaginings, his toy theatre, his escapades with the village children. And all the time, some two years to the best of my remembrance, Mouse's story was slowly, slowly, set down for its supreme arbiter until *The Wind in the Willows* was written.

Kenneth committed himself to the task, characteristically taking it on wholeheartedly, diligently coming up with a magnificent, handwritten manuscript entitled *The Mole and the Water Rat*. In the end, the series of letters made up roughly a third of the story, mostly chapters 6, 8, 10, 11 and 12. Broadly, the letters are skeleton for the book – mostly concerning the hare-brained adventures of Toad (complete with the letters' original catchphrase 'poop-poop!') – which Kenneth fleshed out into a cohesive narrative involving other characters. Some of the early letters are just used as fragments, but by the later letters, Kenneth felt more confident about his subject matter and they were altered just a little before making it into the book. He came up with twelve chapters almost exactly the same length, something he was proud of. Like many novels of the time it has an episodic feel – but unlike those other novels, it was episodic because it began life as a series of letters rather than a magazine serial.

Elsie believed the book was Kenneth's homage to recreating Wordsworth's celestial view of the glory of nature: 'I have attempted to recapture and commemorate,' her husband told her. Kenneth's objective for his new project was to share the wonder of the world he had recovered from his childhood. The fact that he managed to do this so superbly despite the sadness of his past is what made the book one of the most popular of the twentieth century. He told a friend:

> The most priceless possession of the human race is the wonder of the world. Yet, latterly, the utmost endeavours of mankind have been directed towards the dissipation of that wonder… Science analyses everything to its component parts, and neglects to put them back together again… But what is the use of living in a world devoid of wonderment? … Granted that the average man may live for seventy years, it is a fallacy to assume that his life from sixty to seventy is more important than his life from five to fifteen. Children are not merely people: they are the only really living people that have been left to us in this over-weary world… In my tales about children, I have tried to show that their simple acceptance of the mood of wonderment, their readiness to welcome a perfect miracle at any hour of the day or night, is a thing more precious than any of the laboured acquisitions of adult mankind.

Chapter 17

Mr Mole and His Mates

'It is the boys that matter most of all.'
Kenneth Grahame, in a letter
to a father of a young reader

Now retired and approaching 50, Kenneth drew on life experience for character, plot and theme as he reflected what made him most happy in life. 'Retirement and reminiscence are apt to trot in harness together,' he once wrote. While *Pagan Papers*, *The Golden Age* and *Dream Days* depicted childhood with a tartly satirical tinge, his new story had a gentler, melancholic tone. Kenneth mined the recesses of his memory in an entirely different way than previously, giving *The Wind in the Willows* unique and enduring appeal. Julian Fellowes, the Oscar-winning screenwriter who made both a film and musical of the novel believes:

> There is a poignancy about Grahame's writing. An inner sorrow perhaps. There's something touching about Ratty and Mole's friendship; there's something touching about all of it, really. I love that. *The Wind in the Willows* is a happy story and we're smiling as we read it or watch it but there's a kind of poignant quality that makes it stay with you, haunting you, and this increases its value.[1]

The Wind in the Willows is one of the great classics of children's literature, but it wasn't Kenneth's intention to write a book just for the young: he was at pains to explain that he had written about childhood to be read by adults (just as his previous collections): 'A book of Youth – and so perhaps chiefly for Youth, and those who still keep the spirit of youth alive in them: of life, sunshine, running water, woodlands, dusty roads, winter firesides; free of problems, clean of the clash of sex.' Kenneth borrowed a quote from George Meredith's poem *Melampus* to explain what he meant: '...of life as it might fairly be supposed to be regarded by some of the wise small things "That glide in grasses and rubble of woody wreck".' The novel is part of the first golden age of children's literature, which is recognised as running between 1862 and the beginning of the First World War, when writing for young people emerged as a distinct genre. The canon includes E. Nesbit, Beatrix Potter, A. A. Milne and Rudyard Kipling; the influence of these writers on all children's stories published after this time cannot be underestimated. '*The Wind in the Willows* seems as if it were written about the beginning of the modern world rather than at the end of the Victorian era. There's a lack of sentimentality. The animals are very truthful in their representation of human beings,' believes Julian Fellowes.

Anthropomorphism emerged as a key characteristic of the golden age period, and it has its roots in aural folklore. As a boy, Kenneth had been brought up on Scottish ballads and was fascinated by the 1880 book *Uncle Remus*, a collection of African-American slave stories about speaking animals getting up to smart tricks. Some fourteen years before *Willows*, Kipling's *The Jungle Book* was published in 1894, featuring talking animals of the exotic variety, although unlike *Willows*, the story centres around the character development of a human boy, Mowgli, and has less of a sense of humour compared with Kenneth's wit. Irony rather than humour is the tone of writer and illustrator Beatrix Potter, who published *Peter Rabbit* in 1902. Like Kenneth, she sets her stories in the English countryside amongst animals, but these are the only common threads with *The Wind in the Willows*, of which Miss Potter was critical: 'Kenneth Grahame ought to have been an artist – at least all writers for children ought to have a sufficient recognition of what things look like,' she sniped. 'Did he not describe "Toad" as combing his hair? A mistake to fly in the face of nature – A frog may wear galoshes; but I don't hold with toads having beards or wigs!'

Kenneth answered this indirectly when he spoke on the need for readers to willingly suspend belief about animals: 'It is the special charm of the child's point of view that the dual nature of these characters doesn't present the slightest difficulty to them,' he said. 'It is only the old fogies who are apt to begin "Well, but..." and so on. To the child it is all entirely natural and as it should be.' Magical thinking, we remember, is a concept that psychologists recognise as being unique among children – real and imaginary worlds exist in parallel until a person is about 10 years old. Kenneth was unusual because he never lost the ability to slip easily between them. In his own life, regular withdrawal into make-believe tormented Elsie and caused him to misunderstand his son. But writing *The Wind in the Willows* was a safe retreat, and one that was approved by his wife. Actually, Kenneth achieved the reverse – making the real imaginary – by going back into happier times and fictionalising them, trawling the depths of his memory for all those blissful days spent boating on the Cornish sea and rowing in the Thames, alone and with good friends. He used his places and people to create the story, celebrating all his favourite holiday destinations including Cornwall, Venice, Marseilles and Bordeaux. Venice's Grand Canal is described: 'feasting with friends, when the air is full of music and the sky full of stars, and the lights flash and shimmer on the polished steel prows of the swaying gondolas… The Water Rat, silent too and enthralled, floated on dream-canals…' The food Kenneth loved, the weather he enjoyed and the people he met are skilfully amalgamated into the story. The water mill where Rat and Mole have their picnic may well be the picturesque sawmill at Bodmin Pill upstream from Fowey. The Cornish fishing village we remember was fictionalised as the Sea Rat's 'little grey seaside town'. Kenneth also included some of his beloved Berkshire landmarks such as the fine Tudor houses around Hurley, Henley and Pangbourne: 'I have always felt that Toad Hall was on the Oxfordshire side,' wrote Kenneth to a fan, keen to know where Toad Hall was. Ultimately, it was Kenneth's unquenchable love of the water that inspired his greatest character, the riverbank. Whether the river he refers to is the Thames at Cookham, or the River Lerryn at Fowey, or a magical combination of both, he captures it like no other writer.

Similarly, Kenneth searched his memories for characters, fashioning hybrids of his favourite people for Toad, Ratty, Badger and Mole from Q, Atky, Henley, Mouse and Elsie, as well as himself. 'Friendship is one of the most important emotions in our lives yet literature is mostly about romance or hatred and very little is written about friends,' believes Julian Fellowes. 'It fascinated me that Grahame knew that and wrote about it. He correctly identifies certain types of human beings that we are all aware of. We know these people and somehow Grahame finds the truth in them and that's compelling.'

Q is the only real person confirmed by Kenneth as inspiring one of his characters: Ratty. Kenneth wrote this in the front of a signed copy of the novel he gave to Q's daughter Foy. Atky's stately credentials set him up perfectly for the role of Badger, a wise bachelor some years older than Kenneth and a loyal, trusted friend: 'He sat in his arm-chair at the head of the table, and nodded gravely at intervals as the animals told their story; and he did not seemed surprised or shocked at anything...' Atky's home of Rose Bank wasn't unlike Badger's stately burrow, and Kenneth's respect for the gruff publisher W.E. Henley would suggest he is honoured in the character of Badger as well, although as an editor he might have been more careful about grammar: '"I'm very sorry," said the Rat humbly. "Only I think it ought to be 'teach 'em, not 'learn 'em." "But we don't want to teach 'em," replied the Badger. "We want to learn 'em – learn 'em, learn 'em!"'

No matter how arrogant, selfish or bombastic Toad's behaviour, he is always forgiven as he is 'really a very good-hearted animal'. Toad descends into the worst traits imaginable, yet his friends remain loyal to him, just as a parent will ultimately always love their child no matter his behaviour. Kenneth had in mind his son Mouse when he wrote the character, believed Constance Smedley: 'Mouse's own tendency to exult in his exploits was gently satirised in Mr Toad, a favourite character who gave the juvenile audience occasion for some slightly self-conscious laughter.' It is certainly true that Mouse would frighten his parents and nanny by lying down in the road in the way of oncoming cars. We also know from accounts by his friends that Mouse loved talking and was a witty conversationalist. 'I have the gift of conversation,' boasts Toad to his friends. 'I've been told I ought to have a "salon", whatever that may be.'

Toad may also be partly based on Walter Cunliffe, the governor who was a likely cause of Kenneth's resignation from the Bank of England. Other inspirations are said to be King Edward VII, Horatio Bottomley (the larger-than-life financier and editor), Bishop Charles Gore and Kenneth's friend Sir Charles Day-Rose, who was known for his eccentric hobbies including motor cars. Kenneth frequently visited him at his home, the red-brick Hardwick House on the Thames, where he is said to have lain on the river bank watching the water rats.[2]

And what of Kenneth? Turning himself into a character would have seemed the height of vulgarity in his eyes, although the reader cannot help wondering if his complex personality has a touch of Badger's stateliness and wisdom coupled with Mole's conventionality and conservatism. Elsie envisioned her husband as Mole, writing of 'the coming together of Kenneth and Mole', describing her husband in a velvet dinner jacket running out barefoot into their garden to catch a glimpse of a fight between a mole and a robin over a large worm. Perhaps Mole represents the figure of good conscience on Kenneth's shoulder, while Rat is the person he yearns to be. It is Ratty who longs for the South in 'Wayfarer's All' but Mole who pulls him back. And Rat finds an outlet for his imagination through writing, encouraged by Mole: 'The Rat pushed the paper away from him wearily, but the discreet Mole took the occasion to leave the room, and when he peeped in again some time later, the Rat was absorbed and deaf to the world, alternatively scribbling and sucking the top of his pencil.' Kenneth may have included parts of Elsie in the personality of Ratty. She was a confident, sociable animal – always keen to make friends and introductions. Kenneth idealised Ratty as the perfect companion, lamenting that Elsie fell short of his ideal.

Like Mole, Kenneth's personality is characterised by an acceptance of his fate:

The Mole saw clearly that he was an animal of tilled field and hedgerow, linked to the ploughed furrow, the frequented pasture, the lane of evening lingerings, the cultivated garden-plot... he must be wise, must keep to the pleasant places in which his lines were laid and which held adventure enough, in their way, to last for a lifetime.

The futility of going against what nature has sown is a theme Kenneth repeatedly explores throughout *The Wind in the Willows.* Just as his own life had been tied to the ancestral obligations of banking rather than academia, Mole recognises – and accepts – his lines are also set. Perhaps the river is all Mole needs to satisfy his wanderlust; similarly, Kenneth found contentment through his own adventures, following the sun annually to the sea of Cornwall, the fountains of Italy and the water of the Thames, while always knowing he could return to the safety of home.

Obligation versus adventure presents itself to three of the four protagonists; to Mole and then Rat and later, Toad: throughout the novel Toad's constant chafing at the bit for thrill is thwarted every time. Finally, there is a hint of smug contentment after escaping from prison: 'And by this time he was feeling very happy, for the sun was shining brightly… he had had a first-rate breakfast, and he had got money in his pocket, and he was getting near his home. And he thought of his adventures and all the dangers he had escaped…' The comfort of home offers contentment and acceptance for one's lot, Kenneth seems to be saying, especially after the risk of losing it. Ultimately, all the animals are offered a taste of adventure by fighting against the weasels in the final chapter as they defend against the most important thing: home. Kenneth was always drawn back to his corner of Edwardian England no matter how much he enjoyed his holidays: 'What do you find to attract you in this poor drab little country?' asks Rat to a migrating swallow bird, who replies: 'The call of the lush meadow-grass, wet orchards, warm, insect-haunted ponds, of browsing cattle, of hay-making, and all the farm-buildings clustering round the House of the perfect Eaves…' Another swallow answers: 'we shall be homesick once more for quiet water-lilies swaying on the surface of an English stream.'

Home is a central issue in the book, one that Kenneth had previously explored in his essays: we see how Mole misses his own home more than he realises when he catches the smell of it on the wind and returns inside with Ratty. Mole knows on the one paw that he must be brave and embrace opportunities, but at the same time he is reassured by the familiar and the friendly. He is like Kenneth, who retreated into the burrows of his mind but knew he must still get up for work the next day and face duty and family:

> He did not at all want to abandon the new life and its splendid spaces, to turn his back on sun and air and all they offered him and creep home and stay there; the upper world was all too strong, it called to him still, even down there, and he knew he must return to the larger stage. But it was good to think he had this to come back to, this place which was all his own…

For the animals, the river is their physical home and for Kenneth, it was his spiritual one. As an adult, he generally lived within a few miles of the Thames. The river acted almost as a biblical balm to soothe his thwarted aspirations, both professional and personal. If Kenneth was homosexual and had attempted to express this in his story of maleness, it would explain his overprotectiveness for the novel – twice he refused to entertain the idea of an abridged version and he also protested against the fee for foreign rights. *Willows* seems to have a power over him as a sort of cathartic 'water-biography'. Kenneth found his own salvation within the confines of the river; the waters of the Thames offered him the only private space where he could simply be himself, happiest in male company or alone with his thoughts: 'Problems such as present themselves are here of the simplest and least complex form,' he once wrote of the joy of paddling on the Thames. He expressed the feeling of privacy the river afforded him: 'the stream bore me out of hearing, that is one of the special charms of the Thames. The River of Life has remorseless eddies and backwaters which forbid escape from such disputes.'

The mysterious healing power of nature, and in particular, water, is discussed in the 'The Piper at the Gates of Dawn', a chapter that stands out from the rest of the book and is one of only two that don't have their origins in the letters to Mouse ('Wayfarers All' being the other). It reveals Kenneth's most secret, innermost desires and his mystical view of nature aligns with the neo-pagan writers of the *fin de siècle* movement such as Edith Nesbit and the Rossettis. Perhaps Kenneth also saw shades of himself in the character of Pan, who turns away from industrialisation in favour of preservation of the pastoral: 'Both iron road and level highway are shunned by the rural Pan, who chooses rather to foot it along the sheep-track on the limitless downs or the foot-path through copse and spinney not without pleasant fellowship with feather and fur.' Pan, too, seems to be an extroverted introvert given the right sort of crowd: 'nor does it follow from all this that the god is unsocial. Albeit shy of the company of his more showy brother-deities, he loveth the more unpretentious human kind...'

Kenneth had a strong sense of the importance of the land and rural living; throughout his life he cultivated genuine friendships with rural folk – the fishermen of Cornwall and later the farmers and shepherds of Berkshire. Being mistaken for a Cornishman was one of the greatest compliments he was ever paid. 'Pan has been known to appear at times, in homely guise of hedger-and-ditcher or weather-beaten shepherd from the downs. Strange lore and quaint fancy he will then impart, in the musical Wessex or Mercian he has learned to speak so naturally...' he wrote.

The character of Pan is a direct link to a book which runs almost in parallel to *The Wind in the Willows*. *Three Men in a Boat* was written in 1889 by Jerome K. Jerome, Kenneth's friend and neighbour in Chelsea Gardens. Both books have four principal male characters (counting Montmorency the dog) and both use humour to capture the jolly pre-war atmosphere of the leisured Edwardian English riverbank. Perhaps Kenneth saw himself in George, the clerk 'who goes to sleep at a bank from ten to four each day'. At the very least, he suffered from many of the same medical maladies as Jerome's characters perceived they had. Both novels are men's own adventures: 'It is the boys that matter most of all,' Kenneth once wrote to a father. Yet while *Three Men* is largely without political satire, Kenneth's novel can be read as a political statement, criticising the rise of the Victorian bourgeoisie (Toad) and voicing concerns about social mobility upsetting the old order (stoats and weasels occupying Toad Hall). Toad is industrious and ingenious – able to adapt and survive unlike complacent figures who refuse to change. Rat (Kenneth?) shouts after the motorists who destroy Toad's caravan: 'You scoundrels, you highwaymen, you – you – road-hogs!' In the original manuscript he had penned the final insult as 'you stockbrokers!' Clearly he had not forgiven the Bank of England.

Ultimately, what elevates Kenneth's masterpiece is its stunning lyrical quality. For Kenneth, joy is bound up in the beauty of nature that he first appreciated as a boy. His intention for the novel is that it is 'an expression of the simplest joys of life.' Constance praised this: 'The river scenes and country were... woven into the adventures, but from an older point of view,' she wrote, 'that of the man who knew this river, its floating craft, its flower tufts, its deep banks, its quiet upper reaches, and willow-shrouded islands.'

Who can forget the opening chapter of the novel, when the end of winter is celebrated so eloquently?:

Spring was moving in the air above and in the earth below and around him, penetrating even his dark and lowly little house with its spirit of divine discontent and longing.... Something up above was calling him imperiously ... The sunshine struck hot on his fur, soft breezes caressed his heated brow, and after the seclusion of the cellarage he had lived in so long the carol of happy birds fell on his dulled hearing almost like a shout. Jumping off all his four legs at once, in the joy of living and the delight of spring... It all seemed too good to be true... He thought his happiness was complete when, as he meandered aimlessly along, suddenly he stood by the edge of a full-fed river. Never in his life had he seen a river before...

Kenneth delicately employs literary techniques of hyperbole, personification and onomatopoeia to create a master impressionist's watercolour of the riverbank. Not a word is out of place. He admitted that many of the months he spent on *Willows* were dedicated to honing the language of the book – as he put it, 'the pleasurable agony of attempting stately sentences'.

Kenneth's intense thinking had evoked profound memories of his childhood: 'Coming back here wakens every recollection,' he told Constance Smedley, as he offered his story to her as an inspiration to the 'unwondering' world. Constance found the beautifully handwritten manuscript breathtaking: 'Compare *The Wind in the Willows* with *Dream Days* and one sees a maturer set of memories have been drawn on,' wrote Constance, 'although the brisk adventures have been framed to please the child.'

Kenneth had at last broken his ten-year silence, giving expression to an entirely new literary voice that would have lain dormant had it not been for the persuasive Constance. Four months after Kenneth's retirement, they prepared the manuscript to be sent to the editor at *Everybody's* in the United States. Autumn was falling in the Berkshire countryside; the animals of the riverbank at Cookham Dean nestled down to retreat from winter and there was nothing left for Kenneth, Elsie and Constance to do but curl up and wait to hear from the other side of the Atlantic.

Chapter 18

Three Animals in a Boat

'Boats are the only thing worth living for.'
Letter from Kenneth Grahame
to a young fan, Miss Joy, 1909

When Kenneth Grahame's eagerly awaited manuscript landed on the editor's desk in America, there was much at stake. Here was a British author with a respected reputation and huge commercial potential.

But *The Mole and the Water Rat* was rejected.

'Mr. Cosgrave was delighted with it,' said Constance Smedley in *Crusaders*, 'but the owners of the magazine had other ideas. They felt that a fairy story, however beautifully woven was out of character with the style of the magazine… Most reluctantly Mr Cosgrave explained the awkward situation and returned the manuscript.'

Elsie thought carefully about why her husband's story wasn't the instant success she had assumed it would be, writing:

The impasse between what was supplied and what was demanded was great and seemed insurmountable … It is, of course, a known fact that once an author has made a success with one type of book, he must continue to take that as a model… the American publishers were quite at a loss how to adapt themselves to the transmutation of those very realistic boys and girls, such as their readers could comprehend, into animals, and wild animals at that.

Constance similarly explained the rejection:

The form of *The Wind in the Willows* was unexpected, the atmosphere of *Dream Days* and *The Golden Age*, the charm of scene and inhabitants so inevitably blended, the fragrant good sense and philosophy, and perfect understanding of the way a child thinks, were all incorporated therein together with much more of a maturity and universal understanding: but *The Wind in the Willows* had been written for a child, and *The Golden Age* and *Dream Days* had been written for an adult public!

There is no record of what Kenneth thought of the rejection of the manuscript he had put his heart and soul into, only that he asked for it to be sent back to him. But the women behind the *Willows* were far from giving up. Constance Smedley with 'kindly enthusiasm' arranged a meeting with her friend the literary agent Curtis Brown, who read the manuscript excitedly and declared it was 'lovely'. Constance initiated the beginning of a long, successful and mutually respected relationship between the Grahames and the American newspaper man in London. She wrote:

> Kenneth Grahame was to him the supreme artist that he was to me, and the writing of *The Wind in the Willows* had been news of tremendous import ... Mr Brown's keen artistic sensitiveness was combined with a very wide knowledge of the literary markets in England and America, and I knew he would take care of this book as I could not and Mr Grahame could not. The introduction was accordingly made to their mutual liking and *The Wind in the Willows* found a puissant champion.

The editing process began; very little of the stories of the later letters Kenneth had written were changed, and the manuscript was smartly typed up in green ink on cream paper, given the Curtis Brown stamp and sent back to the author for approval. Kenneth carefully read it, his sharp eyes correcting the odd spelling mistake and making small but significant word changes to ensure exact meanings, such as Mole looked 'each side' rather than 'every side' and 'quiet' to 'peaceful'.

Kenneth, we recall, asked for Graham Robertson as illustrator: 'I well remember my joyful enthusiasm when I first read the MSS,' wrote Robertson, who was at first modestly and eccentrically reluctant to accept the commission for the frontispiece (the book would not be fully illustrated for another five years): 'time was lacking and, moreover, I mistrusted my powers, for I could not number an otter or a water-rat amongst my acquaintances though I had once known a mole almost intimately and had several toad friends. I could not altogether forgo the honour of lending a hand, so I drew, hastily and very badly...' Robertson created a beautifully whimsical river scene of an otter swimming through reeds towards a waterfall overseen by three cherubic water nymphs. It was captioned 'And a River went out of Eden' and would become one of Robertson's most treasured pictures: 'It is not worthy – but I am glad, all the same. It's nice of Methuen to say it's charming when I am sure he hates it,' he wrote to Kenneth of the publisher's feedback. Kenneth, too, cherished the image and was interested to hear Robertson's vision of what a fully illustrated version would look like: 'a series of landscapes (rather in the style of Blake's Pastorals) with the merest suggestion of Keats creeping in at out of them. But now the first edition is the thing.'

Kenneth always kept Robertson's ideas close to his heart and was somewhat disappointed with the book's many subsequent illustrators. Paul Bransom was the first artist commissioned for the job, and he depicted the animals literally. Kenneth grumbled: 'My animals are not puppets; they always make them puppets.' The book is one of the most illustrated children's stories (with more than ninety different versions), but it wasn't until it was in its eighth edition that it included any pictures at all apart from Robertson's frontispiece. Kenneth's first choice was Arthur Rackham (an animator for Disney's *Snow White and the Seven Dwarfs*) but this didn't come about until after Kenneth died.

The most well-known illustrations are by Ernest H. Shepard of *Winnie-the-Pooh* fame (thirty-eighth edition). Shepard had worked on *The Golden Age* and *Dream Days* but approached the challenge with caution:

> I hesitated, as I considered it so perfect a work of art in itself that no pictures could do justice to it, but I learnt that it had been illustrated already by various artists, none of whom, to my mind, had made a success of it. I suppose I felt that I could do better than this, anyway, I could try.

Shepard was introduced to Kenneth by a mutual friend and came to visit him in 1930. Kenneth, now 71 and somewhat frail, begged: 'I love these little people, be kind to them.' Shepard had great respect for Kenneth and worked as hard as he could on the project:

I went over to his house at Pangbourne on the Thames, he was very kind but I think he rather feared another illustrator! He told me of the spots on the river where his little animals lived and where to find them all, where was Toad Hall, where Rat kept his little boat. He said he himself would take me to these places but he was too infirm.

Armed with his instructions and my sketch book I set out. It was very peaceful in the meadows by the river and I kept as quiet as possible as I moved along the bank – some movement in the grass might perhaps mean that mole was about or the line of bubbles on the water told me that rat was not far away. I looked for the tiny boat among the rushes and peered into the dark hole in the bank, fancying that I could see a pair of tiny eyes watching me. I stayed and sketched till the light failed, then I picked my way carefully across the fields, back to reality.

I was to see Kenneth Grahame once again. When I had made some drawings for the book I took them to Pangbourne. He was critical but I think he was pleased with my efforts and when he handed the drawings back to me he said, 'I'm glad you've made them real.' I always regret that he did not live long enough to see the new edition completed.

Shepard offered the author one of his original sketches as a gift before they went on exhibition in London: 'I have felt it is a great honour to illustrate your lovely book, and was very much cheered by your kind words of approval on Thursday.' Despite his mindfulness, Shepard made a mistake which can still be seen in some editions – when Mole and Rat go boating, he depicts Rat rowing although in the text it is Mole who takes the oars. (It was rectified but the plates were not thrown away explaining why some editions are still printed with the incorrect images.)

The book's title was discussed at length before it was published remembered Kenneth:

So far as my recollection goes, the book was to have been called *The Wind in the Reeds* [the name of the chapter he had given to 'The Piper at the Gates of Dawn'] and may have been so advertised in advance by Methuen, when it was pointed out that there was already

a book by W.B. Yeats called *The Wind Among the Reeds*. So the title
had to be changed – in something of a hurry!

Kenneth came up with *Mr Mole and His Mates* but when this was also
rejected, he again leaned on his trusted friend Graham Robertson who
had plenty of ideas including Down Stream, With the Stream, The
Lapping of the Stream, The Babble of the Stream, By Pleasant Streams
and By Waters Fair (both inspired by Blake), The Whispering Reeds, In
the Sedges, Under the Alders, Reeds and Rushes, Reeds of the River,
River Folk and The Children of Pan.

'That's as far as I've got at present,' Robertson mused. 'No good... It
may come, as you say, while shaving.'

It is not known who chose the final title, presumably the publisher.
Robertson took a great personal interest in the project, having been
involved in one way or another since Kenneth first began writing those
letters to Mouse. So well did he understand Kenneth's writing and the
public's perception of him that he offered his friend a nugget of advice
that was missed by both Kenneth's agent and his publisher. Robertson
recognised that the book was of an entirely different style from previous
work and suggested it was made clear that the novel is 'not a political skit,
or an Allegory of the soul... or a social satire.' Curtis Brown would have
done well to heed Robertson's advice: the first place he tried, Kenneth's
usual publishing house Bodley Head, turned it down.

Brown then tried offering it to magazines as a serial; again, this was
unsuccessful. Finally, after 'laboring long and hard', Brown persuaded
Algernon Methuen to take it on, although Kenneth received no advance
and was set to make very little money if the book didn't sell well. Brown
was proud of securing 'excellent royalties, in case the book should fulfil
my dreams'.

Just as he had seen the initial MSS, Robertson was one of the first
to see the published novel: 'The arrival of the book was a great delight
to me and the re-reading of it a still greater pleasure... I only wish my
silly little drawing were more worthy of its forward position.' He joked at
there not being a picture of Pan, hinting at frustration of having to have
'appropriate pictures', perhaps in reference to its homoerotic associations:
'In the... picture edition, we won't have a picture of Pan, will we? Perhaps
a little bit of his shadow, but no more.'

It is clear that Robertson still cared for Kenneth, as his professional letter written as an illustrator softens into the personal, that of a friend and admirer:

> I hope that the work may have a most prosperous career, & that, when it attains an enlarged and illustrated edition, you will think of me ... I would like to see it the same size as the big 'Dream Days' & 'Golden Age' – with our windy-willowy cover and appropriate pictures! ... I'm rather sorry that the present cover attempts to show the Heart of the Mystery – it pictures the thing that is always just around the corner.

He closes the letter wistfully: 'How wonderful the autumn is. I do hope you are enjoying it and not messing about with Banks and things.'

Like the Grahames, he had made the tree change with his beloved dogs from city to countryside moving to Sandhills in Witley, Surrey. He drily remarks that as a gay man he didn't exactly fit in: 'The publican in our village won't consult with me. He is an ex-butler & has lived in the best families.'

The Wind in the Willows was released to the general public in the UK a year after it was first submitted to *Everybody's*, in October 1908, with the American edition released by Scribner in New York four days before the English one (the copy that Kenneth inscribed for his son and muse, Mouse, is the American edition). It sold slowly at first and was rudely snubbed by critics as a 'bread-and-butter *Jungle Book*'. *The Times* wrote loftily: 'Grown-up readers will find it monstrous and elusive, children will hope, in vain, for more fun.' A rare positive review ran in *Vanity Fair*, declaring it 'the best book ever written for children and one of the best written for adults'. Journalist Richard Middleton described it as 'wise', noting: 'the book for me is notable for its intimate sympathy with Nature and for its delicate expression of emotions.' The public agreed with Middleton and began buying steadily; a second edition was released within the month. As it turned out, it would simply keep selling, racking up edition after edition – reaching 100 in Britain alone by 1951. Even today, annual sales are 80,000 and it has never been out of print, despite being published more than a century ago – a feat that is impressive for any novel, let alone a children's one. As its original champion, Constance

Smedley, wrote: 'Its success was unprecedented on both sides of the ocean, and it was indeed a matter of rejoicing that such a book should be launched on a favourable current.'

It was to be another connection with America that would help *The Wind in the Willows* to its next level of success. The book had originally been written for an American magazine, then it was taken on by an American agent, and now it landed in the hands of the most famous man in the country. Kenneth knew that President Theodore Roosevelt was a fan of his earlier novels and arranged a copy of *The Wind in the Willows* to be sent to him. He wrote to The White House:

Dear Mr President, – You expressed yourself with such great kindness last year on the subject of my books that I think it possible you may care to have a copy of the English Edition of one that has just been published, so I am venturing to send you one. Its qualities, if any, are mostly negative – i.e. – no problems, no sex, no second meaning – it is only an expression of the very simplest joys of life as lived by the simplest beings of a class that you are specially familiar with and will not misunderstand.

The President replied heartily before he'd even read the novel:

My dear Mr Grahame – The book hasn't come, but as I have never read anything of yours yet that I haven't enjoyed to the full, I am safe in thanking you heartily in advance. Of course it won't have 'any problems, any sex, any second meaning' – that is why I shall like it...

Again heartily thanking you, and with real regret that you are not to come to this side while we are in the White House, believe me,
Sincerely yours,
Theodore Roosevelt

After President Roosevelt had read it, his response was like many others:

My dear Mr Grahame, – My mind moves in ruts, as I suppose most minds do, and at first I could not reconcile myself to the change from the ever-delightful Harold and his associates, and so for some time I could not accept the toad, the mole, the water-rat and the badger as substitutes. But after a while Mrs Roosevelt and two of the boys, Kermit and Ted, all quite independently, got hold of *The Wind in the Willows* and took such a delight in it that I began to feel that I might have to revise my judgement. Then Mrs Roosevelt read it aloud to the younger children, and I listened now and then. Now I have read it and re-read it, and have come to accept the characters as old friends; and I am almost more fond of it than your previous books. Indeed, I feel about going to Africa very much as the Sea Rat did when he almost made the water-rat wish to forsake everything and start wandering!

I felt I must give myself the pleasure of telling you how much we had all enjoyed your book.

With all good wishes

Sincerely yours

Theodore Roosevelt

Kenneth eventually met the president at Oxford, when Roosevelt described him as 'simply charming'. Kenneth was surprised and delighted to know his work struck a chord across the other side of the world: 'It is not exactly logical, but somehow to have given pleasure to readers very far away seems to bring a special satisfaction which one cannot feel about the opinion of the man round the corner.'

Kenneth believed in his characters so powerfully that they were real to him in a sort of parallel world. Constance Smedley summed up the extraordinary strength of Kenneth's imagination:

There was the Banker, not so much alarming as austere, the Scholar, rather remote, the Author, approachable; and then there was the man who was more exactly right than any one I have known about the world of Fairytale... He lived and wrote simply and with dignity. He never seemed interested in himself or his writings. But he was passionately interested in outdoor world; in noble literature; in 'all things lovely and of good repute'.

Constance continued to lend her support for the book's success and Elsie too remained engaged; she loved a good project to keep her happy and inspired, and working on behalf of her husband she revelled in drumming up publicity. She wrote to her many literary contacts inviting them to review the novel including their family friend Anstey Guthrie (who politely declined).

How did Kenneth take the success? With a characteristic pinch of salt, a dollop of melancholy and more than a touch of whimsicality. 'They liked the subject matter,' Kenneth told a friend of the public's reaction to *The Wind in the Willows*:

> They did not even notice the source of all the agony, and all the joy. A large amount of what Thoreau called life went into the making of those many playful pages. To toil at making sentences means to sit indoors for many hours, cramped above a desk. Yet, out of doors, the wind may be singing through the willows, and my favourite sow may be preparing to deliver a large litter in the fullness of the moon.

The novel would be the last book Kenneth wrote.

Chapter 19

A Feeling of Snugness

'The City is there, all the time – only waiting, till one rides up the road, and over the drawbridge.'

Kenneth Grahame writes a metaphor
for his old life in a letter, 1911

As Kenneth's fame grew, so did the number of visitors to his home, both invited and otherwise. A reluctant celebrity, he wrote in a letter to a friend: 'I was very sorry to leave Cookham Dean, but there was really nothing there that suited us at all.' The Grahames didn't own Mayfield (it wasn't unusual for middle-class families to rent in those days) and the landlord wrote to let the family know of his intention to move back in.

It was time to burrow deeper into the countryside, further towards the source of the Thames. Kenneth worked hard to find a suitable new home for his family, and it wasn't easy. But both the wait and effort were worth it – he finally came across a rural farmhouse nestled in one of a string of beautiful villages a mile or so north of the Berkshire Downs not 12 miles from his beloved Oxford. Blewbury has been described as the quintessential Berkshire village (it has since became part of Oxfordshire) and is a tranquil, pretty place with a tiny green, grazing cows and a small stream running into a pond with plenty of willows on its banks. Although the houses these days are a mixture of original farmhouses and newer builds, the surrounding countryside looks the same as it did in Kenneth's time – he would have been delighted that the land has been preserved – with acres of spectacular views spreading out from around the village.

As Kenneth put it, 'Blewbury… is only about 54 miles from London but 5,400 years remote from it in every way.' His romantic sensibilities loved the fact that the village was in the heart of King Alfred's country where 'nothing has really happened since'. William the Conqueror's curfew bell still rang throughout the winter months. 'The village is really a charming one – a mixture of orchards and ancient timbered cottages and clear little streams, and the people are simple and friendly and dignified.' It was January 1910 when the Grahames moved into Boham's, a 300-year-old farmhouse surrounded by an orchard and flanked by barns. Today, with a greater number of dwellings in Blewbury, Boham's lies within the village itself and the road next to it has been named Grahame Close in his honour.

Although some 10 miles from the River Thames, a small trout stream ran along the back of Boham's. The traditional interior included two thick-walled kitchens, a parlour with a carved chestnut mantelpiece from the William and Mary period, and an office for paying the farmhands. The family slept next to the granary and the apple loft; by now, Kenneth and Elsie had separate bedrooms. When the Grahames moved in, they decided not to employ the usual domestic help, so it was up to Kenneth and Elsie to unpack. Now in his fifties, Kenneth remained strong and fit, described at the time as: 'very tall and broad, a massive figure but with no spare flesh... His hair was white, but his face was almost beatifically young, and he had the clear and roseate complexion of a healthy child.' Nevertheless, Kenneth's account of the exhaustion of the move will be familiar to many of us. He wrote to Alan Lidderdale (the son of the governor of the Bank of England who helped him secure his clerkship all those years ago):

> We moved into this little old farmhouse a fortnight ago and have been slaving ever since to get it straight, with very little result – the trouble being that we have got too much stuff for so small a space... This is a very beautiful village, in quite a different way [from Cookham Dean] and the Downs are at one's door. I hope for some fine walking when I have finished picture-hanging and falling over rolls of carpet.

Kenneth was keen to restore the farmhouse to its original state, and had the eight coats of paint on the walls removed to reveal oak, in the linen-folded style. Later, he converted a barn to be his library, reminiscent of the London bachelor pad of his earlier days and indicative of the separate life he was leading from Elsie: 'I have put a good stove in, and most of my books, and it makes a very decent study indeed, and gives us more room, which we wanted...' he wrote to a friend. His many books were crammed into a large converted gun case of dark, carved oak and he displayed his favourite souvenirs from Cornwall; candlesticks, inkstands and a photo frame all in heavy Cornish granite. For Kenneth, the importance of home had always been paramount. As a freelance writer he had composed 'The Iniquity of Oblivion', a piece about recurring dream of the importance of home:

> a sense of snugness, of cushioned comfort, of home-coming... a certain little room, very dear and familiar... solitary, the world walled out, but full of a brooding sense of peace and of possession... ensconced in the most comfortable chair in the world, the lamp lit, the fire glowing ruddily... always the same feeling of a home-coming, of the world shut out, of the ideal encasement. On the shelves were a few books – a very few... On the walls were a print or two, a woodcut, an etching – not many. Old loves, all of them...

Elsie, too, enjoyed decorating the farmhouse with treasures she had collected during her travels in Europe as a girl (it is thought she had been born in Indonesia, although Kenneth still had not taken her abroad), along with carefully preserved family heirlooms. Her taste, unsurprisingly, was eclectic; a silk Japanese folding screen lay next to an old Welsh dresser decorated with Nelson's head juxtaposed with old Bohemian glass and tortoiseshell tea caddies. She decorated the walls of the farmhouse with precious eighteenth-century embroidered samplers, oil paintings and antique fans. Inspired by the river, a soft, willow-green rug lay on the floor.

Boham's was miles from the nearest town, with no driveway to entertain unwelcome voyeurs; Kenneth adored being surrounded by nature and delighted in making friends with his animal neighbours, from sheepdogs to a tame robin who would hop over to him each morning for a currant. Equally, Elsie embraced country life. Although a former London society hostess, she was equally happy tending to her garden as she wrote to a friend: 'A farmer drove up just now with a great basket of Whiteheart cherries for Kenneth and yest. I got such a bunch of sweet peas from another farmer's wife. They really are such kind neighbours.' The Grahames became close to their farmer friends, the Saunders, and would have tea with them most Sunday afternoons.

Kenneth was happier than he had been for a long time, believed his first biographer, Patrick Chalmers. He fell into the rhythm of the seasons and spent his energy forging a deep connection with Blewbury, its countryside and its local families. At the August fete, Kenneth joined in with the country dancing and Mouse had a sweet stall. Both loved discovering the sheep-fair: 'one of the most intoxicating things I have been at,' described Kenneth, 'not an outsider present except ourselves... Mouse was soon in the thick of it, but when I sought him and discovered him bidding at the auction for pedigree rams, I had to haul him out of action.' Elsewhere, Kenneth writes colourfully of going on the train with the locals for Cattle Show Week – a rare jaunt to London:

> Our carriage was crammed with a jovial crew of Berkshire farmers, their wives and children, laden with toys for the children left at home... This country really gets older and more primitive in a sense, a race apart – prosperous, well-to-do, living a jolly life, but among themselves, and intermarrying among themselves and keeping up their old habits and customs.

Kenneth wrote with fascination of the shepherds who roamed the hillsides, their traditions, their ancient work matched by their names taken from the Bible; Kenneth endeared himself to them and they invited him to their harvest home feasts at the end of the summer. Pork, crackling, roast beef, gravy, plum pudding and apple tarts were served with strong, brown ale before the entertainment began of recitation and country songs – surely Kenneth's idea of heaven.

Kenneth published very little while living at Blewbury; most of the writing he did was through letters to friends. He described himself as an author who operated as a pump rather than a spring, and *The Wind in the Willows* had exhausted the flow. Perhaps being further from the Thames had stemmed the tide or maybe he had no need for creative output now his soul was being nourished by nature. As always, he remained connected to his life-blood of the river and Elsie recalls how he took up canoeing again, and he happily spoke of paddling through 'hay-harvest and honeysuckle weather'. In a rare piece of prose, five years after *Willows*, Kenneth wrote about how close he felt to nature in Blewbury. It is called 'The Fellow that Goes Alone' for the jubilee edition of his old school magazine the *Chronicle*. In it, he talks about the joy of walking and the meditation it offers and is worth including in detail here, as it reveals much of Kenneth's singular state of mind during his early fifties:

For Nature's particular gift to the walker, through the semi-mechanical act of walking – a gift no other form of exercise seems to transmit in the same high degree – is to set the mind jogging, to make it garrulous, exalted, a little mad maybe – certainly creative and suprasensitive, until at last it really seems to be outside of you and as it were talking to you, while you are talking back to it. Then everything gradually seems to join in, sun and the wind, the white road and the dusty hedges, the spirit of the season, whichever that may be, the friendly old earth that is pushing forth life of every sort under your feet or spell-bound in death-like winter trance, till you walk in the midst of a blessed company, immersed in a dream-talk far transcending any possible human conversation. Time enough, later, for that – across the dinner table, in smoking-room armchairs; here and now, the mind has shaken off its harness, is snorting and kicking up heels like a cold in a meadow. Not a fiftieth part of all your happy imaginings will you ever, later, recapture, note down, reduce to dull inadequate words, but meantime the mind has stretched itself and had its holiday. But this emancipation is only attained in solitude...

The saying is 'no man is an island', but the closing paragraphs suggest Kenneth still mourned his singledom:

This is as much company as you ought to require, the comradeship of the road you walk on, the road which will look after you and attend to such facts as must not be overlooked. Of course the best sort of walk is the one on which it doesn't matter twopence whether you get anywhere at all at any time or not...

Kenneth always relished the thrill of travelling solo, his experiences intensified without Elsie:

The best adventures of his life were pursued and achieved, or came suddenly to him unsought, when he was alone. For company too often means compromise, discretion, the choice of the sweetly reasonable. It is difficult to be mad in company; yet but a touch of lunacy in action will open magic doors to rare and unforgettable experiences.

The piece is similar in sentiment to the thoughts of his transcendentalist hero Henry David Thoreau, who wrote *Walden; Or Life in the Woods* (1854) about living in a cabin in a forest in New England for two years. Thoreau spent much of his time walking, fishing, paddling and swimming in an experiment to 'live deliberately'. Kenneth wasn't a religious man, but for him, walking (and being in and on the water) was a meditation, a vital exercise to achieve inner peace. Walking became part of him – whatever the weather – and winter exhilarated him. He wrote:

It was a cold still afternoon with a hard steely sky overhead, when he slipped out of the warm parlour into the open air. The country lay bare and entirely leafless around him, and he thought that he had never seen so far and so intimately into the insides of things as on that winter day when Nature was deep in her annual slumber and seemed to have kicked the clothes off. Copses, dells, quarries and all hidden places, which had been mysterious mines for exploration in leafy summer, now exposed themselves and their secrets pathetically, and seemed to ask him to overlook their shabby poverty for a while, till they could riot in rich masquerade as before, and trick and entice him with the old deceptions. It was pitiful in a way, and yet cheering – even exalting. He was glad that he liked the country undecorated, hard, and stripped of its finery. He had got down to the bare bones of it, and they were fine and strong and simple.

Despite the fact that Kenneth wished to be the fellow who goes it alone, he welcomed to Boham's his close friends. Atky from Fowey popped in unannounced, which absolutely delighted Kenneth:

He just dropped from the clouds, without notice, ate a hearty lunch, talked a great deal, and flitted away again into the outer darkness. He seems to have been very poorly all the winter, as the result of influenza, which sapped his strength, but he was distinctly on the mend when he came here, and is probably all right by now.

Sadly, it was one of the last times Kenneth saw his dear friend. Atky drowned in a boating accident in 1911, after almost being rescued by Q's son, Bevil; when their 18-foot yacht foundered, Bevil helped Atky swim to the safety of the rocks at the bottom of a cliff before running to get help. But when Bevil returned, the body had been taken out to sea.

Kenneth was desolate:

> I loved Atky – in perhaps a selfish way first of all because all his special 'passions' appealed to me – boats, Bohemianism, Burgundy, tramps, travel, books, and pictures – but also, and I hope I believe chiefly, for his serene and gentle nature, his unfailing good humour and clear, cheerful spirits, and his big kind heart... always some fresh whimsicality.

To preserve the memory of a man who helped keep his spirits up in a place where the sun always shone, Kenneth considered purchasing Atky's home, Rose Bank, but complications prevented a sale – a shame, as he had always harboured a fancy of retiring in Fowey. Elsie, to comfort Kenneth and Q, painted a portrait of Atky. While it is true that Elsie was frustrated with Kenneth's escapes to Cornwall, boating with his male friends, her compassionate gesture indicates that she had made peace with them.

In 1911, the family welcomed Kitty Cheatham to stay, an American singer and actress who performed popular stories and songs from children's literature. She had connected with the Grahames the previous Christmas, ahead of performing parts of *The Golden Age* in London the following March, embarrassing Kenneth by throwing her arms around him after they were introduced backstage. She described Elsie as being 'devoted' to Kenneth when the pair came to meet her from the London train to Didcot:

> We rode the high cart that took us to the village of Blewbury, where, with his devoted wife and adored young son, he lived in the old world cottage near the downs that he loved so well. All was peaceful, lovely and entirely innocent of modern ways. What beautiful long walks we took interrupted by unforgettable visits to the gentle shepherd who would tell us wonder tales of his flock...

Kitty described Kenneth:

> There he stood, and he was very straight and tall and the sunset was
> in his hair… as he stood there high over me. I never lost my first
> impression of the shy, gentle, ineffably tender, quietly humorous,
> great-hearted childlike man, who lived in a world of his own creating
> with, at that time, shepherds as his closest visible companions.

Elsie and Kitty struck up a friendship which continued through letters.
Kitty had no children of her own, and Elsie helped the American with
her British performances by sharing her knowledge and contacts (she
introduced Kitty to Graham Robertson). In turn, Elsie shared some of
her children's poetry with Kitty, and it is a great shame the poems haven't
survived; Elsie shows in her letters that she had a deep understanding of
children, just like her husband.

Now Kenneth wasn't regularly seeing his old friends in Fowey, he
found a new male companion with whom he conversed prolifically (and
with a wonderfully dry sense of humour) for seven years. An American,
Austin Montgomery Purves was a well-known book collector from
Philadelphia. Kenneth and Elsie had met him, his wife and five sons
when they holidayed in Fowey in 1907. They stayed in touch until Purves'
death in 1915, meeting again just before the First World War. The sons
came to visit several times, to Oxford and when the Grahames were in
Italy.

We learn from the letters that Kenneth was frequently ill at Blewbury,
suffering everything from severe influenza to depressed spirits; it seems
he had befallen mental 'unwellness' just as his wife suffered. In the winter
of 1909, his general health was so poor that even the mildest case of
flu literally floored him. In late 1910 he suffered with recurrent chest
infections:

> I have been laid up in bed with a sharp attack of bronchitis, which
> has interfered sadly with my Christmas duties and pleasures too for
> that matter, and other people's also; but that is over for the present,
> though I have to sit indoors over a fire and not run about over the
> downs, as I would fain be doing. We have not had much fun this
> winter…

Later, Kenneth wrote of how this constant physical discomfort had begun to affect the mind: '"Rundownedness" is quite a specific complaint, and a bad one; and it's apt to be the patient's own fault too,' he wrote, of the importance of practising self-care. For her part, Elsie did her best to beat her emotional demons and cheer everyone up by making the most of the festive season; she always found the energy to send a long list of cards and spent time choosing thoughtful gifts. Always a skilled correspondent, she loved writing to her many friends around the world over the festive season. 'E. is Christmassing for all she's worth,' wrote Kenneth, who became generally disinterested in keeping up with most friends and even his own family – it was Elsie who would write to his cousin and best man, Anthony Hope Hawkins, for example. Even Q accused him of being 'elusive'. Kenneth, always the dreamer, preferred instead to privately meditate on summers at Fowey: 'perhaps some future Christmas we will have a private joint-stock lobster-pot of our very own, and haul it up and eat the proceeds thereof on Christmas day.'

During the dark months of winter, just as the animals in *The Wind in the Willows* reflect on their summer memories, Kenneth relived his holidays to keep his pecker up: '[we] miss the sea and the sunshine,' he wrote to Purves. Kenneth lived for the summer, when he would travel abroad, mostly to Italy (when he tried France – Brittany – he complained he didn't enjoy it as much): 'I want to smell foreign smells again and drink wine in the country where it grows.' He satisfied his Sea Rat side by regularly visiting Oxford; Blewbury was the closest he had lived to the city since his schooldays: 'I had a jolly day at Oxford a short time ago,' he wrote to Purves. 'Everything in full swing and the river covered with men doing "tubbing" practice. The old place was just as beautiful as ever, and I bought some youthful ties and some "Oxford sausages" in the delightful market.' It could have been a scene from *The Wind in the Willows*, and Kenneth loved showing Mouse his favourite city. The two became close again during Mouse's final year at home before being sent to boarding school. Like many boys of the age, he was tutored until he was 11, and Kenneth played his part in educating his son, once carefully writing out a general knowledge quiz (along with scoring method). What do you know about the phoenix? Kenneth asked, surely crestfallen when Mouse answered: 'The phenix [sic] is an insurance co.'

Kenneth was conscious that this would be the last golden year of his only son's childhood before he left to go to into the Wide World.

Chapter 20

An Early Environmentalist

'I *don't* talk about my river,' replied the patient Rat. 'You *know* I
don't, Toad. But I *think* about it,' he added pathetically, in a lower
tone: 'I think about it – all the time!'

The Wind in the Willows

Kenneth constantly thought about nature, and the river was never
far from his thoughts. Unlike Rat, though, he did talk about it – or
at least wrote about it. Kenneth wasn't a political man and he was
unused to voicing his personal views – but the issue of the environment
was so important to him, he made an exception. He wanted to make
it known he opposed urbanisation and *The Wind in the Willows* is his
song of praise for England's fragile rural beauty. An amateur naturalist,
Kenneth had championed the countryside in his earlier essays; now he
drew on his love of animals for this latest work.

The book is Kenneth's water-biography, written in the last year of his
forties, and a culmination of his thoughts on the natural world. It is an
early environmentalist's manifesto, a strong case for preserving Britain's
countryside amidst the unprecedented industrial development of the early
twentieth century.

Britain at the turn of the century was the most industrialised nation
in the world and also the most powerful with an Empire that spanned
a sixth of the Earth's surface. But rapid industrialisation had meant
unprecedented urbanisation with half of Britain's population living
in cities. Some 20,000 miles of railway track was built between 1825
and 1914, and the increasing popularity of the car saw the development
of Britain's first road network. As the environmental impact of
industrialisation began to become clear, groups sprang up to protect the
countryside, including the Society for the Protection of Birds (1889) and
the National Trust (1895). One of Kenneth's most well-known admirers,

President Theodore Roosevelt, set up the National Wildlife Refuge System in the United States in 1903.

Kenneth's conservative prose was a homage to water and the countryside; he was profoundly concerned with the destruction caused by the effects of the post-industrial revolution: 'Year by year I see things I have admired and loved passing and perishing utterly,' he addressed an audience at one of his final engagements. Although he worked for the Bank of England, which funded Britain's railways, he famously hated the train tracks ripping through the countryside. Neither was he a supporter of big business. Like many minds of the time he disliked the squalor of London and Britain's other cities, and although he generally remained apolitical, writing was his way of communicating his views. Man needs nature more than nature needs man, and in a very modern way of thinking, Kenneth recognised that we will leave the planet in a much worse state than when we joined it:

The more one considers it, the humbler one gets. This pleasant, many-hued, fresh-smelling world of ours would be every whit as goodly and fair, were it to be rid at one stroke of us awkward aliens, staggering pilgrims through a land whose customs and courtesies we never entirely master, whose pleasant places we embellish and sweeten not at all. We on the other hand, would be bereft indeed were we to wake up one chill morning and find that all these practical capable cousins of ours had packed up and quitted in disgust, tired of trying to assimilate us, weary of our aimlessness, our brutalities, our ignorance of real life.

Kenneth had previously stretched his creative muscles in 'The Inner Ear', as he writes lovingly and lyrically about his favourite subject:

At intervals the drum of the woodpecker rattles out from the heart of a copse; while from every quarter birds are delivering each his special message to the great cheery-faced postman who is trudging his daily round overhead, carrying good tidings to the whole bird-belt that encircles the globe… To all these wild, natural calls of the wood, the farmyard behind us responds with its more cultivated clamour and cackle; while the very atmosphere is resonant of its airy population, each of them blowing his own special trumpet.

Highways and Hedges was to be a 40,000-word book written by Kenneth about country life, offered to him as a commission by the publisher A. & C. Black. Kenneth was asked to include 'anecdotes, folk-lore, philosophy, political economy, botany, ornithology, and references to anything and everything that rambles in beautiful English country are likely to bring to mind'. Kenneth was the perfect man for the job but understandably refused the shockingly low £50 fee. (It was published in 1911 by Herbert A. Morrah.)

Instead, we must be content with Kenneth's essays about the land, which show his deep – almost spiritual – connection with the earth. Here he writes of the Berkshire Downs surrounding his home of Blewbury:

> Up there, on the windy top of the downs, the turf is virgin still to the share; the same turf that was trodden by the hurrying feet of Saxon levies ere they clashed with the Danish invader on yonder ridge... This year its turn has come late, and the furrows still gleam unbroken, touched each, on the side the share has polished, with warm light from the low, red, winter's sun. The stillness all around, the absence of chirping and singing life...

Kenneth's connection with the land, and the people who worked it, recalls Thomas Hardy; the two men were friends and both preoccupied with the beauty of their particular corners of England. They shared a fatalistic view of man versus the elements and regularly referenced paganism.

Nature was a connection between Kenneth and Elsie; she was inspired by nature to write poetry and some of her early drawings featured flora and fauna. In later life, she loved gardening and her letters to friends would often comment on her garden and the seasons and she got great satisfaction from giving away home-grown bouquets. Many of her remembrances of her husband in her personal notebook of informal jotted memories associate Kenneth with nature: 'He loved to hear the owls hoot at night... Flowers, birds, especially kingfishers, gulls, skycatchers... Animals, fishes, dragonflies, bees, wasps, hornets.' His great love of nature meant that he recognised connections in flora and fauna across the world; for example, he wrote of the Judas trees of both Italy and Cornwall.

Throughout his career, the outdoors was always Kenneth's favoured pontification; remember in his red bank ledger the very first piece of writing that inspired him was a poem by Matthew Arnold, and Kenneth's print debut was 'A Northern Furrow' about the Berkshire countryside. *The Wind in the Willows*, his only full-length novel, gave him the space to write his expansive love letter to nature, including his favourite places across the British Isles, such as Fowey in Cornwall: 'you look down flights of stone steps, overhung by great pink tufts of valerian and ending in a patch of sparkling blue water,' says the Sea Rat. The Wild Wood could be the ancient woods of Fowey's Lerryn River (there are stoats) or Quarry Wood, part of Bisham Woods. Near his former house Mayfield, the acres rise from the floodplain of the Thames. An ancient site now protected by the Woodland Trust, Bisham Woods is recognised for its rare flora (fungi and bryophytes), variety of trees (ash, whitebeam and towering elms cast the place in spooky shadow) and wildlife (including owls but no stoats). More than 500 years old, it is quite possibly one of the oldest wildwoods in Great Britain.

Above all, Kenneth is most successful in his description of that uniquely English beauty spot, the riverbank, a place that he escaped to (both in body and mind) time and time again. It is a rare writer who can capture so evocatively a perfect summer's day by the water:

> white mist… clung closely along the surface of the water… the radiant transformation of earth, air, and water, when suddenly the sun was with them again, and grey was cold and colour was born and sprang out of the earth once more… the languorous siesta of hot midday, deep in green undergrowth, the sun striking through in tiny golden shafts and spots, the boating and bathing of the afternoon, the rambles along dusty lanes and through yellow cornfields…

The Wind in the Willows is littered with water imagery – from the Wild Wood as 'low and threatening, like a black reef in some still southern sea', to an enchanting description of the river at night as a 'silent, silver kingdom'.

The book follows the cycle of the year, beginning in spring and following the seasons. Kenneth's abundantly joyful description of summer could only have been written by a passionate naturalist:

Such a rich chapter it had been, when one came to look back on it all! The pageant of the river bank had marched steadily along, unfolding itself in scene-pictures that succeeded each other in stately procession. Purple loosestrife arrived early, shaking luxuriant tangled locks along the edge of the mirror whence its own face laughed at back at it. Willow-herb, tender and wistful, like a pink sunset cloud was not slow to follow. Comfrey, the purple hand-in-hand with the white, crept forth to take its place in the line; and at last one morning the diffident and delaying dog-rose stepped delicately on the stage, and one knew, as if string music had announced it in stately chords that strayed into a gavotte, that June at last was here.

In real life, Kenneth evoked the beauty of each 12-month, just as the animals settle by the fire and reminisce about their hazy summer memories.

Kenneth was a keen ornithologist who could recognise birds from their feathers, flight, song and habits. 'As for animals, I wrote about the most familiar and domestic in *The Wind in the Willows* because I felt a duty to them as a friend,' he wrote. 'Every animal, by instinct, lives according to his nature. Thereby he lives wisely, and betters the tradition of mankind. No animal is ever tempted to belie his nature. No animal, in other words, knows how to tell a lie. Every animal is honest. Every animal is straightforward. Every animal is true – and is, therefore, according to his nature, both beautiful and good.' Poor Elsie didn't stand a chance when Kenneth explained: 'I like most of my friends among the animals more than I like most of my friends among mankind... Perhaps we ought all to serve a term of two years or so as sheep-dogs... and then we should be better men and women???'

Kenneth quite naturally seemed to confer human qualities to the animals he met daily, whether it was his prize pig, who escaped from the pen in Berkshire and became the subject of *Bertie's Escapade,* or a water vole. Kenneth once wrote to a friend about a water vole near his home who he noticed had gone missing: 'He's quite a friend of mine. Evidently he's gone on some excursion – I shall hear about it one day.' Kenneth's biographer, Patrick Chalmers, notes that Kenneth regaled a humorous story about his sister Helen when they were at the beach:

My sister said that she went along the cliffs and climbed down to a little cove and as she sat there a big rat came out and sat beside her and ate winkles! Said I to my sister, 'Did he buy them off a barrow and drop them into his hat?' But she looked puzzled and said, 'No, he only scraped in the seaweed with his little paws and fetched them out.' Then I began again – 'Was it a black pin that he ate them with?' And she thought I was raving so I dropped the subject. But had I been there he'd have given me some winkles and I'd have lent him a pin out of my tie.

Ultimately, Kenneth was an optimistic environmentalist: he believed that nature will always outlast man, and that humanity is dispensable:

Indeed, it is evident that we are entirely superfluous here; nothing has any need of us, nor cares to know what we are interested in, nor what other people have been saying of us, nor whether we go or stay. Those rooks up above have their own society and occupations, and don't wish to share or impart them; and if haply a rook seems but an insignificant sort of being to you, be sure that you are quite as insignificant to the rook. Nay, probably more so; for while you at least allot the rook his special niche in creation, it is more than doubtful whether he ever troubles to 'place' you at all. He has weightier matters to occupy him, and so long as you refrain from active interference, the chances are that for him you simply don't exist…

Kenneth concludes with a suggestion that mankind would do well to heed more than a century later: 'The least we can do is to make ourselves as small as possible, and interfere as little as may be with these lusty citizens, knowing just what they want to do, and doing it, at full work in a satisfactory world that is emphatically theirs, not ours.'

Chapter 21

Eternal Boy

'By the side of the river he trotted as one trots, when very small, by the side of a man who holds one spellbound by exciting stories...'

The Wind in the Willows

Now 10 years old, Mouse thrived in the freedom of the Berkshire countryside just like his father. There were children his own age to play with and he was invited to their birthday parties. 'Mouse... continues to be very happy and contented here,' wrote Kenneth to a friend. Elsie was delighted to see her son blossoming and proudly recorded his life at Blewbury in her little black notebook. She wrote how he joined in with the local fox hunt, running with the hounds and being blooded afterwards: 'so proud of it that refused to have [his] face washed before bed-time'. Elsie saw Mouse befriending neighbours: 'Old blind Blewbury Cottage woman... kept her door open in hopes of hearing "that voice as he went down the lane".' He became accepted in the village she noted: 'Always known as the "young squire" in Blewbury a great compliment in those parts where from the large landowners were not accorded that title. Intimately acquainted with the villagers, but always treated them with the uttermost respect.'

Elsie wrote about the time when Mouse collected his pocket money for those less fortunate, giving them Christmas gifts of 'baccy', tea, snuff and sweets for the children. Mouse told her the money was for 'people who everyone had forgotten. A fellow can't help being old & a baby can't help being young so why blame him for it.' She was proud of her son's manners and disregard for social class: 'He knew no difference between a Duke & a dustman – & at a very tender age once enquired why the chimney sweep was never invited to tea as he was often at the house,' she wrote. The final quote from Mouse in her black notebook is: 'Why is it that people can be so stuffy & get away with it?'

As Mouse grew older, Elsie drew her strength from him. Without the love of her husband to satisfy her emotional needs, Elsie lavished her affection on Mouse to his great detriment. Elsie seemed to be well again for a time after her debilitating postnatal depression, but her happiness was dangerously dependent on her son's social, academic and sporting success. Elsie was at risk of confusing her own achievements with Mouse's, becoming oblivious to her son's faults and exaggerating his strengths.[1]

When Mouse was small, Kenneth had had a modern approach to parenting (we remember him romping with the toddler on the steps of the Albert Hall), which developed into a close relationship through the 'dearest Mouse' letters. Now father and son spent precious afternoons together, visiting their neighbour Farmer Saunders to buy some fruit: 'first we went up a ladder into the apple-loft, and sampled every sort of apple and filled our pockets – and then we sat in the parlour and discussed circuses, and all three of us agreed that they were the only thing worth living for.' It is a happy memory of a father-and-son moment that Kenneth never had the opportunity to share with his own father nor any other male relative. He relived one of his happiest childhood times by taking Mouse to St Giles Fair in Oxford: 'M and I… had a dizzy day riding around on pink bears, swinging to the clouds in Dreadnoughts,' he wrote delightedly, as he shared one of his greatest passions with his son. They both looked forward to the Blewbury Fair each year: 'the glory and colour of it all, the friendly show-people and their vans, and the maddening whirl of the roundabouts.'

As well as fairs and circuses, it was important for Kenneth to share another of his great passions with Mouse: Cornwall. 'I want Mouse to make the acquaintance of my Cornish haunts, and friends, before he goes to school – then he may like to go back there.' Kenneth took care to make arrangements for a family holiday at Fowey, organising a room at the homely St Catherine's House rather than the grand Fowey Hotel. Mouse was treated to one of Atky's special luncheons and loved pottering about his home filled with books and objects – apparently the man had forty-five telescopes, countless clocks, barometers and binoculars. Another day, Kenneth organised a picnic *The Wind in the Willows*-style: 'One sunny day we all went over there [a farm] with a large luncheon basket, and lunched in the open, off "hoggy pudding" and other good things, in a riot of daffodils and primroses…' Of course, there was plenty of messing about on the river: 'One specially warm and sunny day I took M and his governess up to tea at Lerryn, "on a tide", sailing up and rowing back.' Mouse thought Q was like a hero from a novel. 'Mouse has asked to be taken back to Fowey some day soon, which is a good sign,' wrote a delighted Kenneth.

> I fancy, on the whole, he liked the Lizard best. To be sure he went there first, and we had better weather there, but the wildness, freshness and strangeness of the Lizard, its grandeur and sparkling air, probably impressed him more than the slightly sophisticated Fowey; and he liked the simple, friendly people, who were all so nice to him and let him run in and out of their places, and had him to tea, and called me 'Mr Kenneth' as I was known to them four-and-twenty years back.

Kenneth doesn't mention Elsie in his letters, but the fact that all three of the Grahames went away together is significant because usually Alastair went to Broadstairs with his nanny and his parents to the West Country. Kenneth and Elsie recognised the importance of spending time as a family, and made an effort to go on holiday together again after realising how much it meant to Mouse.

It was their last break before Mouse was sent away to school in the summer term of 1911. He attended The Old Malthouse in Langton Matravers by the sea in Dorset, newly set up by former England footballer Rex Corbett. The family visited it together, when Kenneth admired 'the beautiful bathing'. Mouse was looking forward to the independence: 'he made the plunge last Monday, going off very manfully and composedly and, from what we hear, he is falling into the new ways of life very well,' wrote Kenneth to a friend. 'It is very quiet here now without him.'

Kenneth's letters from this period are unfailingly positive whenever the subject of Mouse and school turns up: in February 1912 he writes: 'We are alone here once more, Mouse having departed school-ward, undaunted and in high spirits. We have excellent accounts of him and his progress.' Mouse flourished at The Old Malthouse although it was the only educational establishment that he was happy at, and, significantly, the only letters from his childhood that Elsie kept. Mouse's notes are housed in the Bodleian Library and are a very sweet collection of a young child's thoughts, complete with cartoon pictures and gradually improving handwriting. Mouse's letters indicate he was becoming closer to Elsie, writing to her as 'My dear Madame' and his father as 'Inferiority', a nickname Elsie seems to have unkindly encouraged.

Now their Mouse was out of the house, the couple began to grow further apart. As well as their separate bedrooms in the apple loft, they began to occupy different parts of the house and got out of the habit of conversing with each other; Kenneth preferred to sit for an hour lost in his silent dreamworld rather than have Elsie dominate the conversation. This proved rather awkward for visitors, and Kenneth tried to dissuade people from coming to stay. (If they insisted, he told them not to bring evening clothes.) The couple dramatically reduced their socialising outside of the village, and Kenneth's friends complained that he hardly came to London. It seems they were in danger of becoming eccentric recluses as Elsie rarely got up before 11 am and often went to bed in her clothes – a uniform of baggy cardigan, hand-knitted tights and old navy coat and skirt. She became something of a curiosity in the village as she clattered around with a stick, 'hunting' – searching for dead chickens, and trying to persuade the farmer's wife to give her provisions for free 'which they refuse to do', wrote Kenneth frankly to a friend. He was embarrassed about her miserliness, and quite why the Grahames lived servant-less in such a rudimentary way is a mystery. Although Kenneth had not received his proper pension nor Elsie her full inheritance, the rising royalties of *The Wind in the Willows* alone should have been plenty for a retired couple to live on comfortably. Elsie's deteriorating mental health might explain her illogical concern about money as she lapsed into her old ways of lying on her duvet, sipping hot water. She had no appetite and grew thin. In the recesses of her mind she clung to the glamorous life of her girlhood, gazing lovingly at her beautiful satin dresses and precious rolls of silk she carefully preserved in her wardrobe. She harked back to her carefree days before a lifetime of depression engulfed her and the sadness of irretrievable love overwhelmed her – of Kenneth's disinterest, of her lost baby. Elsie would tell anyone who listened about the famous literary friends of her youth but was laughed at behind her back. She wrote spitefully in her notebook of one of her neighbours: 'Elderly woman with face like turnip and hair like carrots'!

With no writing project nor bank work to occupy his mind, Kenneth finally had all the time in the world to tend to his wife. But despite her pitiful state, scant emotional affection for her would come. After being married for more than a decade, he still preferred to spend time away, happiest outside on the Ridgeway when his daily walk in the fresh air and freedom helped him come alive again. Perhaps the depression and anxiety that his doctor diagnosed on his departure from the Bank of England meant he had no reserves left to help her. Exercise is known to improve mood and Kenneth was a familiar figure on the Downs, dressed smartly in knickerbockers, a soft shirt, and a baggy coat of tweeds (unlike Elsie he never lost the urge to dress well). He made an effort to bridge the gulf between them with travel, holidaying with Elsie in Brittany in 1912; it was only the second time he had taken her abroad. The year before, Kenneth had finally taken her to Europe (previously he preferred to go on his own), but that February they went to Switzerland and Italy and returned in the spring. Travel was an important part of Kenneth and Elsie's relationship: it was a bond that tied them together without Mouse at home. (In later years when the First World War broke out and they were not able to travel, Kenneth wrote to a friend: 'E. keeps pretty well. In normal times we should now run away somewhere where it was dry and sunny, with a cheerful restaurant or two in the foreground; as it is we have to stay at home and talk about the places we would have gone to if we could.')

The vacuum their son left while away at school was vast. Yet when the opportunity arose to be reunited with their Mouse, Kenneth and Elsie failed to take it. Unfathomably, he was regularly left at school for the holidays, as the poor boy wrote sadly in June of his first year: 'nearly every boy in the school is going home for the coronation [of King George V] so there will be only 5 left here including myself.' His letter a week later indicates he is trying to be brave about everything: 'I do not mind not going home for the exeat at all, indeed next to going up to London itself, I would rather stay where I am for the present.' But being left at school while his parents went on holiday to France was one step too far for Mouse. At the beginning of his second year he addressed his letter as To the Artful and Extravagant One:

I hear that you have taken advantage of my absence to make a bolt for France, and I have no doubt that before long you will be in Gay

Paris or Montecarlo. I am at present staying in a little island known as England of which you may have heard. You will find it on the map of Europe, to the west of France. Nothing doing here, at present, England is a dull little place.

Another time he writes a spoof letter from 'prison': 'His Majesty's Prison, Dorset', signing off as Prisoner 99999, with a drawing of a window with bars in a brick wall.

His father had befallen the same fate as those Olympians he had written so disparagingly about all those years ago; for all Kenneth's understanding of children he had become unwittingly cruel and out of touch with his son. 'A saddening doubt, a dull suspicion, creeps over me… Can it be that I also have become an Olympian?' he wrote in the prologue of *The Golden Age*. Little did he know.

Many of Mouse's letters from The Old Malthouse are sweetly affectionate, including one on a Good Friday:

Dearest Mummy

I am sending you this little brooch as a small Easter present. It is only a penny one, but I thought it would be better than nothing. Wishing you both a very, very, VERY, happy Easter. Yours affectionately Tittywillow.

His father sent him adventure books by Alexandre Dumas, Elsie sent him valentine cards and limericks, and posted honey and stamps for his collection.

The sea at Dorset turned Mouse into a water rat, aping his father's great love. He mastered handling a boat and learnt to swim in the glorious sea-swimming pool that had been made from the rocks at Dancing Ledge near to Langton Matravers (look hard and you can still find it now, although these days it is no larger than a rock pool). 'Why did not I learn to swim last summer?' Mouse asks his parents. 'I had my first lesson last Tuesday; since then I have been having lessons every day. It is simply glorious!' Halfway through the summer term he writes: 'On Wednesday I swum across the bath, and yesterday (Sat) I swam about half way down the length, so I expect that by next Sunday I shall have done my length. I am rather excited about it, as I have always been very keen about swimming.'

By the end of the school year, Alastair was good enough to compete in the annual gala:

> Yesterday (Saturday) we had some heats of the learner's race. The final has not come off yet. I have no chance of being in it, I am afraid, as I was knocked out first heat (we swam down the bath in couples)... Don't be disappointed it about it, please. It isn't worrying me much, as I don't consider that sort of race a very certain test of one's swimming powers, not do I think speed the most important thing in swimming, and, anyhow, I came in quite a good second.

In later years, Mouse could never live up to his parents' impossibly high expectations; is this letter an early warning to them not to criticise?

Generally Mouse's letters suggest that as a youngster he was a jolly, sporty boy who loved golf, hockey, acting, roller skating, rugby and swimming. 'We have lots of picnics and cricket,' he notes (he was the last boy in the second XI). Typically for a child, he mentions food a great deal, once carefully enclosing a drawing of a sausage! Mouse's letters are generally quite formal, either an indication of the punctilious relationship Edwardian children had with their parents, or a suggestion of the emotional detachment growing between them. He usually addresses them as 'my dear madam' or 'dear sir'. Kenneth wrote formally too.

Significantly, the Grahames holidayed together again that summer in Scotland. It would be Kenneth's last visit north of the border and he looked upon it fondly: 'it was really an immense success. The weather was magnificent and we were, even for the Highlands, in the most beautiful country. The boy was simply drunk with it all and grieved sorely to leave it. There was a joy of colour everywhere.'

As Mouse neared the end of prep school at 14, Elsie and Kenneth were agreed that he should have the finest education they could offer him. Q helped them with their research on which school would suit their son best, although they chose Rugby against his suggestion. Mouse managed to scrape through the common entrance exam and began in September 1914. He was completely unprepared for the realities of public school, having mostly grown up with adults in a world of imagination of talking animals, Cornish pirates and fairies. 'For the first time in his life Alastair was going to be confronted with harsh and unimaginative realism... He was gruff-voiced, spotty, appallingly shy, and much given to waving his arms about in moments of excitement,' wrote Peter Green, Kenneth's biographer. 'Alastair was what his parents had made him; he had always struggled desperately to live up to their myth.'

Immediately, Mouse knew School House at Rugby wasn't for him. And the teachers sensed it too: in the very first week, Kenneth was asked up to the school by Mouse's tutor who discussed his concerns about the new pupil. The teacher gently and sensitively proffered his care, even offering books for Mouse to read. 'Come in and talk to me as long as you like,' he encouraged the boy. But despite this, the school was a poor fit for timid little Mouse. Rugby is known for its sport and he was a weak sportsman, albeit an enthusiastic one. He didn't do well at 'fagging' for the older boys and even tried the junior military corps like his father but was teased for holding the rifle upside down. He preferred instead to write home to his mother and make her a tiny chest of drawers from matchboxes and compose an accompanying poem: 'made by the little paws… Of one of the Boham's mice.' One of his contemporaries described him as infuriating, and remembered Mouse constantly playing with a cup and ball toy, which irritated the other boys. He was bullied for being a 'bumbler', and it is highly likely was teased for his connection with Mr Toad in *The Wind in the Willows*; Christopher Robin was a famously unhappy teenager after being bullied because of his association with *Winnie-the-Pooh*.

Mouse lasted just half a term at Rugby: 'How can one talk to people whose only powers of conversation lie in their elbows?' he argued with his parents, refusing to go back.

Kenneth, a former head boy, could not quite understand it:

So far as I could gather, the pace and the pressure were altogether too much for him and I fancy that the new boys, with whom he naturally had to spend his time, happened to be a roughish lot. Anyhow though he stuck it out for six weeks, he got no better, and in the end I thought it right to take him away.

It is clear he was disappointed: 'I took great pains and trouble to assure myself that that was the best school he could go to.'

Elsie asked her brother about Eton (he was an old boy) and also wrote to family friend Graham Robertson about his experience there, and received a thoughtfully written, humorous and fulsome reply (running to more than nine pages):

> I was not unhappy at Eton and I do not expect that Mouse will be … But he will be bored… It's a splendid thing for Mouse that he is good in a boat and can swim. It will make a tremendous difference, as a Wet Bob has so much more liberty… He can get away in a boat and be by himself. One of the most maddening things about school is never being by one's self.

And off Mouse went to Eton in January 1915. It was Kenneth rather than Elsie who saw him off; perhaps it was too painful for the emotional Elsie to say goodbye. She later exaggerated her son's settling in: 'he seems to have won very good opinions in the short time he has been at Eton,' wrote Elsie naively to her brother. Mouse told of swimming, sport, making friends and getting into adventures. He continued to play cricket but his parents didn't come to watch, Mouse covering any disappointment by snidely remarking: 'The Parents were as numerous, as arrogant and as over-dressed as they always are.' His housemaid was called Anna Gregory, and, typically, Mouse endeared himself to her – she being of a different age and class: 'He was the only boy in his tutor's house that I ever even thought of cutting the bread-and-butter thin for,' she remembered.

Unfortunately, Mouse could find no such endearment amongst his contemporaries. He stuck it out a year before leaving school for ever halfway through the Lent term in 1916. It seems that nervous, unsporty, quirky, visually impaired Mouse could never live up to his parents' expectations, no matter how accomplished they convinced themselves he was. Elsie tried to rationalise her shock: 'Once, as a big Etonian, he said to me, "Scratch us, we are all barbarians but it happens that I prefer curios and they prefer cricket bats."' But she and Kenneth were devastated and simply could not understand what had gone wrong: they had given their son everything he asked for and sent him to the finest schools in the land. They could not see beyond their own disappointment and were at a loss to accept that their son wasn't the child genius they believed. As their only child, they had heaped misguided devotion on to Mouse; Elsie especially had treated him with great sentimentality. He had inherited his mother's anxiety and in later adolescence could not bear his Elsie's smothering love.

So frequently had Elsie boasted of her son's popularity and his accomplishments, she had convinced herself the myth of Mouse was true. Kenneth had had Mouse in mind when he wrote the character of Mr Toad, an animal who exasperates everyone he meets yet, ultimately, has charm enough to be forgiven. It seems the real Mouse didn't possess enough redeeming features. Elsie wrote to her brother Courtauld after Mouse left Eton:

> Mouse really was getting into a settled unhappiness there which was harming body and mind & the more he got used to the place the less he could endure it… We do not profess ourselves to understand exactly why a Public School life is so uncongenial to him for he is by nature the most spartan & most uncomplaining creature possible… It is so great a disappointment to us that it makes me unhappy even to write about it… K. was really splendid in trying everything in his power to buck him up with plenty of pocket & subscription money & good clothes & orders on the shops & anything that cd hearten & help him – & attach him to the place & life there – but we cd do no more than we have done & it was not of any avail as things are.

Again, like Mouse's nurse Stott, she characterises him as being uncomplaining, an unheeded warning sign.

Elsie remained desperate to apply her son to a top-brass education, and used her social network to do what she could: she and Kenneth wrote to Q again, who had briefly been a professor at Cambridge. He suggested a tutor, pointing out that Mouse's eccentricities turned him against being public school material. A tutor would prepare him for Oxford and suit his propensity to wit and politics while remaining sensitive to his poor eyesight. Elsie hunted for the very best she could find and secured one who had high references. Before the new term started, the family holidayed together in Somerset where Alastair delighted in the swimming and developed a love of riding. He had lessons at home in Berkshire and then at his tutor's in Surrey: 'The Trainer told us that he "never saw anyone take so naturally to a horse,"' wrote Elsie in 1917, still pitifully boasting about her son whenever she could.

In the end, a tutor suited Mouse well and it all worked out; he achieved a high enough academic standard to be accepted at Oxford, the hallowed institution of learning that his father had so longed to attend. Kenneth and Elsie must have been thrilled that their only son, despite a visual impairment and interrupted education, had achieved the pinnacle of academic excellence. It was the Wayfarer's dream of the Wide World that Kenneth had never had the opportunity to realise and he could not be prouder of his Mouse, now on the brink of manhood.

Chapter 22

Like Summer Tempests Came His Tears

'[His] noble ideals, steadfast purposes and rare promise remains only a loved and honoured memory.'

Words inscribed on Alastair Grahame's headstone, written by his father

When Kenneth Grahame wrote *The Wind in the Willows*, never could he have imagined the novel would come to represent the fragile innocence of an Edwardian England that was to be shattered just six years later. With the disruption of world peace and the start of the First World War, the novel's snapshot of that golden period in Britain's history also captured a precious memory of a more personal sort; Kenneth's only son. Now 18, Alastair began to swim away from the safety of the river bank as he entered into the unknown waters of his next phase of life.

Those unknown waters would, tragically, turn out to be fatal.

Mouse (he would never lose his childhood nickname) attempted to sign up for active service but was rejected twice, probably because of his poor eyesight. The colonel of his local OTC and Cadet Corps in Oxford said he would not be fit for A Class until he was older. Mouse was saved from becoming part of that lost generation of brave and beautiful men who were sacrificed on Flanders Fields and beyond, yet he would be cruelly taken in another way.

Kenneth, too, was unfit to fight because of his age, but was able to play his part by setting up a factory in Blewbury for surgical supplies; it is not recorded whether Elsie helped him, but it is probable she did. Her keen sense of obligation would surely have extended to the war effort. She was always influenced by her beloved brother, Courtauld, who served with the Red Cross as chief commissioner in France and also in Malta, Egypt and the Near East (for which he was decorated). Elsie's sister, Winifred, served as a nurse.

Kenneth still had the energy to take on the role of drill sergeant for the village; because of his experience with the London Scottish as a young man, he was asked to get the local Home Guard boys and men (aged between 14 and 90 years old!) into shape in a farm barn. Blewbury, like English villages across the country, struggled to comprehend the devastation of world events. With a population of 500, some 70 souls bravely went to fight. When many didn't return, Kenneth took it upon himself to write a tender tribute to the young men as a small comfort to their grieving families. For the fortunate few who returned, he organised a welcome feast.

In 1918, Alastair embarked on his studies as an undergraduate at Christ Church College, reading Greek, Latin and scripture. He may have been given a helping hand by Kenneth's cousin and Oxford alumni Anthony Hope Hawkins (and perhaps war had made getting in slightly easier because of a reduction in the number of young men able to attend). College life allowed Mouse to be an individual, but he remained unhappy despite the greater freedoms. He was a dreamer and a loner, locked in his own fantasy world like his father. Unusually for a student, he didn't join any societies or clubs.[1] His tutor, Professor Sir Keith Feiling, remembered him as constantly miserable. A girl who met him during this time recalls him as being reserved, sardonic and, unfortunately, unattractive with acne. He didn't offer to dance with the girl, Beatrice Brown, the daughter of Kenneth's agent Curtis Brown, but would only talk 'interminable dullness' to her father.

The war made for a very different undergraduate experience; Kenneth once remarked that his son was 'starved' of social interaction. Mouse would stay up late discussing politics (apparently in a rather abstract way rather than with any expertise). Father and son differed on matters of politics – Mouse had matured into his mother's Liberal views while Kenneth was far more conservative. Apparently Mouse threatened 'with fists' a woman who said that 'Gladstone was a wicked old man.'

Mouse had always hated exams and didn't do well under pressure and found the academic demands a serious challenge. He failed his scripture, Greek and Latin exams three times during his first year. In 1919, his tutor gave him an ultimatum: pass or go. If he didn't get through on his fourth attempt, he would not be allowed to continue at Christ Church. He failed his First Public Examination again and was asked to leave. His parents were devastated – again, they simply could not understand why their beloved Mouse wasn't sailing through academia. But the examiner gave them a glimmer of hope: because of his poor eyesight Mouse was eligible to apply for an amanuensis (someone to whom he could dictate his exam answers). In March 1920, he retook Greek and Latin literature and passed; he had just one final scripture exam to get through, which would allow him to rejoin Christ Church as an undergraduate.

Not a single letter survives from Mouse to his friends or family during his time at Oxford; only three pieces of correspondence sent to him remain. The first is a reply from his former tutor, A.W. Dall on 1 March. His letter indicates the theology student had written to him about denouncing spirituality: 'Your letter interested me very much. I am not surprised at your Agnosticism. A logical and strongly introspective mind which takes life seriously always passes through this phase. P.S. I think your writing has improved.' Another letter survives from a friend, who wrote to Alastair on Palm Sunday of 1920:

> I hope you are enjoying a holiday, with the consciousness of that the bogey of Pass Mods [his exams] has been settled with for ever. Of course I was not surprised at the news, for we were both determined that nothing else should happen, were it only for the Toad's sake! But now you have satisfied yourself that 'will' means 'can' you will go on to success in the subject of your choice.

Significantly, Kenneth and Elsie had recently sent their son a Cruden's Cordance – an index to the Bible. It was forwarded to him by a friend who wrote:

> I trust you have settled down comfortably in your new rooms and find everything as you wish. I am wondering what you have decided to go in for. Whatever it is, I wish you all success. In any case you will have to work jolly hard... As in a way you are making a new start at Oxford, I hope you are arranging your life there on practical lines. You have much to do and time is short.

Those words were a tragic portent. On the evening of 7 May 1920, less than a week before his twentieth birthday, Mouse had his Friday supper in hall as usual (he was still entitled to dine there as a commoner of Christ Church). An undergraduate who ate with him remarked that it was unusual that Mouse asked for a glass of port (Kenneth had apparently bribed him with £100, to refrain from drinking alcohol until he was 21). After draining his drink, Mouse left alone for a walk across Port Meadow at sunset.

The next morning his body was found on the railway line at the level crossing near Oxford station. It had been decapitated and was almost unrecognisable after being damaged by six trains that had run over him between 10 pm and 2.45 am. In his pocket survived a fistful of religious tracts.

The inquest was held on 13 May, when the medical officer, Dr W.D. Sturrock, noted that the position of Mouse's body on the line indicated that it was suicide. When he examined the body he reported: 'The cause was decapitation, and that was compatible with being run over by a train. The right arm was fractured below the shoulder, the left leg four inches above the ankle, and all the toes of the right foot. There were also numerous bruises on the body.' When the coroner asked if the injuries were compatible with being knocked down and then run over, he answered: 'I could not answer the first part of the question as to being knocked down, but certainly they are compatible with being run over.'

Just as if he were an idealised character in *The Wind in the Willows*, Mouse recognised that his parents had built him up to be a myth, and one that he knew he could never live up to. He had an eccentric personality, encouraged by his mother and father, which had turned him into an outsider. He was a spectacular academic failure, unable to go on at university any longer. He could not fight in the war because of his blindness. Finally, he had lost his faith in Christianity. Described by Elsie as 'a real Stoic, who would never complain, or plead his own cause in any way,' Mouse felt the only way out was by ending it all. Was his suicide an act of revenge on his parents?

In sheer desperation at the hopelessness of his life, the poor young man had lain across the track in a diagonal position, his neck and one shoulder on one rail and his right foot and left leg on another rail. As a child, we remember, like the character of Mr Toad, how he lay on the road in the path of oncoming cars. A tragic portent too, is seen in *The Wind in the Willows* when Portly the little Otter goes missing: 'They were silent for a time, both thinking of the same thing – the lonely, heart-sore animal, crouched by the ford, watching and waiting, the long night through...'

The coroner was a kind man; clearly not wishing for Kenneth and Elsie to be forever haunted by the agony of a suicide verdict, he quietly sidestepped the evidence of foul play and instead focused the jury's minds on the fact that Mouse had a good relationship with his family, was in no financial difficulty and was blind in one eye. A don of Christ Church described Alastair as 'a very quiet and reserved man', admitting 'I never got to know him well.'

The jury reached a verdict of accidental death at the railway crossing.

Kenneth and Elsie, utterly devastated, convinced themselves the death of their only son was the result of a tragic accident. Anything else was beyond their comprehension. His father inscribed the gravestone with the words: 'Here was laid to rest on his twentieth birthday, 12th May 1920, only child of Kenneth and Elsie Grahame, of whose noble ideals, steadfast purposes and rare promise remains only a loved and honoured memory.' Kenneth scattered white lilies over his coffin. Alastair's body lies in the churchyard of Holywell Cemetery, Oxford, the city that held such complex emotions for both him and his father. It had been the place of their greatest aspirations and now their deepest sorrow. Port Meadow, the place of the tragedy, had been where Kenneth once played cricket; surely, his son's words that he recited as a child would come back to haunt him: 'death is a promotion'.

Almost exactly 100 years to the month it was written, a previously unseen letter from Kenneth expressing his grief over Mouse's death was uncovered in London. It was written to his agent, Curtis Brown, on 26 May 1920:

Dear Mr Curtis Brown
Just a line of true appreciation of your most kind words of sympathy with us in our overwhelming sorrow.

The dear boy went back to Oxford this term so full of new plans and interests, with 'Mods' safely behind him, and liberty to follow a wider range of thought and reading. From all we can glean, his last days were specially happy ones. He was laid to rest in Oxford on his 20th birthday.

You may like to know, that his little visit to you was a matter of constant pleasant recollection.

Owing to the war, he had led so secluded a life, socially speaking, that this was a real 'event', and the memory of it was cherished by him.

Yours most truly
Kenneth Grahame

To have failed so spectacularly as a parent must have been a horrendous shock for Kenneth, already at risk as he was of mental illness. He had never been able to learn how to heal the vulnerable child within himself, so what hope did he have to bring up his son to be a healthy, functioning adult?

Madness threatened Elsie as grief tormented her fragile mind. Despite receiving hundreds of letters of condolence, she became fixated on anyone who dared to suggest Mouse had committed suicide. Q privately believed this, writing an obtuse remembrance for *Oxford Magazine* the month following Alastair's death: '…there is nothing to accuse, if a boy – with as he had, some defect of eyesight – chooses to stray, at night, across the complicated metals of two railway lines. Aware of it or no, he had run the risk, and there's an end.' This was hugely upsetting for Elsie and Kenneth, despite the rest of the obituary, with its tender remembrances of Mouse such as: 'he found delight and gaiety and wisdom in the simplest happenings of animals and people. Above all he was gentle…' Q had also lost a son too soon; Bevil survived the war but succumbed to the Spanish flu shortly before his wedding.

Kenneth and Elsie became united against the world and those who believed their son had committed suicide; they clung desperately to the verdict of accidental death. They retreated into themselves, just as Kenneth had done during other traumatic events in his life, such as when his father rejected him, he took refuge from 'the rubs and disappointments of a life where things go eternally askew' and instead went to 'our imaginary world, where we have things exactly as we want them'. He used an avoidant coping method by hiding behind fantasy, his 'shred of self-heal', and taking excessively long walks. Without domestic help, Boham's became dishevelled (rumours suggest there were mice in the pantry) and the couple developed strange habits and fixations. Elsie grew eccentric, insisting Kenneth wear a strange sort of undergarment that was only changed once a year. Their grief hung heavy over them, as they took to: 'Staying in bed half the day and breakfast at all hours and the place in such a mess it's not fit to be seen.' These words from *The Wind in the Willows* had been written in happiness. But now they had developed a bitter taste that threatened to poison the devastated Kenneth and Elsie.

Chapter 23

Dino and Minkie Rekindled

'In fact, you mustn't think at all, but sit in the sunshine and let things just happen before your eyes and don't ask yourself why they happen, or any other conundrum. Nature will do her work all right, if she's given the chance and a free hand.'

Kenneth Grahame, in a letter to a friend

The months after Mouse's death were unbearable torture for the bereft couple, both of whom had a history of mental illness. Kenneth was described as 'a broken man' by one who knew him during this time.

It is ironic that the last piece of writing Kenneth had published before the tragedy concerned the subject of death. He wrote the preface of *The Cambridge Book of Poetry for Children* in 1916 and edited the selection:

It is surprising how largely the subject of death is found to bulk [poetry for children]. Dead parents, dead brothers, dead sisters, dead uncles, dead puppies, dead kittens, dead birds, dead flowers, dead dollies – a compiler of Obituary Verse for the Delight of Children could make a fat volume with little difficulty… I have turned off this mournful tap of tears as far as possible, preferring that children should read of the joy of life… above all [poetry] should proclaim that there is joy, light, and fresh air…

For the first time in their marriage, Kenneth and Elsie were united; the death of their son was something they finally had in common and their grief brought them closer as they despondently clung to one another against the world. They were tightly bound by their belief that Mouse had not killed himself, no matter what anyone else thought. They had grown emotionally distant during Mouse's lifetime, yet after his death they began to rekindle Dino and Minkie of their courtship. The Grahames had always loved to travel; now they realised getting away from it all was essential if they were to survive, and threw themselves into preparing for four years of travelling to escape the torment of their loss.

Four months after Alastair's death Elsie found the strength to write to an auction house with a long and detailed description of the domestic possessions they wanted to dispose of, to heal the past and look to the future with a clear head. Although emotionally fragile, Elsie screwed up her courage to do something practical and filled two pages with her wiggly handwritten scrawl, every part of the paper crammed with description as she attempted to make the family's heirlooms as appealing as possible. Typically, Elsie was keen to befriend or at least build up a relationship with the auction representatives: '& wd be glad if he wd lunch with us this being quite a country place.' It must have been a wrench for Kenneth to part with his beloved souvenirs, which included his forty sailor's farewells (glass rolling pins offered by Cornishmen to their sweethearts). As the Grahames were not short of money, it wasn't lack of funds that inspired the purge, but a hope of moving on from their sad past and looking towards a happier future. As well as getting rid of her own belongings, Elsie gave all Mouse's clothes and personal possessions to the Blewbury jumble sale. Such a drastic action carried out in haste just months after her beloved son's death would surely have been cause for heartbreaking regret later.

But there was no turning back: with their house emptied and let for eighteen months to a Mr Davies, Kenneth and Elsie became Dino and Minkie again as they embarked on 28 October for an extended convalescence, or rather perhaps, a long overdue honeymoon. Mouse's death finally gave Kenneth the impetus to explore the Wide World at length – rather than gazing at holiday souvenirs in his study, he at last heeded the Sea Rat's call of the south. Until now, Kenneth had preferred to be the fellow who goes alone, but for his longest and possibly most significant journey, he had Elsie by his side and, for the first time, wanted her there. Unlike Elsie, who was always very close to her brother Courtauld and sister Winifred, Kenneth had broken all ties with his blood family; he had not spoken to his sister Helen since he married Elsie, nor his brother Roland after a seven-year disagreement. Purves, his American pen pal, had passed away.

The couple travelled to London and two days later boarded the boat SS *Orvieto*. It was Italy that they went to first, for three years – the country that Kenneth had fallen in love with as a young man and which had fascinated him all his life. It had come to represent both happiness and sadness; it was the place of his first holiday as a young bachelor in London when he visited with his cousin, Annie; Italy had been where he regained his strength after his many bouts of illness; and now it was the country where he sought solace after Mouse's death. He joked he went to see beggars, fleas and vines, but really it was because he adored 'the feel of the warm sun striking hard between my shoulder blades'. Water fascinated him the most, of course – he spent hours wandering the streets of Rome finding new fountains, idly throwing pennies to make a wish – but he also found comfort in the peace of the churches and the beauty of the palaces and became an expert on architecture. He befriended English-speaking archaeologists who later described Kenneth's 'great glorious boyish joy' of exploring and how he took tremendous pleasure in the beauty of art. Throughout 1921, the couple spent much of their time together, exploring every nook of Rome as a pair, stopping at local shops for bread, cheese and a bottle of wine for sustenance. They were agreed they would not reply to the many calling cards that were left at their hotel.

Kenneth gradually regained his appetite, and food, as usual, provided him with a comfort, as he enjoyed the rich tastes of the trattorias, feasting on gelato, porchetta and mortadella. Elsie was concerned that ice cream was bad for her husband's health, so he indulged in it in private, and when she stayed behind in their hotel, he quietly drank in taverns. Gradually, he began to accept one or two of the countless requests for new writing. The American ambassador in Rome asked him for a five-minute tribute to John Keats in recognition of the hundredth anniversary of the poet's death. The British ambassador then invited Kenneth to lecture at the Keats-Shelley Association, and the talk was a great success: 'surely it is by seeing things as better than they are that one arrives at making them better,' Kenneth bravely professed.

It wasn't long before Kenneth heeded the call of the wild and in August he and Elsie swapped the city for the countryside of the Dolomites. It was a far cry from the Berkshire Downs, but hiking through nature once more refreshed his senses. A witness saw him out walking one day and described the Kenneth we know of old:

He was a remarkable-looking man, striding across hill and dale, his Inverness cape swirling around him, his hair all swept up by the wind. On and on he went, solitary, absorbed in his own thoughts, until he vanished in the distance. I think he was deeply grieved over the loss of his son and I hesitated to intrude on this self-imposed isolation.

The next phase of the Grahames' physical and metaphorical journey was Rapallo in Genoa before seeking out Kenneth's favourite season, the spring, at Lake Garda. Capri was to follow, where Kenneth developed a nasty bout of bronchitis. By the following spring, however, he felt well enough to go back to his beloved Rome. Elsie wrote of their spending so much time there: 'we wintered in Rome, and summered there, and Eastered, and Christmas'd and knew every one of the 400 old churches.' They were profoundly moved by a significant historical moment they witnessed together as they saw Mussolini march through Rome in 1922: Elsie's description of it to her brother is shockingly raw: 'we used to hear the Fascists cracking the skulls of the Socialists at street corners, with cannons at both ends of the bridges and snipers shooting over the high wall surrounding the courtyard of the G.P.O.'

Florence was next, where they 'were regaled on biscuits from china bowls and delicious golden wine in blue Venetian glasses'. They spent their final winter at Ospedaletti before gathering the strength to return home briefly in early 1924. The final trip they made in 1926 was an eventful one as together they experienced adventures such as viewing the ruins near Mount Etna, and in Palermo somehow sneaking into a trial of a man charged with thirteen accounts of murder! Elsie remained enraptured with Kenneth's sense of wonderment, when she writes of how even as an older man he always managed to turn an ordinary day magical: '[he] found himself in the midst of every sort of adventurous scene,' she wrote in *First Whisper of The Wind in the Willows*.

There is a fairy-tale of which I was often reminded by this power of his; that in order to gain access through some secret gate, its key must be sought... Kenneth appeared to possess this golden key, so carefully concealed from most mortals. Sometimes we found ourselves the only 'outsiders' at a bandit's trial in Sicily, carefully guarded by armed soldiers standing behind our chairs, or in the more peaceful scene of a ball in Brittany in honour of a quite unknown peasant's wedding...

Kenneth and Elsie were still interested in – and capable of – making new friends, and while abroad made the acquaintance of a J.B. Mussey who remembered their holiday: 'Mr Grahame's white hair and moustache seemed to light up the room; and the first impression he made was always one of distinction.' He describes Kenneth showing him around enthusiastically, despite his walking cane, and called his knowledge of Amalfi ('and of almost everything else') encyclopaedic. 'I remember him saying, 'The strongest human instinct is the desire to impart information, and the second strongest is the desire to resist such teaching.' Kenneth, at 67, was fascinated with any new fact or idea, and remained humbly modest. 'It all wound up in a grand party to which we invited everyone in town, native or foreign. Mr Grahame sat in a corner, as he had when we first saw him, and enjoyed it all in silence.'

Time spent together had drawn Kenneth and Elsie back to life; perhaps the extended period of travel was the foreign honeymoon they had never had, more than twenty years after their wedding. Finally, after almost a decade away, they were ready to face England together again and made preparations for their return. Their hasty departure had left Boham's in somewhat of a mess (although, in truth, it was probably as tidy as it ever had been). Their tenant, Mr Davies, had written to them while they were away complaining of mouse-nests in the larder and 'a good deal of litter and disorder'. Mr Davies chose not to renew his contract, and Kenneth offered the place to A.A. Milne who regretted he could not take it as he was looking for somewhere permanent. In the end, Kenneth and Elsie sold Boham's while they were abroad; the farmhouse held painful memories after being Mouse's home for ten years and their sorrow was too well known amongst the small local community.

Kenneth was heeding the call of his beloved River Thames; as he had written in 1915: 'one can only remember that troubles mostly pass, sooner or later, and that, when one has sailed into smooth water again, perhaps the pleasant harbour and its sunny shores look more smiling and peaceful on account of the breakers left behind.'

Chapter 24

The End

'O and a lot of other things, little and big, they all come back to me...'

Kenneth Grahame

Still today the soft leaves of the huge weeping willow tree peacefully brush the gentle waters of the River Pang as it flows through Pangbourne village before joining the Thames between Whitchurch Lock and Whitchurch Bridge. How Mouse would have loved swimming on this appealing stretch of water.

It was not half a mile from the river that the Grahames found peace on their return from their European exodus. It seems Kenneth and Elsie were strong enough to enter back into the world again and rejoin English village life. Church Cottage is a beautiful red-brick house with gabled windows framed in white. It stands in the centre of the village next to the church of St James the Less with its matching tower of red brick. Kenneth, indifferent to Christianity for his adult life, may have gained comfort living next to a place of worship after his son's death. Although still in the countryside, Pangbourne is much less rural than Blewbury being directly connected by rail with London as well as market towns such as Reading.

The couple bought Church Cottage in 1924 but didn't settle there until 1930, when they had reached their mid-sixties. Kenneth's study was characteristically decorated with nursery ornaments and curtains with dwarf motifs; he also put out his cricket bat, tennis rackets, jigsaw puzzles and packs of cards. 'Like the Treasure Trove of some darling child,' Elsie later wrote. Her bedroom (the couple again slept in separate chambers) was of smart mahogany with Sicilian marble bathroomware, and pretty Wedgwood, decorated with a tapestry screen of French brocade.

The house had three bedrooms, a maid's room, a cosy drawing room and a large dining room with a distinctive stained glass window inscribed with the words 'vigilante defend' (keep awake) depicting a rooster and a man holding a club in the Classical style. Elsie's bohemian taste decorated the entertaining area with exotic crimson rugs, green upholstery and Japanese lampshades. Their fine collection of glassware was on display – and had a functional purpose; it is recorded that large amounts of claret and Champagne were delivered to the cottage, indicating that the couple was heavily consuming alcohol. Kenneth's father had been an alcoholic and the disease is known to be hereditary, although medical records do not suggest Kenneth had befallen the same fate. The locals at Pangbourne thought the couple somewhat unusual; the famous author was regarded as quiet but pleasant, tall and white-haired who took pleasure in dressing well, wearing red Harris tweeds with a checked monochrome scarf. For his rare visits to London by train he would dress in elegant trousers and smart coat, looking 'a handsome and dignified figure of an elderly city man.'[1]

But old age didn't become Elsie. A lifetime of anxiety was laid bare on her tired, lined face, and her grey hair was unstyled, left a thin, frizzy mess. She had not looked after her skin during her time abroad and was described by a local as: 'a chinny woman of leathery countenance.'[2] Pitifully thin, unlike her husband, she still seems to have remained strangely fixated on saving money – Kenneth would turn away ashamedly as she regularly haggled at the butcher's over a meagre piece of meat. Some locals say she dressed poorly, others suggest she too wore tailor-made tweeds. They both made an effort to join in with local life, with Kenneth introducing lectures for delighted groups such as the Pangbourne Arts and Crafts Society, and the Pangbourne Literary, Dramatic and Musical Guild. Elsie made new friends who enjoyed hearing charming stories of her literary past as they swapped gardening tips and birthday greetings. But the bossiness with which she treated Kenneth had also seeped into her friendships and she became pushy with her neighbours, press-ganging them into doing all sorts of errands for her. One who knew her at this time wrote that Kenneth looked as if he 'suffered from the wearing personality of his wife… [who] talked stridently and interminably, laying down the law about her preferences in literature and art, and never taking much heed of what anybody else has to say.' This over-confident woman is a far cry from the nervous new mother who spent extended periods at Woodhall Spa. One wonders if there was ever a period in Elsie's life where she felt balanced and comfortable in her own skin.

If Kenneth and Elsie had grown closer whilst abroad, it seems their affection for each other all but disappeared again when they were back in England. Perhaps their relationship had always been based on a holiday romance (after all, it was from Cornwall that Kenneth had courted Elsie). The balm of the sun and the thrill of exploring foreign climes was lost in Pangbourne as the couple once more grew divided. Writing continued to play a large part in their daily routine; the house had at least three writing bureaus, including a polished oak writing desk in Kenneth's study, which were all put to good use. Fan letters regularly came in from around the world and Elsie took it upon herself to conscientiously keep up with correspondence (Kenneth wasn't as diligent – he handpicked the most interesting ones). Kenneth was regularly asked to take on writing projects, including a biography of Dr Barnardo, but politely declined, until finally, a spark of energy was lit by a writing project that piqued his long-standing interest in the circus. In 1925, he accepted a commission to write the introduction to George Sanger's reissued biography, *Seventy Years a Showman*. It would be the last thing he published and, overflowing with nostalgia, wit and joy, shows his sense of wonderment of the world never diminished: 'the most eternal feature of a fair is the Roundabout. As the highest expression of the emotion of joy, we would all of us naturally choose to spring upon a charger and ride forth at top speed...' He meditates on his own life, the conundrum of his double-existence: 'Show-people are a contented folk... because they rarely want to be anything but what they are... Illusion, as the showman knows, is nearly everything,' he concludes.

Kenneth consistently refused to write a follow-up to *The Wind in the Willows*, unlike his Olympians series. 'Sequels are often traps which the wise author does well to avoid, if he wants to go, like Christian, on his way singing!' he wrote to a fan after she begged for more. And when asked for his approval to abridge the novel for schoolchildren, he would not give it. Not writing a sequel is one of the great mysteries of Kenneth's life, believes the Oscar-winning screenwriter Julian Fellowes, who thought about this carefully while making the film version of *The Wind in the Willows*.

Grahame set the characters up, it sold incredibly well and I can't understand why he didn't bring the characters back. None of the characters were dead, there was nothing to stop him. It is my speculation that it was too difficult to write for children after his own relationship with his son turned out so badly.

After losing his child, and possibly another (if it is true that Elsie suffered a stillbirth) a sequel was impossible.

Kenneth's oldest friend, Graham Robertson, put it another way:

In Kenneth Grahame's work there is no need to remove the wheat from the chaff; he has left us nothing but the purest golden grain, and his mere handful of writings have swept round the world on a gathering of love and admiration for the man who would give nothing short of his best...

Kenneth had given his best, and had nothing left in his pen or his mind for further creative writing.

By 1929, he was slowing down, hibernating like an animal, and described his days as sleeping in 'with head on pillow very late on a thoroughly wet morning', only to end the day in a similar way: '[in] my armchair of evenings, with closed eyes', taking gentle afternoon walks in the woods. Memories of his life flashed before him: 'It bought the Villa Lante back to me very vividly... a lot of other things, little and big, they all come back to me...' he wrote aged 70, of his holiday with romantic Annie all those years ago. This was the same year that his brother, Roland, died, from whom he had been estranged for years after a quarrel over money. It was his sister, Helen, who wrote to him with the news. He had also been alienated from her since marrying Elsie. The couple was well and truly alone in the world.

Kenneth had developed lower-back pain and walked with a stick, slightly hunched and growing overweight as he constantly turned to food for comfort, which didn't help his arteriosclerosis (cardiovascular disease). His obsession with nursery treats such as ice cream is an indication of his emotional need and an attempt to cling to childhood happiness. '*Do* let me have something to eat!' he begged to his doctor as Elsie put him on yet another strict diet.

During these later years, Kenneth drew pleasure in bringing nature closer to him; he and Elsie regarded the outside of their property as more important than the inside – we deduce this because a gardener was the only domestic help they sought. (Hang spring cleaning!) The large garden with its fertile soil made for a gorgeous oasis, and Kenneth in particular was taken with its outdoor amphitheatre. The couple often ate outside together, and Kenneth's favourite pastime was reading in the garden within earshot of the church bells as he spent his days revisiting his favourites – Shakespeare, Shelley, Robert Burns, Tennyson and Henry Fielding (he had keen eyesight even as an older man and never lost his love of reading). Kenneth refused to let go of his interest in childhood, his bookshelves overflowing with almost a hundred volumes of boys' and girls' adventures that he had collected throughout his life. Childhood may be short in years but it was a subject that fascinated him until the end.

One of the final occasions Kenneth left Pangbourne was to see A.A. Milne's production *Toad of Toad Hall* in London. The experience nourished him with pride and happiness as he saw his novel come to life on stage: 'I arrived in London stiff as an icicle with cold. I returned glowing with warmth, and with the merry tunes of Toad and his friends dancing through my head,' he wrote to his agent Curtis Brown at the beginning of 1931. How fortunate that Kenneth lived long enough to witness the next phase in his book's life; Milne's play did much to keep *Willows* in the public consciousness and continue its successful momentum. Milne wrote:

> It may be that to turn Mr Kenneth Grahame into a play is to leave unattractive fingermarks all over him, but I love his books so much that I cannot bear to think of anybody else disfiguring them. Of course I have left out all the best parts of the book; and for that, if he has any knowledge of the theatre, Mr. Grahame will thank me… we are not going to add any fresh thrill to the thrill which the loveliness of '*The Piper at the Gates of Dawn*' has already given its readers.

Ultimately, the playwright had such high regard for the novel that he placed it above criticism:

> One does not argue about *The Wind in the Willows*… The book is a test of character. We can't criticise it because it is criticising us. But I must give you one word of warning. When you sit down to it, don't

be so ridiculous as to suppose that you are sitting in judgement on my taste, or on the art of Kenneth Grahame. You are merely sitting in judgement on yourself. You may be worthy: I don't know, but it is you who are on trial.

Since Milne, *The Wind in the Willows* has been brought to life on stage across the world. One man who has been instrumental in dramatising the novel as well as Kenneth's life at home and as far abroad as Australia is David Gooderson, who co-wrote his first adaptation as a full-length musical with David Conville and music by Carl Davis. His second version is a small-scale one-hour play, unique in the way that it is almost entirely follows Kenneth's text word-for-word. It was commissioned by and first performed at the Bank of England as well as The River and Rowing Museum in Henley. Gooderson appeared as Mole in his musical version of the play.

In 1931, Kenneth entered into his last full year of life, punctuated by frequent visits from his GP Dr Bourdillon who delivered the devastating news that he should not go on any more long walks. Kenneth remained overweight, had high blood pressure and his arteries were under strain after a lifetime of rich food and wine. Kenneth, who had enjoyed making curries, had to make do with his favourite Mediterranean salad of lettuce, chervil and tarragon mixed with olive oil and vinegar.

His final outing was to London, on 25 June 1932, to a bookshop for a celebration of 100 years since Lewis Carroll's birth. Less than two weeks later, he died.

Kenneth passed away in the early hours of a summer's morning on 6 July 1932 at home in Pangbourne. He had spent all afternoon at the river, walking there after filling out *The Times* crossword (complaining it wasn't difficult enough). When he died, he was holding Sir Walter Scott's *The Talisman* novel. Life had come full circle; Kenneth and Scott had been born in within a stone's throw of each other in Edinburgh.

Elsie was shocked. Her husband, aged 73, had seemed quite well. He had gone to bed early after supper but there had been nothing unusual in that. In death, as in life, he had simply turned and moved away from her, that fellow who goes alone, even in his final hours. Despite a lifetime together, she had never properly understood the secrets that lay deep in his heart.

Typically, Kenneth had put his affairs in good order and in his will had bequeathed all the royalties from his works to the University of Oxford for the benefit of the Bodleian Library. He also donated many papers and materials to it, including the most precious copy of *The Wind in the Willows*; the one dedicated to Mouse. Kenneth's foresight has allowed the library to gain many books and manuscripts for lovers of children's literature to appreciate for all time.

For all her grief, Elsie was practical enough to organise Kenneth's funeral in just three days, no doubt helped by her eminent brother Courtauld. On a sunny Saturday, the funeral was held next to Church Cottage, at St James the Less, which was decorated just as Kenneth would have wished, with a gloriously abundant display of nature's finest flora including delphiniums, roses, cottage flowers and branches of willows taken from the river that morning. Kenneth always had a keen sense of smell, so it was fitting that thousands of fragrant sweet peas (they grew at Church Cottage) were placed lovingly on his coffin as it was lowered into the ground. Flowers and wreaths flooded in from around the world, from Cornwall to Scotland, New York to France, as well as from almost every villager in Pangbourne. Most touching were the ones with cards handwritten by the children who loved Kenneth's work so dearly. One of the wreaths was red, sent from his sister Helen, now 76 and too frail to make the journey from the Lizard for the funeral. In a gesture of reconciliation she sent Elsie the string purse she had treasured all her life that Kenneth had made for her at school.

Kenneth was temporarily buried in the churchyard before being laid to rest in peace beside his beloved Mouse in a quiet corner of Holywell Cemetery next to St Cross Church in Oxford. The eulogy was delivered by Kenneth's cousin and best man, Anthony Hope Hawkins. His words were later added to the gravestone: 'To the beautiful memory of Kenneth Grahame, husband of Elsie and father of Alastair, who passed the River on the 6th July 1932, leaving childhood and literature through him the more blest for all time.'

Sir Hope Hawkins wrote to Elsie shortly afterwards, summing up the overwhelming regard and admiration in which Kenneth was held:

It must be some solace to your grief to receive so many [letters]...
It is not only the numbers of them but the quality of the people

from whom they came that are so striking. He will be more than a memory… he will still be a living presence and an enduring friend…

It would be one of the last letters Sir Hope Hawkins would write, as he died shortly after, suffering a stroke. Elsie carefully noted his letter, as she did with the hundreds of others, from handwritten notes written by children: 'From two little boys, David and Stephen/Who love *The Wind in the Willows* and the hand that wrote it' to the highest dignitaries in the land. Many of the letters came from local friends in Pangbourne, including one who presciently noted: 'That he succeeded so well in capturing and preserving on paper the spirit and viewpoint of childhood is a valuable service that posterity will, without doubt, appreciate even more than we who honour Kenneth Grahame's name today.'

Another, from Pangbourne Lodge, expressed the sentiments of the entire village: 'It is a sorrow which will be widely felt, and particularly in this place, where Mr Grahame had a very special place in the hearts of all his neighbours.'

Constance Smedley sensed that that Kenneth would have been prepared for the end: 'he believed that beyond what he saw now lie wider revelations.' Graham Robertson, his oldest friend who had shared a part of Kenneth's life that may never be fully understood, was, of course, deeply upset. He laid tribute to his friend as an 'exquisite and only too occasional writer'.

Other letters reveal as much about Elsie as they do about Kenneth, including one from the nearby village of Goring:

My husband… has been privileged to know such a wonderful personality as Mr Kenneth Grahame. He has always spoken of him with such affection. He has told me how you have devoted yourself to his call and service and this must be a great comfort in this hour. I shall never forget the loving sympathy you gave us when we lost our baby last year and your letter is still treasured by me among the few that I have kept.

Elsie was alone now, for the first time in her life. Kenneth had been her world; putting aside her own dreams of becoming a writer, she had always supported her husband in his creative work, bravely bringing up

Mouse while suffering mental ill health, and caring for Kenneth during his many bouts of illness. It was true that as they grew old together she had expressed her love in dominating ways, by forcing him to wear strange underwear, contradicting him in public and dictating a strict diet. Nevertheless, Mouse's death had brought them closer and they had spent a lifetime together as husband and wife; Kenneth had died days from their thirty-third wedding anniversary. What was she to do now, a white-haired woman of 70?

'A new world is being born… And one cannot grieve for the old, the new is all so wonderful,' Kenneth had written to a reader some years previously. Elsie comprehended her new world, one that she would not have been able to cope with as a younger, anxious woman. But she was stronger and braver now, and ready to face the future alone.

Chapter 25

Elsie Lives On

'He walked into people's hearts, and there are locked hearts as well as locked doors.'

Elsie of her husband Kenneth,
First Whisper of The Wind in the Willows

Elsie woke suddenly, sitting up in bed with a start. She had been dreaming, reliving the moment when she discovered Kenneth had gone. She remembered hearing the thump of his book falling on to the wooden bedroom floor and rushing into his room at one o' clock in the morning. He was still alive at that moment, in a coma after suffering a haemorrhage of the brain. She sat by his bedside in shock as he breathed shallowly for almost five hours, his silver hair spread across the pillow, his childlike face peacefully resting. When he finally stopped breathing, after a lifetime together it was as if he had simply slipped away without saying goodbye.

As she faced another day without her husband, Elsie took a deep breath and resolved not to let her mental fragility get the better of her.

From 1933, it is arguably because of Elsie that the popularity of *The Wind in the Willows* continues today, more than a century after it was written. After her husband's death, Elsie conscientiously took on Kenneth's affairs, without, so far as we know, any secretarial assistance nor need for financial gain. Curtis Brown remained the professional agent and the first point of contact for literary enquiries about Kenneth's work, but Elsie took an enthusiastic role in liaising with the agent as well as replying to enquiries directly. (Receiving the pilgrims who came to Church Cottage to pay homage to the author would have been enough to occupy her.)

There was a great deal to keep up with: terms for new editions to be discussed, broadcasting deals from the BBC and serialisations. Requests for performance rights came in from around the world and there was the long-running correspondence with Roy Disney about the movie of *The Wind in the Willows*. Elsie took an active role in the negotiations and it was released as a double feature in 1949 as *The Adventures of Ichabod and Mr Toad*, introduced as 'the most fabulous character in English literature'. It later inspired a Disneyland ride. Disney also paid for the rights for *The Reluctant Dragon*, released in 1941.

Elsie, in her seventies, would have had to spend considerable brain-power to keep up with the mountains of correspondence regarding all matters of her late husband's work. She genuinely cared about his stories and their future; she took the time to make sure they were being properly managed and enquiries thoroughly followed up. Her mental faculties were still working well – perhaps it was the intellectual activity she needed to get back the long-lost spark from her youth, the effervescence that attracted Kenneth to her in the first place.

Elsie was particularly supportive of charity requests, for example, the transcription of *The Golden Age* into Braille (surely a homage to Mouse?) and ensuring royalties were not claimed for toys made for disabled children. It is not completely clear from correspondence, but it might be true that Elsie had the idea of manufacturing toys inspired by *The Wind in the Willows*; she certainly investigated the possibility with a toy manufacturer along with Curtis Brown. As a woman without a formal education, she was smart enough to recognise the concept of a brand extension and articulate enough to take advantage of the opportunities it represented.

The Wind in the Willows remained an international success; a French translation was made, which Elsie took the time to check herself, and she helped get the novel translated into Danish, Norwegian, Italian and Czech, as well as editions released in Brazil and Argentina. Elsie realised the commercial importance of being published in the US after countless magazines enquiries.

She continued to keep abreast of business correspondence until she died, despite becoming blind and suffering bronchitis in her later years. Elsie would have someone to read letters to her and dictate her reply. She bore her disability with the same strength she bore being a widow, becoming childless and possibly suffering a stillbirth or miscarriage. She refused to let it define her. The shaky figure of a new mother on the sofa sipping water was long gone. Instead: 'with spirit undimmed by age or infirmity, she carried on a world-wide correspondence,' said her admiring brother, Courtauld.

A year after Kenneth died, Patrick Chalmers got in touch with Elsie. He was a banker and a writer, who had heard one of Kenneth's lectures to a local society at Pangbourne. He requested a meeting with Elsie to discuss writing a biography in tribute to his hero. Elsie agreed to help – as long as she received half of the royalties. She loved being involved, characteristically working hard to build a personal relationship with Chalmers and his wife. She provided Chalmers with invaluable contacts and took on the painstaking graft of writing to Kenneth's friends and family with a conscientious energy. But Elsie's heavy involvement was to the detriment of factual accuracy. It was the academic Peter Green who unpicked it all a quarter of a century later – and he never quite forgave Elsie for her patchwork of fabrication (his account of her is savage!).

Being involved in the biography after Kenneth and Mouse's deaths provided Elsie with a purpose in life – she always loved a project. Although she and Kenneth had convinced themselves that Mouse's death had been an accident, without her husband's reassurance, Elsie became anxious to obtain further proof that her son was resting in peace. In the Bodleian Library lies a letter from a medium replying to Elsie's enquiry, which claims Alastair is 'sorry he failed'. Elsie wrote for further comfort to the Council for Psychic Investigation at the University of London, which advised her not to trust disreputable mediums.

Elsie continued to compose poetry and wrote of her experience of the Second World War in *Straphanging* when she rode on a bus during the blackout. The mood of the verse is of complete exhaustion and suggests life had made her weary:

> The last bus and the furthest stop,
> Not a seat or a strap to be found,
> And I so weary that I might drop
> A hapless heap to the ground.

One of the reasons why Elsie was attracted to Kenneth (and made friends with people such as Constance Smedley) was because his sense of childish wonderment never left him. Without him to remind her of the magic of life, Elsie must have found it difficult to endure her dark moments. For most of her adult years she had put aside her own literary ambitions to support her husband, and now finally she had an opportunity to express her voice as she wrote the biography of her husband. *First Whisper of The Wind in the Willows* was published in 1944 by Methuen, an impressive accomplishment for an 82-year-old. Finally, fifty-six years after publishing *Amelia Jane's Ambition* (and in a new century under her own name – she had used a pen name for *Amelia*) her personal writing ambition had been realised.

Elsie did well to negotiate a £200 advance on account of a royalty of 12.5 per cent to 500 copies and 15 per cent thereafter. She inscribed a first edition for her agent, Curtis Brown, acknowledging their long and happy relationship – impressive, as few agents and authors get on for almost forty years. Always a keen correspondent, much of Elsie's research for *Whisper* was based on re-establishing connections with Kenneth's many friends. Her eyesight was extremely poor, yet somehow she retained her characteristic handwriting style and wrote merrily and comprehensively off to them all. Elsie got in touch with Graham Robertson, requesting that he illustrate her book and the character of Pan. He writes: 'All should be gay – young – alive – and… drawn by a young man – I'm too old.' Do Robertson's final words hint at an opportunity missed? 'I felt that it should be a song of innocence and not in any way a lament.' But he was eventually persuaded to take on the project, eccentrically joking that he could only paint a nude: 'The "radiant" boy was the devil & all of a nuisance. He wouldn't wear any clothes, though I told him that publishers were most particular… Well – I mean to say – what is one to do? I'm through with radiant boys – cannot manage them at any age…' Robertson, himself now in his eighties, was incredibly supportive of Elsie's book: 'I do hope that you will keep it very much in your own hands and write it yourself throughout – using letters, of course, and further appreciations, reviews etc. in an appendix. You have the writer's gift and the intimate knowledge and can produce a real record with all sympathy and understanding.'

Unsurprisingly, Elsie was heavily involved in the editing process: 'I am not quite comfortable about the deletion or alterations here and there of words and phrases in the letters,' she wrote to Methuen. A difficult author she may have been yet Elsie's commercial instinct proved correct to the financial gain of the publisher; her clever idea to renew interest in *The Wind in the Willows* for a new generation meant *First Whisper* was an instant bestseller, with 10,000 sold at once (other unlucky readers had to wait for their copy until the war's paper shortage eased, when a further 3,000 were printed). Although slim, *First Whisper* reveals almost as much of Elsie's muddled, creative, sentimental personality as Kenneth's unfailingly honest one. It doesn't read particularly logically and in places is confusing – for a start, it is credited as being authored by Kenneth Grahame when the man had been dead for twelve years. Elsie's 'little preface' as she terms it runs for almost half the book. Yet it is full of vivid reminiscences about Kenneth and Mouse, colourful anecdotes about *The Wind in the Willows* with the bonus of premiering the Dear Mouse letters and *Bertie's Escapade* (later she successfully encouraged Bodley to publish *Bertie's Escapade* as a separate story).

Elsie's micro-opus has been heavily criticised for being inaccurate; in it, she indicates she was the person who came up with turning Kenneth's letters to Mouse into a novel, although, as we remember, it was likely that Constance Smedley was the driving force behind the project because of her professional publishing experience and international business connections. The tone of Elsie's book similarly has been disregarded as cloying and exaggerated; Elsie's descriptions of her genius son, for example, are painful to read in hindsight. Her charm is hard to resist though; who can argue with her anecdote of two little brothers who knocked one day to ask to see the 'sugar man'.

'Why do you always call him the sugar man? He never gives you any sweets,' asks Elsie.

'No, but he's the sweetest man in the very whole world, so he must be made of sugar.'

The truth or Elsie's fabrication? She doesn't let the facts get in the way of a good yarn although seems to have forgotten she was meant to be producing a piece of non-fiction rather than another penny dreadful, which makes it difficult for a biographer (or any reader) to decipher reality. More concerning is the suggestion that Elsie destroyed the family's written history by disposing of Kenneth's diary, letters between them and much of Mouse's unhappy correspondence from school.

Whether it is accepted simply as a product of time or criticised as Elsie's attempt at rewriting the truth behind Brand Grahame, *First Whisper of The Wind in the Willows* remains a useful historical document for anyone interested in Kenneth and his writing. The memoir shares some important connections that might have been otherwise lost and, at the very least, survives as one of the only remaining documents that records Elsie's voice. Her husband always refused to write his autobiography, protesting to his agent: 'My chief trouble is that I have kept no diaries or memoranda at all and since the War my memory seems to have gone all to pot. I doubt much if I could ever get as much as a book together...' If he wouldn't, why shouldn't she? *First Whisper* was written with an impressive amount of energy, enthusiasm and comprehensiveness for a widow in her eighties who was almost blind and perhaps she can be forgiven if in her final years her greatest sin was that she had come to genuinely believe she was the inspiration for her husband's work. Incidentally, Elsie was writing her own memoirs when she died, although these have never been found.[1]

Notwithstanding her advancing years, the grand dame remained involved with village life, and kept herself busy accepting engagements beyond Pangbourne when her brother invited her to his country estate, Dorneywood in Buckinghamshire, for summer luncheon parties (where she was described as having a fascinating personality, 'so full of charm, intelligence and vitality'). Her brother, now director of the Red Cross, welcomed army officers to Dorneywood for rest and recuperation. Elsie donated her tiny rations of sugar and tea to help the army men. In 1942, her brother wrote to her: 'I always feel you are far too generous in the gifts you send us and I do hope you don't deprive yourself. Anyway you know how grateful we are.' She maintained her ability to make friends even as an older woman, making the effort to stay in touch with new people she met. She still enjoyed entertaining at home: 'I shall never forget her kind hospitality in her garden – sometimes when the white roses were showering their petals on the grass,' said one guest. 'She had so much personality and her life was so full of various interests that she was to be envied – and admired.' Elsie was a vivid storyteller to the end who didn't need encouragement to share tales from her past especially her travels and famous friends; an acquaintance writes: 'How we enjoyed listening to her delightful stories, & to hear of the distinguished people she had met in her long life.' Although unable to travel, she never tired of hearing of new places and delighted in asking questions. Her brain remained sharp and her memory good. And after living at Pangbourne for twenty years, Elsie always remembered what it was like to move to the village and made an effort with newcomers: 'Mrs Grahame was the first and kindest of our visitors,' wrote one local. 'I shall never forget her kind hospitality.' Another remembered: 'She was so kind, after Aunt Annie died.' Another friend wrote: 'Mrs Grahame's wonderful old home at Pangbourne should belong to the nation, like Thomas Hardy's... it has seen so many visits of her friends and is stored with the priceless treasures she had collected in the course of her long life.' (When she died she donated her belongings to Dorneywood.)

It seemed Elsie always needed someone to care for. As a young woman she had devoted herself to her politician stepfather, taking on responsibility for entertaining his important friends. She had fallen quickly and heavily in love with Kenneth, before becoming a doting mother (if a misguided one). Now all she had left in the world was her brother, Courtauld, who had taken his seat in the House of Lords the same year as *First Whisper* was published. She lavished her attention on him – as he did her, albeit to a more measured extent. That word – devoted – is again applied to Elsie and her relationship with her brother: 'you meant such a lot to her and I know how devoted she was and that you were her first interest,' wrote a mutual friend. Courtauld needed Elsie too, for their sister, Winifred, had died in 1944. They had been a small but united trio; without a wife of his own Courtauld was close to both of them and missed Winifred, with whom he had lived for forty years, immeasurably.

Courtauld, now in his late seventies, was Elsie's latest source of pride; she talked constantly of him and openly admired all he had achieved. One of her greatest joys was to write to him and she adored hearing his letters read to her. He was especially loving to her in her later years and spent a great deal of time considering her health and happiness, which allowed her to be much more comfortable than she otherwise would have been. He thoughtfully sent her a wireless radio, for example, which she loved listening to, and shared with her the minutest details of his social engagements with the great and the good of the day. Elsie had always been close to her brother but now leant on him for emotional as well as practical support, a demand which he took seriously.

As loyal to her friends as she was to her brother, Elsie never forgot a birthday and remained an avid letter-writer; she was described by her friends as a charming and interesting correspondent, and was always interested in new topics. She was incredibly supportive in all sorts of ways to those she loved, offering practical help such as bags of old clothes, and not taking offence at petty trifles ('I cannot get to the funeral I fear, – but she wouldn't mind that,' wrote one friend of her after she died).

Elsie was fiercely independent; now completely blind with her bronchitis worsening, she refused to have any home help at Church Cottage, despite Courtauld's begging. (He was concerned that she would die alone in the middle of the countryside.) Courtald helped her put her affairs in order, and in 1943 she donated many of her important letters and papers to the Bodleian Library, just as Kenneth had done. (She had become a great supporter of the Friends of the Bodleian Library.) Gradually, Elsie sensed she was coming towards the end of her life and eventually agreed to move to London. She spent her last days being cared for by her beloved brother and as late as 3 May 1946 she was still composing poetry.

Elsie died in London on 19 December 1946 following a stroke, fourteen years after Kenneth and just two years after publishing *First Whisper*. She was 84. Courtauld arranged for her body to go back to Dorneywood, the place she had so enjoyed in her later years, and she is buried a mile away in the churchyard of St Anne's, Dropmore. 'She loved and was loved' is inscribed on her gravestone, and a stained glass window inside the church is dedicated to her, Kenneth, Winifred and Courtauld. An inkwell and quill feature.

In 1942, Courtauld had handed over the deeds to Dorneywood to Winston Churchill at 10 Downing Street, for use by the prime minister or others in the cabinet. Today it is often used by the Chancellor of the Exchequer for his country home.

Courtauld received an extraordinary number of condolence letters, from No. 10 Downing Street to Queen Victoria's granddaughter Helena Victoria. The list of Who's Who might be a reflection of his own status rather than Elsie's, but nevertheless the sentiments expressed in the letters are a testament to her vivid personality. Courtauld, in his obituary for *The Times*, wrote: 'Although largely generous and intensely interested in the well-being of others, she cared nothing for her own comfort. Elsie just lived in her brilliant and cultured mind, in her gentle soul, and in the hearts of those she loved.' A family friend summed up the unique Elsie as 'gallant and gifted', offering her bereft brother words of comfort:

I hope that you will be helped by the pride you must feel in the brave and uncompromising way in which she triumphed over her physical difficulties. I have often been touched by what you have told me of her invincible courage and resource. That indeed was an example of how to live.

Elsie's determination to see the best in things and make the most of her final years of life would have pleased her husband. Perhaps he would have been surprised by her strength. 'History may be told two ways: backwards or forwards – just as a river may be traced from its finish… or from the all but untraceable trickle of the river to its ending,' wrote Elsie in the opening lines of *First Whisper of The Wind in the Willows*.

Both she and Kenneth were guilty of rewriting their own personal histories yet Kenneth's recognition of the magic in life, and his ability to articulate it, has enriched literature for ever.

Elsie dedicated her life to showing the world her husband's belief in wonderment. As a maiden she had fallen in love with the ideal of Kenneth the writer, an ideal that the unfortunately repressed Kenneth could never live up to. After his death, Elsie gained the emotional comfort she had always sought by fuelling the memory of Kenneth and sharing him with readers across the world. She wrote this poem as a young woman in love, and it is apt to conclude with the last verse. It seems Elsie, in the end, has the last word over her husband:

Give Me a Kiss That Will Last For Ever

You must give me a kiss that will last for ever
A glance from your eyes that I shall not forget
A clasp of your hand which time cannot sever
That the force of remembrance may vanquish regret

Bibliography

By Kenneth Grahame
Pagan Papers, John Lane, The Bodley Head, 1893
The Golden Age, John Lane, The Bodley Head, 1895
Dream Days, John Lane, The Bodley Head, 1898,
The Wind in the Willows, Methuen & Co, 1908
The Cambridge Book of Poetry for Children, Cambridge University Press, 1916
First Whisper of 'The Wind in the Willows', Methuen, 1944
Bertie's Escapade, Methuen, 1949

The most comprehensive bibliography of Kenneth's works including his essays which appeared in periodicals is found in *Kenneth Grahame: A Biography*, Peter Green, 1959, John Murray.

Bennett, Alan, *The Wind in the Willows* (play), Faber & Faber, 1996
Chalmers, Patrick, *Kenneth Grahame: Life, Letters and Unpublished Work*, Methuen, 1933
Dennison, Matthew, *Eternal Boy*, Head of Zeus, 2018
Duke Cox, Nicholas M., *Taking the Waters at Woodhall Spa*, Woodhall Spa Cottage Museum, 2020
Gooderson, David, *My Dearest Mouse: The Wind in the Willows Letters*, Pavilion/ Michael Joseph, 1988
——, *The Killing of Mr Toad*, Finborough Theatre, 2009

David Gooderson's two adaptations of *The Wind in the Willows* are not yet published but are available for public performance. Enquiries: David Gooderson (www.david-gooderson.co.uk) or Mike Sharland at The Sharland Organisation (tso@btconnect.com)

Green, Peter, *Kenneth Grahame: A Biography*, John Murray, 1959
——, *Beyond the Wild Wood*, Grange Books, 1993
Hunt, Peter, *The Making of the Wind in the Willows*, Bodleian Library, 2018
Jerome, Jerome K., *Three Men in a Boat*, J.W. Arrowsmith, 1889
Milne, A.A., *Toad of Toad Hall*, Scribner, 1929
Morrah, Herbert A., *Highways and Hedges*, Adam and Charles Black, 1911
Needle, Jan, *The Wild Wood*, Andre Deutsch, 1981
Oxford Dictionary of National Biography, Oxford University Press

Parkes, Roger, *Herries: A History of a Happy School*

Prince, Alison, *An Innocent in the Wild Wood*, Faber & Faber, 2009

Rawlings, Antoinette, *The World of The Wind in the Willows*, Pitkin Guides, 2012

Robertson, W. Graham, *Time Was: The Reminiscences of W. Graham Robertson*, Quartet Books, 1981

——, *Pinkie and the Fairies*, Heinemann, 1931

Sanger, George, *Seventy Years a Showman*, Dent, 1926

Sharp, Evelyn, *Unfinished Adventure, Selected Reminiscences from an Englishwoman's Life*, Faber Finds, 1933

Smedley, Constance, *Crusaders*, Duckworth, 1929

Steven, William, *Scottish Storytrails*, NWP, 2017

The Oxford Companion to Twentieth-Century Literature, Oxford University Press, 1996

Thoreau, Henry David *Walden; Or, Life in the Woods*, Boston: Ticknor and Fields, 1854

Watson, J.N.P., *Dorneywood*, Robert Hale, 1993

Notes

The primary sources I have drawn from are held at the Special Collections section of the Bodleian Libraries, University of Oxford; the Bank of England Archive and at Dorneywood, Buckinghamshire. Secondary sources are referenced in the text and below:

Chapter 1
1. *Pagan Papers*, 1893, John Lane, The Bodley Head

2. The town is well described by Kenneth's biographer Patrick Chalmers, who was helped by Kenneth's wife to collate the first full-length memoir, *Life, Letters and Unpublished Work*, 1933, Methuen

Chapter 2
1. 'A Funeral', published in *Life, Letters and Unpublished Work*, Patrick Chalmers, 1933, Methuen

Chapter 4
1. *Life, Letters and Unpublished Work*, Patrick Chalmers, 1933, Methuen
2. Ibid
3. Ibid
4. Ibid

Chapter 5
1. *Life, Letters and Unpublished Work*, Patrick Chalmers, 1933, Methuen

Chapter 6
1. Account by Mary Richardson in *Kenneth Grahame: A Biography*, Peter Green, 1959, John Murray
2. Letters by Mary Richardson in the Special Collections section of the Bodleian Libraries, University of Oxford

Chapter 8
1. Account by Mary Richardson in *Kenneth Grahame: A Biography*, Peter Green, 1959, John Murray
2. *Unfinished Adventure, Selected Reminiscences from an Englishwoman's Life*, Evelyn Sharp, 1933, Faber Finds

Chapter 9
1. *An Innocent in the Wild Wood*, Alison Prince, 1994, Allison & Busby

Chapter 12
1. *Time Was*, W. Graham Robertson, 1931, Hamish Hamilton. It was published the year before Kenneth died

Chapter 14
1. Bank of England Archive

Chapter 15
1. *My Dearest Mouse*, David Gooderson, 1988, Pavilion/Michael Joseph

Chapter 16
1. *Crusaders*, Constance Smedley, 1929, Duckworth

Chapter 17
1. Interview with Julian Fellowes by the author, 2018
2. Hunt, Peter, *The Making of the Wind in the Willows*, Bodleian Library, 2018

Chapter 21
1. *The Killing of Mr Toad*, David Gooderson, 2009, Finborough Theatre

Chapter 22
1. Interview and research by David Gooderson

Chapter 24
1. *Kenneth Grahame: A Biography*, Peter Green, 1959, John Murray
2. Ibid

Chapter 25
1. Letter from Courtauld to Elsie, 'I hope you have begun your memoirs'. 8 September 1942, Special Collections department of the Bodleian Libraries, University of Oxford

Index